On December 16, 1998 . . .

. . . Manhattan District Attorney Robert Morgenthau announced murder charges against Sante and Kenneth Kimes. The 84-count indictment accused mother and son of second-degree murder, conspiracy, robbery, attempted robbery, burglary, grand larceny, attempted grand larceny, forgery, eavesdropping and possession of weapons, stolen property, and forged documents. If convicted of all charges, they faced up to 131⅓ years in prison.

"These are two very competent, very cold criminals," said Police Commissioner Howard Safir. "I think in my experience, I have not seen people who have such disregard for other people as the Kimeses."

They Call Them Grifters

Alice McQuillan

AN ONYX BOOK

ONYX
Published by New American Library, a division of
Penguin Putnam Inc., 375 Hudson Street,
New York, New York 10014, U.S.A.
Penguin Books Ltd, 27 Wrights Lane,
London W8 5TZ, England
Penguin Books Australia Ltd, Ringwood,
Victoria, Australia
Penguin Books Canada Ltd, 10 Alcorn Avenue,
Toronto, Ontario, Canada M4V 3B2
Penguin Books (N.Z.) Ltd, 182–190 Wairau Road,
Auckland 10, New Zealand

Penguin Books Ltd, Registered Offices:
Harmondsworth, Middlesex, England

First published by Onyx, an imprint of New American Library,
a division of Penguin Putnam Inc.

First Printing, March 2000
10 9 8 7 6 5 4 3 2

Copyright © Alice McQuillan, 2000
All rights reserved

REGISTERED TRADEMARK—MARCA REGISTRADA

Printed in the United States of America

To my parents, Julie and Frank

ACKNOWLEDGMENTS

Tracking the exploits of Sante and Kenny Kimes was a far-flung adventure that I could not have attempted alone. So many people helped me pull this book together, especially my colleagues at the *Daily News*. Thank you, Editor-in-Chief Debby Krenek for green lighting the project and generously giving me time and resources to tackle this coast-to-coast story. Reporters who run our "police shack" never let me feel overwhelmed. Special gratitude to the ever-calm and savvy John Marzulli, Michael Claffey, Patrice O'Shaughnessy, Michele McPhee (who traveled to the Bahamas for this book with wonderful results), and Henri Cauvin. Criminal Court reporter Barbara Ross, thank you for uprooting key documents and always being wonderful to me. Columnist Juan Gonzalez shared his impressions of Sante Kimes, gleaned from two exclusive interviews. Civil Court reporter Sal Arena and investigative reporter Willie Rashbaum helped me solve problems. Our crack staff of librarians, who can find anybody in America, were a godsend, particularly Shirley Wong, Alain Delaqueriere, Faigi Rosenthal, and Scott Browne. Editors Richard Rosen, Dean Chang, Wendell Jamieson, and Richard Pienciak encouraged me. Vice President Ed Fay and Photo Sales Editor Angela Troisi, thank you for the *Daily News* pictures.

I was lucky to find nine researchers who tracked down people and documents from Hawaii to Florida.

They are: Rebecca Boyd of the *Sacramento Bee*, Caren Benjamin of the *Las Vegas Review Journal*, Evelyn Poitevent of *USA Today* in Washington, D.C., Mary Ann Oros in Honolulu, Christian Berthelsen in Los Angeles for the *New York Times*, Lucia Hwang of the *San Francisco Bay Guardian*, Frances "Frenchie" Robles of the *Miami Herald*, Jennifer Burns at Fordham Law School, and Annia Ciezadlo of New York University. Thank you all for covering so much ground under a tight deadline, especially Rebecca, Caren, and Evelyn, who patiently said yes, no matter how often I called with another request.

Journalists who tackled the Kimes case were generous with contacts and documents. Topping this list are the folks at *60 Minutes*, producer Richard Greenberg and executive story editor Vicki Gordon. Richard applied his awesome skills and discerning eye to this story long before anyone else. Vicki, with the patience of a marathon runner, engineered the first TV interview of mother and son. Many, many thanks to you both. To my friend, the indefatigable WPIX-TV investigative reporter Jonathan Dienst, I owe a lifetime debt for all your insights and bursts of humor. CBS-TV reporter Michael O'Looney was among the first to follow the Kimeses' path in the Bahamas and kindly showed the way. The wonderful John Miller, ABC correspondent and former NYPD spokesman, expanded on his *20-20* Kimes broadcast and gave me entrée to producers Olive Talley and Dean Tsouvalas. *New York Observer* columnist Michael Thomas, Irene Silverman's former tenant, I appreciate your thoughts on structuring this tale. From the *New York Post*, retired court legend Mike Pearl and reporter/author Kieran Crowley shared their wisdom. Reporter Rick Catline of the *Caymanian Compass*, and *Nassau Guardian* managing editor Oswald Brown helped explain the bank collapse. I'm also grateful to reporters Dan Morrison, Leonard Levitt, and Mary Voboril of *News-*

day and Tom Hays, Donna DeLaCruz, and Samuel Maull of the Associated Press.

Police Commissioner Howard Safir and Deputy Police Commissioner for Public Information Marilyn Mode, thank you for insights on the Silverman case and for granting me access to the task force detectives. Special thanks to Inspector Joseph Reznick, 19th precinct detectives Tommy Hackett and Tommy Hovagim, and Manhattan North homicide detectives Danny Rodriguez and John Schlagler. I appreciate the help of Barbara Thompson and Wayne Brison in the Manhattan District Attorney's Office, Patrolmen's Benevolent Association trustee John Flynn, Lori Corral of the Illinois Attorney General's Office, Johnette Hardiman, Florida assistant state attorney, Special Agent Walter Deering of the State Department, and Supervisor Douglas Hanna and Detective Sergeant Mosey Evans of the Royal Bahamas Police. Others in law enforcement went out of their way to assist me, but wish to remain anonymous. I'm lucky to have them as sources.

The members of the Kimes defense team were always gracious with their time, ideas, copies of court transcripts, and impressions of their clients. Many thanks to attorneys Mel Sachs, Jose Muniz, Robert Silverberg, and Matthew Weissman, and private investigators Les Levine and Lawrence Frost.

My book research trips to Nevada and California went smoothly due to contacts like Las Vegas Police Chief Ray Flynn, retired FBI agent Tom Nicodemus, attorney and now Las Vegas mayor Oscar Goodman, Nevada state archivist Guy Rocha, private investigators John Doty, Leslie Schifrin, and Graham Howard, Fay McMillan and Grace Waters at the U.S. District Court in Las Vegas, Lori Doan, Walter Cannon, and Kira Wirges.

My deepest gratitude to the loved ones of the missing and dead, especially Linda and Steven Kazdin,

Dan and Ken Holmgren, Judy Weidlich, and friends of Irene Silverman, including Helen Pandelakis, who translated an epic poem about Irene's ancestors, as well as many others whom I can't thank publicly.

Dick Blood, I am grateful for your friendship of 15 years, your words of encouragement, and the expert eye you turned on this manuscript. Every change you suggested improved this book immensely. You're a tough but true wordsmith. Other friends kept me going, especially Berenika Cipkus, with her priceless advice and unflagging support; Michelle Caruso of *People* magazine in Los Angeles, a fountain of hospitality and warmth; playwright Darci Picoult for advice on organizing this saga; and Tom and Caroline Law for Fed Ex and other support.

My incredible agent, Alice Martell, took a chance on me and made this book happen. Now I know why all your writers include such glowing tributes to you. Alice, you deserve every compliment.

At New American Library, this project was in the expert hands of Carolyn Nichols, a joy to work with. I'm grateful for her shrewd editing, wise choices, enthusiasm, and care. And thank you to Valerie Andrewlevich, editorial assistant, and to Gina Anderson, deputy general counsel. Attorney David Korzenik went beyond the call in checking this manuscript in what felt like the most thorough vetting process on the planet. I appreciate all your hard work.

I wish to pay tribute to my wonderful family: Julie, Frank, Mary Ann, Paul, Peter, and Debbie, for always being there. To my soulmate, John Gillespie, who caught so many typos and read the copy until he was bleary-eyed, thank you for being my rock. Your patience and support made this all possible.

CHAPTER 1

Image Counts.

"Please don't make me look like a monster," defendant Sante Kimes whispered to a courtroom artist who was sketching her.

"I'm a mother, not a monster," she said, enunciating each word as if she were center stage in a Broadway play.

All eyes in Part 50 on the 11th floor of the Manhattan Criminal Court building were staring at this so-called Dragon Lady, this woman of many names and schemes. Waiting for her arraignment on fraud charges, Sante (pronounced Shan-tay) found herself seated momentarily next to courtroom artist, Jane Rosenberg. Image counts under the spotlight, so Sante began posing for the artist. She had tried to look her best that afternoon of August 5, 1998, although her efforts fell a bit short. Her painted eyebrows were crooked, as if she'd applied liner without a mirror, and the rouge on her face blazed too red for a grandmother who had just turned 64. Swept up into a messy bun, her dyed black hair was so thin that patches of scalp were exposed. She wore black slacks under a long-sleeved fitted jacket, this rare attempt at conservatism concealing most of her ample bust.

In 20 years of covering trials, Rosenberg was accustomed to defendants looking terrified at their arraignments. Not this defendant. Sante was behaving as if she owned the place. Along with her appearance, Sante focused on her codefendant, the love of her life, her son Kenny. Her eyes lit up when court officers escorted the 23-year-old to the defense table. She gazed up in adoration at the muscular six-foot-tall young man, all jaw and forehead under a head of full thick brown hair. His angular features made him look vaguely like a model from Eastern Europe, although his ancestry was a mix of Irish and Indian.

With their lawyers standing between them, mother and son craned their necks to lock eyes with each other, as two rows of newspaper, radio, and TV reporters watched their every move. It was a brief arraignment, not enough time for the 90 minutes of handholding and whispered secrets the pair indulged in at their last court appearance the month before. As soon as their handcuffs were removed that time, mother and son reached for each other. They clasped their hands tightly together, sometimes resting the mound of fingers on top of the defense table. They were a team, in a huge mess together, fused so closely that the spectators wondered about the depth and nature of their bond. Months later when they faced the nation via an appearance on the TV program *60 Minutes*, they held hands again throughout the interview.

All the reporters were staring at them that August afternoon because it seemed that everywhere they went, people vanished. Or died. A lawyer disappeared in 1991 after telling federal agents he torched Sante's home in Hawaii in an insurance scheme she'd hatched. An auditor at a Bahamas bank where the Kimes family had accounts vanished after dining with mother and son in 1996. Their acquaintance, David Kazdin, ended up dead in a Dumpster in Los Angeles on March 13, 1998, after mother and son allegedly used his name in a fraud. Finally on July 5, 1998, millionaire landlady Irene Silverman vanished from her Manhattan town house. Under an alias, Kenny had rented an apartment there and, authorities said, plotted with his mother to take over Silverman's $7 million home on one of the best blocks of the exclusive Upper East Side.

The annals of crime had never seen a pair quite like the mother and son team of Sante and Kenny Kimes. Once they had lived in a world of riches and privilege, but now ended up outcasts who dupe and intimidate others. Along the way they graduated from stealing confidences to taking lives, investigators believe. Crisscrossing the country, using aliases, filing lawsuits and insurance claims, allegedly leaving missing and murdered people in their wake, they appeared to be instigating their own crime wave. Law enforcement was always one step behind them. No detective ever connected all the dots, linked them to all these unsolved mysteries until they were arrested, almost by accident, in Manhattan on July 5, 1998. The public had never heard of them before. Suddenly they were practically household names, the focus of national news shows, subject of a British documentary, inspiration for a segment on the hit TV drama *Law and Order*.

If the allegations were true, she was Mommy Dearest and Ma Barker rolled into one and Kenny was her deadly creation. They represented family life gone terribly wrong. She seemed to exercise unnatural control over her son. When she ordered him to stay inside a room in the Silverman town house as punishment for a few hours, like a slave he obeyed. A control freak, she was the brains behind their schemes. She had a mind like a computer gone wild and apparently was compelled to write down her every move and keep copious notes. Unfortunately for her, those notes ended up forming the best evidence against her.

Why she felt the need to plot and, as prosecutors allege, kill, is not entirely clear. Obsessed with money, a legacy of an impoverished childhood, possessions filled a deep need in Sante. Under this theory, anyone who stood between her and riches was an enemy. However, no pot of gold was ever big enough. As companion for nearly a quarter century to a millionaire, Kenny's father, motel builder Kenneth Kimes, Sante had plenty of money for life's luxuries. Instead she stole items like furs, which she easily could have afforded, and enslaved her maids, forcing them to work seven days a week without wages. Something else was going on here. Logic didn't always apply, for she worked from different sock drawers than most other housewives and mothers. She seemed to like the thrill of breaking the law, living on the edge. Conflict and controversy were like card parties for her. Her past is an avalanche of lawsuits, which she started or defended herself against. Either she had the world's worst luck with the employees and lawyers who sued her or she created trouble wherever she went.

She liked to try to exercise control of people and events in her life. Psychologists said she excelled at the art of manipulation, driven by a personality disorder that made her feel as if others were out to get her. Paranoid, she pounced first but was not crazy. She knew the difference between right and wrong, but chose to ignore the conventions of society. The experts said she was clever and willful to the extreme. She got what she wanted through charm, deceit, or force. Her packaging was impressive. Once a dead-ringer for Elizabeth Taylor, she also had a mind that lured, or intimidated, and seemed to enjoy bending people to her will, fooling others, "getting over."

Like a potter shaping clay, she molded the destiny of her son Kenny. Raising him in a gilded cocoon of sumptuous homes and resorts and with private tutors, she became the center of his universe. For the most part, he grew up isolated from his peers. His mother even tried to select his friends. As a boy, he had one shot at independence when she spent four years behind bars. During her absence, he attended regular school and grew close to his late father, a successful businessman who seemed strangely passive around Sante. There were signs the couple drank too much alcohol, worsening Sante's personality disorder. Her return from jail brought back the controls, and after a brief teenaged rebellion, son bonded with mother into a single force that stayed one step ahead of the law from Hawaii to the Bahamas.

As clever as Sante was, her run finally screeched to a halt on July 5, 1998, when a bounced check for a Lincoln Town Car brought a lifetime of deceits crashing in on her and Kenny. A Utah warrant sworn out by the car dealer she allegedly swindled was the humble means to hold the mother and son in Manhattan. A month later, prosecutors also accused them of credit card fraud. Despite these relatively petty charges, they couldn't get out on bail. Authorities were preparing to accuse them of Irene Silverman's presumed murder. They were unique defendants, and the homicide case against them was unprecedented. Silverman vanished without a trace. The case lacked all the elements of a standard murder: no body, witnesses, forensic evidence, or a confession.

It did have a wily defendant in Sante, who personally ran a public relations campaign from jail. In jailhouse phone calls and face-to-face chats through the iron mesh at the attorney-client meeting room in the Criminal Courts building, Sante presided over her version of meet the press. Newspaper columnists and TV shows carried her claim that she and Kenny were innocent, that a corrupt system framed them, that the police beat them. Her timing was perfect. She wept and complained of being a Kafkaesque figure, just when the New York City police department was reeling from two of the worst human rights violations in its 153-year history. One cop in Brooklyn confessed to ramming a stick up a prisoner's rectum and four others in the Bronx faced murder charges for shooting at an unarmed man 41 times. The police looked like monsters. Sante took advantage of their public-relations disaster. After all, when under the spotlight, image counts.

CHAPTER 2

"Where is Irene?"

Stanley Patterson watched the Manhattan skyline unfurl in all its glory, but in his funk, the majesty of steel and glass cutting through the morning clouds hardly inspired him. Even in good times, his thin lips could barely curl upward in a convincing smile. He was anxious that morning of July 5, 1998, and his mouth pressed into a grim line as he thought about the FBI agents and New York City police detectives who would soon meet his America West red-eye from Las Vegas. Patterson, 53, small-boned and balding, delivered pizzas at night in the city of high rollers and lived in a trailer park. He had lost his job as a hotel boiler man a few years ago after arguing with his boss. Ever since, he worked maintenance jobs for smaller buildings but that had begun to wind down. On that plane, he was mired in the deepest swamp of this bad-luck streak. Foolishly he had supplied guns to a mother and son who seemed to be wealthy eccentrics. He could kick himself for getting mixed up with Sante Kimes and her son, Kenny, by answering their handyman want ad and running errands for them for several months.

This mother and son had deceived him, as they had so many others. Wealthy widow and college student were just some of the many roles these alleged con artists slipped into at will. She had at least 22 aliases. In fact, Patterson knew her as "Ellen" until cops clued him into her real name and criminal rec-

ord. Dating to the Kennedy Administration, her rap
sheet ranged from stealing lipsticks and furs to enslaving alien maids in her luxurious homes.

Patterson hadn't known any of this. He hadn't
known why the mother and son wanted guns, which
they called "toys." He hadn't known they were suspects in one murder in California and scams on both
coasts. Now to save himself from gun charges, he
flew to New York that Sunday in July to set a trap
for the unlikely suspects.

It was Sante's idea to meet Patterson in Manhattan
that July, giving Los Angeles detectives an unexpected break. Ever since March 13, 1998, when David
Kazdin had been shot execution style and thrown
into a Dumpster near the Los Angeles International
Airport, detectives had been searching in vain for the
mother and son. Through the gun purchases, they
had tracked down Patterson and told him the facts
of life. Help find the alleged killers or face jail. Sante
made it easier when, in hiding, she telephoned Patterson, offering him a job managing a fancy building
on Manhattan's Upper East Side. She told Patterson
a retired ballerina lived there. "She said I would
enjoy the woman's dances in the hallway at 11
o'clock at night; she was in her negligee," Patterson
said. "She said, 'I want you to manage an apartment
building.' She was calling me about three times a
day. I said, 'Sounds good to me, how much does it
pay?' and she said, 'More money than you can
imagine.' "

Worried about the sting operation, and scared of
the Kimeses, Patterson had arrived at John F. Kennedy Airport wearing a bulletproof vest under his
plaid shirt, which annoyed his handlers on the
NYPD-FBI Joint Fugitive Task Force. It's illegal in
New York for civilians to wear those vests. Besides,
it was too bulky for summer, a giveaway for an informant. They made him take it off and instead wear a

black baseball cap with the words "Lucky Dogs" on the brim. "I look like a jerk," Patterson complained. If and when Sante and Kenny arrived at the appointed meeting place, the Hilton Hotel five blocks from Central Park, Patterson was to signal the task force by removing his cap. Legal grounds to hold the pair was a Utah warrant charging that they had bounced a check to pay for their 1997 Lincoln Town Car.

Patterson and the task force waited six hours by the pay phones in the Hilton lobby for Sante that Sunday. Talking with Patterson on her cell phone, she kept promising throughout the late morning and afternoon that she would arrive momentarily. She claimed her car broke down on the Garden State Parkway in New Jersey. Finally, breezing in at five p.m., she surfaced alone, her once beautiful face packed with pancake foundation, black eye shadow, and neon pink lipstick. As eight undercover agents and detectives trailed them, Patterson and Sante waited for Kenny at the Hilton bar. Walking away from Sante to order food, Patterson whispered to the antsy undercovers, "Kenny is coming." Sante griped about paying $7.50 each for her three Seven and Sevens, and they walked outside looking for another place to drink. Across Sixth Avenue, at the Warwick Hotel on West 54th Street, they sat down inside Chao Europa, where Sante downed three glasses of wine and munched on appetizers.

Drawn to a street fair on Sixth Avenue, she strolled outside and began haggling with a merchant offering two T-shirts for $10. Although she was carrying more than $10,000 in cash, Sante bargained him down to three shirts for $10 and continued browsing. Mingling with the crowd, the undercovers saw Kenny on Sixth Avenue, a few feet behind Sante and Patterson. Kenny stayed back a few minutes, looking around to make sure they weren't being followed. Unaware of the dragnet, he walked up to his mom, and they hugged. It was shortly before seven p.m. Kenny stood by patiently as she kept bargain hunting among the stands. Patterson removed his "Lucky Dogs" cap, and the task force pounced, slapping handcuffs on Sante as she sorted through a rack of clothes. They also arrested Patterson so as not to tip off Sante and Kenny that he was an informant.

Kenny was so startled that he wet himself, soiling his black jeans.

Immediately, Sante tried to distance herself from the black vinyl purse in her hands, according to authorities. "This bag isn't mine," she said. Then she began demanding answers.

"What's this all about?" she said. "I didn't do anything. What are you doing to my son? He didn't do anything. Stanley didn't have anything to do with it." Turning to Patterson, she apologized, "I'm sorry, Stanley, I'm sorry."

Riding down to FBI headquarters at 26 Federal Plaza, a black and gray 41-story box in lower Manhattan, Sante kept insisting that the bag with $10,580 inside wasn't hers. "The bag belongs to a friend," she told Detective Michael Ryan. "The money is mine. I need the money because I'm on vacation in New York. You can't be on vacation in New York without $10,000. Who are you? I want to see the warrant. I have the right to see the warrant because I went to paralegal school. I used to be a paralegal. I know that I don't have to tell you anything."

The bag Sante tried to disown held a lifetime of paperwork and identification belonging to other people, wealthy landlady and former ballerina Irene Silverman and her late mother, Irene Zambelli. Their names appeared among seven passports, five bankbooks, three payroll stubs, and five checks. Kenny Kimes was also carrying Irene's papers, including her social security card, tax form, and American Express charge plate. He also packed a knife and brass knuckles.

Recovering his nerve after soiling his pants, Kenny gave investigators cocky answers. "This is only about the car?" he said to Detective Ryan. "If that's all this is about, I'm very happy. Sometime after I get back from Utah, I'll buy you a drink." He bantered with FBI Special Agent Emilio Blasse, but refused to answer the simplest questions.

"What's your name?" Kenny asked Blasse.

"Special Agent Blasse. What is your name?"

"Okay, Special," Kenny said. "I'm not sure I should give you my name."

"We have an arrest warrant for Kenneth Kimes," Blasse said. "Is that your name?"

"What if it's not?"

"Then we will let you go," the agent said.

A little while later, Kenny asked, "How's my mother doing? Can I speak to my mother?"

"She's fine," Blasse said.

"Mom, is everything okay?" Kenny shouted to the next room.

"Yeah, Kenny, I'm fine," Sante replied.

"Are all these cards yours?" Blasse asked him.

"Well, Special," Kenny replied, "not out of any disrespect, but I refuse to answer that."

Unknown to Blasse and Ryan, at that moment 100 city blocks to the north, other detectives were searching for the true owner of those cards in a town house jammed with Baccarat crystal, white gardenia plants, and a rainbow of textiles lovingly collected over a lifetime. Former ballerina Irene Silverman, all of five-feet and 115 pounds, hadn't walked the streets of Manhattan alone in 15 years. Petite but feisty, she owned a five-story beaux-arts mansion on East 65th Street. For extra income and companionship, she had converted her home into luxury apartments, which she managed. "Interesting tenants, short-term," she told *New York Times* real estate columnist Christopher Gray in 1990. "Something between posh hotel and grand boardinghouse." Like a queen bee, she stayed close to home. Although a millionaire, the 82-year-old didn't even own a car. She hired limousines and did errands accompanied by someone from her nine-person staff of maids and handymen.

That Sunday evening, July 5, 1998, nobody had seen her at home since late morning. Dressed in a floral-patterned nightgown, she had been reading and chatting on the phone in her first-floor bedroom office. Also missing was a new tenant who had been rude to her, a young man named Manny Guerrin renting a first-floor apartment just 35 feet from her quarters. At first glance, he had seemed respectable when applying for the $6,000 a month rental in mid-June. A green-eyed Gen-Xer, he wore a suit, neatly slicked back his thick brown hair, drove a Lincoln Town Car, and dropped the name of a mutual friend. He called himself a Web-page designer and paid cash for the first month's rent. Still, Irene noticed his limp, his boxer's nose, the way his eyes blazed and later joked to a friend, "he looks like he just got out of jail." Usually she checked references or relied on gut instinct. Although her assets totaled $9 million, Irene had a cash flow problem that month after paying about $34,000 in real estate taxes and insurance fees. Momentarily hungry for cash, she gave Manny Guerrin the keys to Apartment 1B on June 14, 1998.

It was the last apartment she would ever rent.

Although a landlady for the past 41 years, ever since her rich husband bought the landmark building, she had diluted the exclusivity of living at 20 East 65th Street. When her realtor husband died of lymphatic cancer in 1980 and her mother died five years later, Irene expanded the rental space in her turn-of-the-century mansion. It was an illegal conversion, since her building was zoned only for five apartments and a doctor's office. She wanted to raise money for a worthy cause—a public museum, dedicated to the sewing arts and garment workers, in memory of her late mother, Irene Zambelli, an expert seamstress. Instead of a few carefully screened tenants who stayed for years, Irene turned her home into a 10-unit hotel open to a parade of well-heeled guests paying about $200 a night. Her Depression-era youth made her cautious with a buck. Renters were a great way to defray costs and pay for her large staff. Her prices were competitive with Manhattan hotel rates, and she provided maid service; unlike the hotels, she offered privacy and the intimate feeling of staying in a French salon. Each of the 10 apartments bore her love of design and comfort. Soft velvet chairs and richly embroidered pillows hand sewn by her mother, seamstress Irene Meladakis Zambelli, filled the rooms. Guests became loyal repeat customers. Brokers at Feathered Nest, her realtor, dubbed Apartment 3M the "Jennifer Grey" room, because the actress famous for the film *Dirty Dancing* stayed there so often. Like all the rooms, every detail radiated warmth, from the wood-burning fireplace, to the fabric floral walls to the green-and-white striped carpet to the upholstered chairs.

Manny Guerrin clashed with this ordered world from the start. According to prosecutors, each time he opened the mansion's black iron doors, he ducked to avoid two security cameras trained on the entranceway. He ushered in other people, including an older woman and a younger Latino man, who also hid their faces. He didn't sign the rental agreement that asked for employer information, date of birth, social security number, and authorization for a credit check. Spending entire days in his room, he stared through the peephole for hours. His spying was obvious to anyone in the first-floor hallway because his feet showed through a space between the floor and the bottom of the door to Apartment 1B. Catching Guerrin there, one of Irene's staffers used to cover the peephole with his hand as he walked by.

A weird game of cat-and-mouse began between Irene and Guerrin. Irene started jotting notes about the newcomer, who in turn secretly kept a diary of her movements and habits, including the time she awoke and retired.

Guerrin tried to sow discontent among the staff, telling one Ethiopian immigrant that he had no future there and urging another staffer to quit because Irene had bad-mouthed her. The strange new tenant refused to allow the staff inside to clean his room. When one maid managed to open the door and saw an antique cabinet in pieces, Silverman considered evicting Guerrin. But she was a butterfly facing an F-16.

The Sunday that prosecutors say was Irene's last day alive, the mansion was empty that afternoon except for one maid and Guerrin. The night before, Irene served hot dogs to several friends to mark Independence Day. That Sunday, July 5, was a typical summer morning on the Upper East Side, where most of the rich had already fled to beaches on the eastern end of Long Island. Irene's lone tenant still in town, TV producer Peter Jacobson, husband of *Nanny* sitcom star Fran Drescher, left around noon. One of the maids, Marta Rivera, had slept over. Around 11 A.M., Irene buzzed her. Marta visited Irene in her first-floor bedroom office, copying down some phone numbers and brushing the older woman's hair, a beauty ritual they practiced every Sunday that often included a manicure and pedicure. The maid left to walk Georgie, Irene's boxer, on the garden rooftop and do chores in the basement, which had been converted into a giant kitchen and washroom. Irene placed her last phone call shortly before noon to a girlfriend in Fairview, New Jersey, who was suffering heart problems. According to a note Irene jotted down, Guerrin walked into her office just down the hall from his apartment around that time and asked her for a copy of *Barron's*, the financial weekly, or *The Wall Street Journal*, papers Irene didn't have. She noted the teeth marks left by the comb he used to slick his hair.

Around 1:30 P.M., another girlfriend called Irene and assumed she was sleeping when she didn't pick up. Shortly afterward Guerrin, the tenant who never let anyone inside his apartment, suddenly clamored for maid service. Telephoning Marta, he asked her to come up from the basement and clean his apartment. She said there was no maid service on Sundays but would check with Mrs. Silverman and get back to him. A short time later Guerrin called again, now insisting the maid straighten up his place, promising her a good tip. Marta refused, saying she didn't want to disturb Mrs. Silverman. On the security monitor in the basement, Marta spotted a figure in a white shirt leaving the mansion and assumed it was Guerrin, the only one left inside at that point besides Irene. Sometime between three and four p.m., the phone rang and a strange voice began giving Marta orders. Sounding like a man but calling herself "Lucy," the caller gave Marta instructions purportedly from Irene. The maid was supposed to say nothing to any tax men who might come by, and she was to take the dog home with her.

Spooked now, Marta went upstairs to the first floor and pounded on Irene's door. No one answered. The maid called Irene's girlfriend back, who in turn contacted the rental agent and headed to the mansion herself. When the rental agent heard the message on his answering machine, he ran to the 19th police precinct and then sprinted over to Irene's. Detectives arrived, and Marta and the others convinced them that something was dreadfully wrong, that Irene never ventured outside alone. She didn't just wander away. And they told the cops about the strange new tenant who also vanished that day. Patrol cops began searching the neighborhood and checking area hospitals, while Detective Tommy Hovagim manned the phones all night inside the mansion.

Back at 26 Federal Plaza, FBI agents had tracked a parking ticket stub Kenny was carrying to the Kinney garage at 100 West 44th Street. Arriving there about 10:30 Sunday night, Special Agents David Stone and Robert Bendetson found the forest-green Lincoln Town Car the Kimeses were accused of stealing. On the floor by the front seat lay an empty box for a stun gun, stuffed plastic bags jammed the backseat. A peach comforter covered the bags. In contrast, the car trunk was completely empty, the spare tire and jack switched to the backseat. Without a search warrant, the agents didn't comb through the bags in the Lincoln that night but drove it to FBI headquarters. Through the evening, other agents continued to question the mother and son. Sante was more talkative.

"Is this really only about a Utah warrant?" she asked Detective Ryan about 8:30 P.M. "It says on here (the warrant) one of my names is 'The Dragon Lady.' Okay, I'll tell you my name. My real name is Sandra Louise Walker, and I'm from Oklahoma."

"The cell phone is not mine," she said about 11:15 P.M., then a short while later added, "We'll clear all this up. It's just a misunderstanding. I have all the paperwork." Just before midnight, she said, "Irene Silverman is a friend of mine. She's a ballerina. She lets me hold her papers and documents sometimes."

Somehow the FBI agents and cops who arrested Sante and Kenny and found them with Irene's papers didn't check to see if the former ballerina was all right. They didn't hear about the manhunt at the mansion for Irene and the mysterious tenant. This embarrassing communications breakdown lasted another full day as body-sniffing dogs combed the town house and a police artist interviewed the staff to prepare a wanted poster for the tenant with the slicked-back hair, known as Manny Guerrin.

Deputy Police Inspector Joseph Reznick, commander of Manhattan North detectives, displayed this sketch during an eight p.m. press conference Monday, July 6 when appealing to the public for anyone who had seen this man, wanted for questioning in Irene's disappearance, to come forward. "We have an elderly female who has disappeared very mysteriously," he told reporters assembled at the 19th precinct on East 67th Street. "We have an occupant of an apartment—who she rented to less than three weeks ago—who has also disappeared mysteriously. We are looking at two individuals who have just vanished."

Well, Irene had vanished. Manny Guerrin was right under the nose of law enforcement, though nobody realized it at first. Hearing the name Irene Silverman on the news, it dawned on a member of the Joint Fugitive task force that Kenny Kimes was Manny Guerrin. Reznick screamed over the screwup and sent 19th precinct Detective Thomas Hackett rushing down to 26 Federal Plaza to question the Kimeses first thing on Tuesday morning. He showed Sante the *Daily News* front page for July 7, 1998: "EAST SIDE MYSTERY." The subhead added "82-year-old millionaire missing from her mansion" alongside Guerrin's sketch and Irene's photograph. "How do I know that this is a real newspaper?" Sante said. "You could have printed this newspaper up yourself. I think you should put your energy toward finding this woman. Maybe she's out walking her dog. Maybe after I speak to my lawyer, I can tell you what you need to know."

Irene Silverman's body was nowhere to be found. From garbage dumps in the Bronx, to trash bins around the airports in Queens, to the swamps of the New Jersey Meadowlands, to the wooded areas and fields of Central Park, searchers came up empty. At One Police Plaza, the 14-story headquarters for the NYPD, New York City Police Commissioner Howard Safir began each staff meeting with this pointed question to his chief of detectives, "Where is Irene?" There would be no answer.

Scrambling to recover lost time, the NYPD threw 50 detectives onto the case. Despite a paper trail to Irene's demise as obvious as the yellow brick road, New York authorities faced an awesome task trying to get enough evidence to bring to trial and convict the Kimeses. Without a corpse, the murder case against mother and son hinged on circumstantial evidence minus two crucial pieces usually present in rare no-body cases: forensic evidence or a confession, either by the suspects or overheard by an informant. Barring a surprise saved for trial, there was no forensic evidence. No hair, fiber, DNA, or the like connected Irene to the pair. Any confession seemed a long shot. Mother and son barely gave cops their names and then launched a publicity blitz proclaiming their innocence.

The country's top journalists angled for interviews with the Kimeses. The case fascinated the public. It had all the ingredients of a classic crime tale: mystery, intrigue, great wealth and glamour, and suspects whom the authorities considered truly evil. On the surface, they seemed the flesh-and-blood versions of Lilly Dillon and her son Roy, the con artists unmasked in Jim Thompson's brilliant 1963 novel, *The Grifters*, made into a film noir classic in 1990. Headline writers soon gave the Kimeses that title as well. They were more complicated than grifters, however. Scam artists rarely graduate from taking things to stealing lives. The pride of the con man is to fleece his marks without them realizing it, luring victims to participate in scams in hopes of a payday that never comes. Murder is not this slick and is never smooth. Also the Kimeses weren't poor, but they were accused of being cold-blooded in the quest for riches. The dynamic between mother and son seemed as murky as the suspense tale they brought to Manhattan. It was set in motion a lifetime ago, in a past filled with signs of all that was to come.

CHAPTER 3

"She was very vivacious, sparkling eyes, always had a smile."

Candy. That's the name Sante liked when she was 20 years old and college senior Bill Truman* was happy to oblige when a girl looked that sweet. Cascades of black hair fell like a veil of soft cashmere around her face. It swept across her forehead in a small wave that framed gray eyes and round cheeks that photographed so well when she modeled. Then there was her figure, what men had in mind when they said hourglass. Tight sweaters made her breasts rise like hills above a tiny waist that looked even smaller next to the flared skirt flowing to her ankles. Later, Truman learned about her trick, a corset that hooked up the back.

Sitting behind "Candy" Chambers in journalism class at the University of California at Santa Barbara, he flipped her pigtail. That started the laughing, teasing, flirting, joking, dating, and loving that filled his senior year with such crazy joy. She was his first real girlfriend, and they romanced on one of America's most beautiful campuses. Set on a lagoon on the Gold Coast, UCSB had secluded spots where ducks swam under hanging palm trees. This being 1954 and he being a conservative guy headed for military duty with the ROTC, desire was left wanting. "Certain parts of my anatomy ached for hours," he remembered. "I was just excited to be around her." After

*Not his real name.

more than a year together, they had sex just once, he said, in what he thought was a brief, careful encounter.

They talked so much during those first months, her words spilling forth in a low sexy lilt that held him because she was as clever as she was beautiful. A good student who earned B's or better, she matched the grade in geology class of his buddy who became a geologist. The one area she seemed dense about was her effect on men. "She was a good tease, and when men would chase her, she acted as if she didn't know why," Truman said.

As infatuated as he was, Truman saw that Candy was a tempest of emotions. At a party, he said she threw a fit when he shared an innocent dance with another girl. Behind the wheel once, she sped like a maniac to wake him from a nap in the backseat just because she wanted some attention. Another time as he drove, she tried to pry open the door and jump out at 40 miles an hour after he talked about breaking up. Handsome, athletic, and smart, he had everything but money. Six feet three and 195 pounds, he was on a basketball scholarship and also made the varsity football team. After finishing ROTC, he planned to get his master's in physical education.

" 'I want to land you,' she'd always say," Truman recalled. "And I said, 'What do you mean by that?' And she'd say, 'I just want to land you.' " With other men chasing her, including a high school boyfriend back home in Carson City, Nevada, Truman instead held back. Although smitten, and perhaps in love, he listened to his rational side, which found her too needy, jealous, impulsive, and willful to marry.

By early 1956, they were moving in different circles. She had transferred to the University of California at Berkeley, while he reported to Fort Benning, Georgia, for four months of basic officer training. Then, according to Truman, a letter from Candy a few weeks later changed his life. "It said, 'I'm pregnant,' " Truman recalled. This emergency overrode all rational objections to marrying his beautiful impetuous girl. His commanding officer let him have leave, and on May 9, 1956, he wed Sandra "Candy" Chambers in her parents' living room. The couple hid the pregnancy, telling the relatives that he was a lonely soldier boy who couldn't live without her.

However, in truth, there was no pregnancy, Truman soon learned. This news did not shock him. He did not accuse Candy of lying or jumping to conclusions or forcing him to the altar. Instead he was relieved and viewed the false alarm as the excuse he needed to follow his heart and be with her.

She had other ideas.

Honorably discharged from the army, Truman continued as planned to graduate school at California State University at Long Beach. Candy had dropped out of college and was keeping house for him. He worked at a paint store during the day and took classes at night. She knew her young husband planned to coach high school sports, but she began talking about how much more money he could make going into sales. "She said, 'Go sell insurance, it has a better future,' " he remembered. "There was somebody willing to bring me into sales. For me, I didn't want to sell, and I said that."

Just as he was about to graduate in the spring of 1957, a job at a local high school opened up and Candy accompanied him on the interview. He was hired, and she promptly left him. Without warning, she just called from the road and said she wasn't coming back. "I wasn't going to be rich teaching, and I figured she said to herself, 'Hey, I'm not going to stick with this,' " he said.

Under oath for many lawsuits in later years, Sandra Santee Sante Louise Singhrs Chambers Walker Kimes has time and again neglected to mention her brief first marriage when asked for her biography. Perhaps she is ashamed of what happened, but the marriage is telling about what shaped her model-pretty youth and led to such notoriety in her golden years. Driven to have her own way, she either lied or exaggerated about a phantom pregnancy. Equating money with security, or maybe even love, she tried to manipulate Truman into changing careers. Throughout her life, she's been accused of lying and trying to control others. Her pattern is like an old tattoo. Time may fade its beauty and color, but the outline stays on the skin. She's followed it for years.

Born July 24, 1934, on a farm in Oklahoma City, Oklahoma, she was the youngest of three children from an unlikely marriage. Her mother Mary belonged to an established Dutch-American family from Illinois, the Van Horns, while her father had a more exotic background. His name was Prame Singhrs, identified on her birth certificate as a farmer from India. Years later, Sante called her father variously a Hindu religious leader, a teacher, and "an important man." She was only two or three years old when he died or, in another telling, abandoned the family. "I have memories that he was very kind, and I have memories that he was very, like you, handsome and dark and just very nice-looking," she told an attorney during a 1989 deposition. "I was so young, I'm not sure I am right. I was just a little girl, just a baby."

When Sante was born, her mother Mary Van Horn, then 36, and Prame Singhrs, 44, must have made an unusual couple in Depression era Oklahoma, a time and place nature and man both made miserable. Dust bowl winds whipped the plains into a fury, while America's economic nosedive bankrupted farmers like Singhrs. Just as the Joads in John Steinbeck's epic novel, *The Grapes of Wrath*, had, Sante's family journeyed west to California in hopes of a better life. It's difficult to confirm Sante's version of her early life because as an adult she kept changing details of what sounded like a dreadful childhood on the streets of Los Angeles. Fending for the kids by herself, Mary Van Horn begged for food. Sometimes Sante described her mother as an alcoholic who became a prostitute to feed her kids. "I would have to say I hated my mother," she said in a 1986 sentencing report. "She was never home, and it seemed like when she was, she was drunk or had a different 'date' with her. She was hard on us kids; she'd hit us when she was drunk. I just remember being starved and hungry all the time, and there was never any money. We didn't even have a refrigerator, just a little hot plate that we used to warm soup up and things like that." Yet a few years after giving this account, she wavered when asked if her mother was involved in prostitution: "I am told by attorneys or specialists, when they are talking, they think so," she said in 1989. "I never really saw it, no."

Picking up the long narrative she gave about her life in 1986, Sante described a childhood tragedy worthy of *Les Miserables*, the novel about a hungry man whose life is ruined when he steals some bread. Caught at age 10 trying to steal cheese, Sante said the shopkeeper called the police. At first the patrolman seemed kind, didn't arrest her, and returned to take the street urchin to parks and the movies. In the first of many sexually charged allegations she has lobbed at people throughout her life, Sante said this cop began molesting her, the abuse lasting three to four months. "All I can remember is that he was a very nice man who was very kind to me, except for wanting to fondle me," she said. "I knew it was wrong and it bothered me quite a bit and I went to some friends to get help."

Those friends were Dorothy Seligman and her husband, Kelly, Los Angeles merchants with a soft spot for the olive-skinned street kid with the sweet face who kept hanging around their malt shop and movie theater in the mid 1940s. The couple started feeding her, gave her money for busing tables, and turned her life around. They confronted the cop, and he disappeared from her life, Sante said. Then the Seligmans arranged for Sante to be adopted by Dorothy's sister in Carson City, Nevada, a town of 5,000 people that still had the feel of the Old West. From the turn of the century until 1963, it was America's tiniest state capital. Sante says that she boarded a bus in Los Angeles and looked out the window as her world changed.

Passing through the Mojave Desert, the 12-year-old gazed up as the peaks of the Sierra Nevada jutted out of the wasteland. Juniper and piñon pines lined the rising road that followed Carson River. The final leg of the journey through alfalfa farms and cattle herds ended in an all-American ranch-style home, brick with redwood siding. "It was the most important thing that ever happened to me," Sante said. "I went from nothing to everything. I had my own room and new clothes and very nice parents."

Mary Thelma Cunningham Chambers and her husband, Nevada Army National Guard Colonel Edwin Paul Chambers, couldn't have children of their own. Both were in their mid-40s, also the adoptive parents of a boy six years younger than their exotic-looking new daughter whom they welcomed to their home at 1602 North Division Street in Carson City.

Like Sante, Colonel Chambers was an Oklahoman, hailing from the town of Shawnee. As a teenager, he rushed to join the navy in World War I. He enlisted again during the Depression and stayed through World War II, rising through the ranks of the Army Air Corps as a maintenance, supply, and ordinance officer at various airbases. Promoted to major by war's end, he started a full-time job with Nevada's

Army National Guard in 1947, in charge of all their
equipment, maintenance shops, and federal appropri-
ations for basics like munitions, jeeps, tanks, and uniforms. His wife Mary, who had been a script girl in
Hollywood and told stories of Bing Crosby getting
drunk on the set, worked as a bookkeeper for the
Guard.

If not for his stutter, the colonel could be taken for
a silver-haired Clark Gable, with his thin mustache,
proud bearing, and way of appearing always as if he
just left a haberdashery. "I swear I'd see him out
mowing the lawn, and he looked like he was going
to the finest party in the world," said Thelma
Kaweski, his secretary in the Guard. "When he wore
jeans, it was like he stepped out of *Esquire* magazine." Sante said he looked like Walter Pidgeon, only
better. "He was the handsomest man I ever met. He
was almost like an Englishman, tall, very immaculate
in his dress and proper in his manner."

In the 1950s, Carson City seemed more a village
than a state capital, with people knowing everything
about their neighbors. "It was a close-knit community," said Jo Ann Foster, Sante's high school classmate. "My mother had a grapevine that would have
made the Russians envious. There were a lot of do-
gooders who felt it was their duty to call your parents and tell what you were doing before you did it,
so you didn't have the opportunity to get into trouble." When the olive-skinned girl, known in those
days as Sandy Singers and then Sandy Chambers,
suddenly joined their class, kids at Carson High
School realized she had been adopted. Some knew
about her rough childhood in Los Angeles and others
heard gossip about her natural mother.

At Carson High, Sante had only 41 other students
in her class. As a 14-year-old freshman, she wasn't
late or absent the entire school year and earned four
Bs, an A in vocal music chorus, and a C in math.

Maintaining a B average throughout her four years, she joined all the standard clubs of the day: 4-H, Future Homemakers of America, and the Girl's Athletic Association. In her junior year she was secretary of the Spanish club and became coeditor of the school's paper her senior year.

She bonded with classmate Ruth Thom, daughter of the town's favorite doctor, and wherever Sandy ventured, Ruth followed. They rode horses together, double-dated, wore the same clothes, and joined the same clubs. When Sandy wrote for the school's weekly, called "Chatters," Ruth became the staff typist. "She was great, we were the best of friends, we always had a lot of fun," remembered Ruth. "She joined groups, she loved working on the Carson 'Chatters.' " Sandy wrote a column called "I am Carson High," which assumed the voice of the building and happily witnessed hay rides, proms, track team victories, student operettas, and the like. Once she chided the kids about vandalism. "Why, do you know that in one day alone I was plastered with gum on my back and on my desks?" she wrote in the issue of October 20, 1950. "That really makes me feel sad! So please stop sticking gum on me, and also please stop cutting me up! A building can only take so much!" Mostly she noted happy events with a carefree air. "Hi, everyone!" she wrote when she was 16. "Happy Spring Fever! Seems as though lately all of you have that faraway look in your eyes. Oddly enough, this strange-airy-wanting-to-get-away-from-it-all feeling is not a strange sickness; it's just spring fever!"

"She was very vivacious, sparkling eyes, always had a smile," said classmate Duane Glanzmann, president of their senior class. "She had a sense of humor, but at times there were off-the-wall comments. Sometimes we were serious in a class and she'd raise her hand and she'd say something and it seemed to us, it was off-the-wall, but it did lighten things up."

While her beauty attracted boys, beyond Ruth, she had trouble making girlfriends. She wore gobs of powdery white makeup over her olive complexion, which was noticeably darker than her classmates' skin. She even shaved her forearms, as one girl discovered when she bumped into her in gym class. Her steady boyfriend was Edward Walker, a track and basketball star a grade behind her. "She sort of dominated him, controlled him," said Georgia Myers, the prom queen in Sandy's senior class of 1952. "She always said what they would do and where they would go." Walker said Sandy had trouble making friends. "During the time she was in school, she didn't have many friends," he said in court papers. "It seemed like she was afraid to trust people and was afraid to let people get close to her. I think that extended even to her stepparents. They were warm people; although she liked them, they didn't have the closest relationship. She never talked about her early life."

Myers and classmate Jo Ann Foster said Sandy alienated other students by being too pushy and several run-ins left her somewhat shunned. She ran for office her freshman and sophomore years, but lost each race. "She was very manipulative, she liked to sort of control people, what they did," said Myers. "She liked to cause trouble between friends. She tried to break up friendships before people got onto her and sort of drifted away from her, saying things about a person to another person." Jo Ann remembered that she and another student were voted cheerleaders in the eighth grade, but Sandy pulled an end run. On their own Sandy and Ruth bought uniforms and ran onto the basketball court before the designated cheerleaders arrived. Once she promised the junior prom committee that her famous aunt could help with the festivities. The phantom aunt never showed.

"She ruled Ruth with an iron hand," said Jo Ann. "Ruth would do nothing until Sandy okayed it. That's why all of us branched away from her. Sandy was a control freak who wanted to own all of us. It was why we moved away from her except for and during school activities."

Mary Chambers fussed over Sandy's clothes and schedule, and worried about her daughter. She hinted to friends that Sandy was rebellious and always wanted her own way. "I was fussing about my little girl, who was six at the time," said Thelma Kaweksi. "And Mary said, 'Don't worry, Thelma, little problems get to be big problems.' Sandy was a teenager then, not doing what her parents thought she should be doing."

Kathryn Etchart was the chief requisition clerk for the Army National Guard and close to Mary Chambers, who organized her wedding shower. "Mary did tell me that she did adopt Sandy from the streets of Los Angeles and she was a street child of Hindu descent," said Kathryn. "I think with Sandy, she adopted her because she felt sorry for her. All I remember about Sandy is that she was a chronic liar. You couldn't believe anything she said. You never knew if she was telling the truth about anything."

In her senior year, Sandy followed the Carson tradition and "bequeathed" items to the junior class. For a woman whose life became a magnet for trouble, her will is ironic. "I, calm-natured Sandy Chambers, do hereby will to Mazey Smith my celestial-like ability of being able to avoid all types of trouble and embarrassing predicaments. To (another student), I will my outstanding ability to oversome (sic) the temptations of intoxicating beverages, a difficult assignment for some of my masculine classmates."

Her senior year, she participated in "Girl's State,"

a weeklong conference where the best students throughout Nevada pretend to be political candidates, hold an election, and start a mock government. Jo Ann Foster was the choice from Carson High, but a scheduling conflict with a 4-H event let Sandy go instead. At the fancy dress dinner capping "Girl's State," Sandy looked beautiful and happy in a flowing off-the-shoulder gown with bows on top of butterfly sleeves. From the wide smile on her face down to the white sandals on her feet, she was the essence of young womanhood circa 1952.

This happy picture of her life in Carson City was just a façade, she claimed years later. Sante said she had been keeping a terrible secret about her time in Carson City. After being convicted of enslaving her Latina maids, in 1986 at the age of 52, Sante Kimes was angling for therapy instead of jail time. Seeking mercy from the court, she charged that her adoptive father, Colonel Chambers, had been raping her throughout her seemingly carefree years in Carson City. Friends of the family couldn't believe this happened. They doubted that the small town's mighty grapevine and Sante's best friend failed to uncover this alleged abuse. Colonel Chambers was an honorable man, they said. Sante varied on the dates, saying the rapes started when she was 11, lasting until she was 18 or, in another telling, from ages 12 to 17. Colonel Chambers, the man who rescued her from poverty on the streets of Los Angeles, had been dead for six years when she branded him a rapist, weeping as she told this story in 1986. Mary Chambers had been dead for almost 17 years when Sante would say these words:

"I matured at an early age and looked years older than I was when I was 12 or 13," she began. "I was aware that older guys looked at me, and looking back on it, I can see where my father took advantage of things. I never told anyone for years, probably because I was starved for attention, and it's hard to explain, but I really liked him.

"I know it sounds like a terrible thing to say, but I've had mixed feelings about this all my life. I'm mixed up to this day on my feelings about this because I really loved my father. He was incredibly handsome and so perfect in many ways. I told my adoptive mother after four or five years, and the news turned the family into a bad situation. She never forgave me or her husband, and they often quarreled after that. I ran away several times because she got very strict with me, and totally changed the way she acted toward me.

"I can understand how she must have felt. If my father tried to stick up for me, she attacked him for protecting me. Right after I graduated from high school, she told me that she wanted me out of the house and called me a tramp. I feel terrible for what I did to her, she treated me with love and I hurt her."

CHAPTER 4

High Times with Kimes.

The rape and incest Sante cried about later in life did not seem to affect her grades or attendance during the years she was allegedly violated. She finished 12th in her class of 42 seniors, earning two A's and three B's and missing only two and a half days of school. Now coeditor of "Chatters," she joined the yearbook club and also auditioned and won a supporting role in the senior class production of *Minick.* She played the wife of a friend who talked sense into Minick, an old man trying to mimic the life of his newlywed son. Active in the chorus, she joined in singing "Thank God for a Garden" and "In the Time of Roses" during graduation ceremonies held Friday evening June 6, 1952, in the school's gymnasium. Judge Charles M. Merrill, associate justice of Nevada's Supreme Court, called his commencement address "Open Door to Opportunity."

Ruth Thom remained her sidekick for two years after they graduated and left Carson City. Both took a six-week secretarial course in nearby Reno that summer of 1952, then roomed together in the nearest large city, Sacramento, California's capital and a magnet for Nevada's young people. Both women landed clerical jobs. Typing by day, Sante, known as Sandy in those days, wrote short stories and poems by night, with faithful Ruth taking dictation. She had a flair for fiction, said her friend. "She would talk, I would type away," Ruth said. "She was a very good writer, very imaginative, and would try to do short stories, fiction. Her themes were things that she knew when she was with Mary and Ed Chambers in Carson. She would make up things that happened to her in the family." She set her heart on a writing career but only collected rejection slips from magazines. "I liked to write poetry, but never published anything," she said years later.

Determined to write, Sante decided she needed the polish of a college education. In September 1952, she and Ruth enrolled at the San Francisco College for Women, a small Catholic school atop Lone Mountain Hill. "She and I were just like Ethel and Lucy," said Ruth. "There were just the two of us, and we were on the town and having a ball. In San Francisco we were in the Salvation Army Hotel for women." However, Sante wanted more journalism courses and transferred to a bigger school, the University of California at Santa Barbara where she met her first husband.

When she left him in the spring of 1957, she returned to the arms of her old high school boyfriend, Edward Walker. He became her second husband on November 9, 1957, and they moved to Sacramento. Walker built homes as a general contractor while she constructed a new identity and role. With a personality as effervescent as champagne and looks that turned heads, she was a natural born saleswoman. She started working in promotions, public relations, and sales for various firms and did well, Walker said.

Now calling herself Santeé, with an accent on the last "e," she started a welcoming service called "Hi! Welcome to California." (She eventually settled on Sante, which is how she will be referred to hereafter.) According to its incorporation papers, this nonprofit civic league's purpose, "shall be to welcome new people, bring in industry, and generally engage in activities to encourage progress, stimulate interest, and foster goodwill, for and throughout the State of California." Adept at public relations, Sante landed in the *Sacramento Union* on August 12, 1960, with a cheery blurb for her company. Dressed in a scoop neck peasant blouse and flowing skirt and smiling as she posed with a dog, she plugged her business. "Sacramento's Top Welcomer, Santee Walker shows off a unique member added to her greeting staff—a wire-haired pooch called Martian. A girl dog, Martian's name fits in with Sacramento Welcoming Center's slogan: 'Sacramento Is Out of This World.' And that, says Santee, is what she's trying to teach the dog to say. Santee and her 18 greeters—plus Martian—plan to open a new welcoming center soon near American River Junior College."

As with her first husband, she urged her second, Edward Walker, to earn more money. He began in his father's plastering business, but Sante pushed him into studying architecture. She talked about finances so much, Walker began to feel like his marriage had become a series of business meetings. "She has an extreme fear about being poor or not having any money," Walker said in court papers. "She has always been absolutely obsessive about it. This led to problems between us because she felt that I wasn't bringing in the money fast enough, and she was always pushing me to get up the ladder faster." Yet for all her talk of getting ahead, she could wildly overspend, as Walker discovered one Christmas. "About 1960 or so, she went out and spent about $13,000 on gifts for everybody," he said. "I can't tell you how shocked I was when I found out. That was the equivalent of a year's wages or more back then, and she blew it all just for Christmas gifts. We paid off all the debts because most of the items she bought had been given away. It took a long time and caused real problems." Walker began to think his generous but money-hungry wife had a split personality.

"She's attractive and intelligent, but sometimes she's just totally out of control, and she can't help herself," he said. "I'm convinced she does these things without much deliberation."

Less than a year after Ed and Sante moved into 4931 Hemlock Avenue, an accidental fire "partially damaged and destroyed" their home on December 18, 1960. Walker sued to increase the $10,000 settlement their insurance company offered. This was the first known lawsuit linked to Sante. Seven months before the fire, Walker claimed he reached an agreement with Farmers Insurance Exchange to insure the structure for $10,000, the contents for $4,000, and living expenses for $2,000. The company paid the $10,000 but balked at the extra $6,000, suggesting that coverage was only discussed, not sealed by a contract. Walker filed the suit on July 23, 1962, but let it languish, and the court dismissed the claim four years later.

Tensions in their marriage flared on February 21, 1961, when police arrested Sante for stealing a hair dryer she could have easily bought. "We went out shopping one day in Sacramento, and we were in a store together when she disappeared," Walker said. "I looked all over for her and finally went to the manager of the store to find out if he had seen her. I found out that she had been arrested for trying to take a hair dryer. I just couldn't believe it. We had plenty of money to buy a hair dryer or almost anything else, but for some reason she just took it. As time went on, it happened several more times, and it seemed like her compulsion began to get worse." This petty-theft charge against her at age 26 was the start of bizarre encounters with the law throughout her lifetime. Time and again authorities accused Sante of stealing inexpensive items like lipstick or lifting luxuries she didn't need or could have afforded.

Walker stayed in the marriage, despite an even bigger embarrassment. In her divorce, the wife of a millionaire publicly labeled Sante the home-wrecker. The case grabbed headlines in the *Sacramento Bee*. Worse still, the millionaire husband was a prosperous land developer who had hired Walker. This developer, Everett Earl Wagner, met Sante's husband in September 1961 at his office at Winding Creek Way in Fair Oaks. Wagner asked him to build three homes in a new residential development, called Sleepy Hollow Acres, in nearby Placer County, just east of the capital. Sante's husband spent the first six months of 1962 making sure the homes were just right, doing extra landscaping and electrical work that Wagner wanted. The millionaire could have been a great contact for the young builder. He owned 3,900 acres of property near Folsom Lake outside of Sacramento and elsewhere in the area. In Canada, he controlled 17 oil wells and a 16-unit motel. However, 17 days after Wagner's wife filed for divorce on January 4, 1963, Walker also sued the developer, claiming he refused to pay $7,856.63 owed on the Sleepy Hollow construction. Then on Valentine's Day 1963, June Wagner added this bombshell to her divorce papers, claiming that her husband and Sante had sex for about two years in the Sleepy Hollow development and in Edward Walker's office:

"That on or about the first day of September 1961, and at diverse times thereafter, at Sleepy Hollow, Placer County, California, and at Winding Creek Way, Fair Oaks, California, the said defendant committed adultery with one SANTEE WALKER, and ever since the said date has been and still is, living in adulterous intercourse with the said SANTEE WALKER, in the state of California."

In a written reply, Wagner, then 39 years old, denied the affair, but he did not contest his wife's divorce action. The court file does not contain any response from Sante, who couldn't have been pleased that the *Sacramento Bee* headlined her alleged role as the other woman, identifying her as "operator of a welcoming service." Complicating this soap opera further, a month later, Sante and her husband sued Wagner for $220,000, alleging that he assaulted them at 11:30 P.M. on March 18, 1963, prompting another newspaper story. "Woman Named in Triangle is Involved in Suit," said the headline. In the end, the court granted June Wagner, 35, an uncontested divorce on the grounds of extreme cruelty, not the adultery charge. She won custody and child support for their three kids, ages 7 to 14, as well as 30 percent of the couple's considerable holdings, the motel, and a home in Canada, $250 a month in alimony payments, and attorney's fees. Ed Walker won his suit for nonpayment against developer Everett Wagner, who was ordered to pay a total of $8,774.96 to cover the principal, fees, and court costs. Court records don't indicate what happened to the assault case Sante and Ed Walker filed against Wagner.

In the midst of all this, Sante became pregnant and at the age of 29, she gave birth to her first child on September 27, 1963, a boy the couple named Kent Edward Walker. Years later Sante would claim to a court-appointed psychiatrist and a sentencing consultant that Kent's real father was her secret lover, a businessman 20 years her senior from Southern California. Then in subsequent depositions, she switched and said Edward Walker fathered Kent.

The Walkers left the scandal in Sacramento, opting for a fresh start in Southern California. Untamed by motherhood, Sante lapsed into bad habits. Three times over five days surrounding New Year's 1966, police charged her with stealing in Los Angeles, Norwalk, and Beverly Hills. "I got home from work and found the house full of cops," said Walker. "They had raided our place. I was flabbergasted. Come to find out, she had been charging items on other people's accounts and had bought coats, shoes, and various clothing. There were other things too, that weren't clothes." She eventually pled guilty to a misdemeanor and paid a $200 fine.

By this point, their marriage falling apart, the couple separated. Walker returned to Nevada while Sante stayed in California, filing for divorce on November 21, 1967, in Los Angeles County, citing "extreme cruelty." Walker claimed she tricked him by filing these papers, while at the same time saying she didn't plan to enforce them. Sante had a friend telephone him in Nevada with news his estranged wife was desperately ill and that he must come to California immediately, Walker said. He dropped everything, rushed to her side only to be served with the divorce papers. Despite this, he claimed they reconciled, living together until August 1968. A year later, Walker claimed, Sante reneged on her promise, went to court, and won a divorce settlement by default of $300 for child support and $700 in alimony each month. Walker balked at paying $12,000 a year, which he claimed was three times his annual salary.

In court papers, he charged Sante with fraud. She countered with a smug motion that noted Walker's three years of college, successful completion of written contractors' exams, and experience in prior lawsuits to emphasize that he can read legal papers and was duly served. "No fraud was ever practiced by the plaintiff upon the defendant. If there has been any fraud, it has been by defendant who has never paid plaintiff any child support in the past 20 months since the interlocutory judgment was rendered." Walker won another hearing on the divorce settlement, lowering child support payments to a percentage of his income and slashing the alimony by a third.

According to court records, Kent lived with his

mother until he was 14 years old, but she set a poor example when it came to staying out of trouble. On November 25, 1968, she was arrested in Glendale, California, for allegedly bouncing a check; the case was dismissed for lack of prosecution. Ten days later in Riverside, California, police charged her with shoplifting; the disposition of this case is unavailable.

She moved to Palm Springs, the desert resort two hours south of Los Angeles. Ever since the 1930s, Hollywood stars searching for privacy brought waves of money and power that turned the Palm Springs desert into a mecca of golf courses, elegant homes, and fancy resorts. Apropos of her fancier surroundings, Sante moved upscale for her next adventure, the fine apparel department of the I. Magnin store in Palm Springs. Two saleswomen fussed over Sante on January 22, 1972, when she expressed interest in a fur coat, selecting one worth $1,650. She also chose a $310 evening gown, according to a criminal complaint. When it came time to pay for both luxuries, Sante pulled out a sales slip from another I. Magnin store, instead of a credit card, instructing the clerk to use the charge account number on the receipt. The account number belonged to Mrs. Edwin G. Chambers of Santa Barbara, almost the same name as Sante's adoptive father, Edwin P. Chambers. Sante told the clerk she had just driven in from Santa Barbara.

Sante's saleswoman took down the information from the sales slip and cleared the purchase through the credit office. The store manager even signed off on the sale, which was the core of Sante's defense. The law caught up with her by the following month, and she was charged with grand theft. At a four-day trial, Sante and her adoptive father both took the stand. The jury deadlocked after two-and-a-half days of deliberations, so the judge declared a mistrial and dismissed the charges.

* * *

By the time of the I. Magnin fur saga, Sante had less incentive to steal than any period in her entire life, having landed a wealthy lover in Palm Springs. Like other women, she fawned over millionaire Kenneth Kimes, considering the divorced motel builder a great catch. Unlike the competition, Sante pounced like a corporate raider leading a takeover. A sponge for information about Kimes, she discovered his favorite color was white and then dressed like a snow princess. Learning that he liked the smell of gardenias, she drenched herself in that heavy sweet scent. She made sure his glass of Jack Daniel's was always full, but she only pretended to swallow hers, sometimes secretly dumping it, the better to concentrate soberly on her conquest. She built up the ego of the older Kimes, a self-made man who started out in California as a field hand picking peas and melons. They met when Sante was in her mid-30s, still a beauty able to sexually excite the businessman, who was at least 16 years her senior. His family members also believed her wild criminal side fascinated him, dovetailing with her apparent need to steal. "He found it amusing and somewhat thrilling," said a member of his family. "What thrilled him was that there were no two days alike. She put him on a pedestal. His whole life was like a blow job."

Kimes made his fortune building a string of 40 motels along California's coast just as America's postwar boom in jobs, babies, and highways put more families on the road looking for vacation spots. His journey from farm boy to construction kingpin was a classic bootstrap tale, when he told it, cloaked in nostalgia for his upbringing in Oklahoma, also Sante's birthplace. "The memories of my childhood should be experienced by every child today," he wrote in a 1986 court document. "Along with my mother and father and five brothers and sisters, we lived in a rural district between Oklahoma City and Norman, on a 140-acre farm. We were a happy family, doing all of the normal chores required to maintain a farm. When I was 12 years old, I owned my first car, a 1925 Model T. The *Oklahoma Daily News* gave me a paper route, which was 25 miles per day. My subscribers paid me with chickens, eggs, butter, vegetables, and fruit."

The third of six children born to farmer Charles Roger Kimes and his wife, Neoma Brant Kimes, Kenneth Kimes has no official birth certificate because his mother had him at home. Baptismal records aren't much help because the family lived so off the beaten track and priests were scarce in that part of Oklahoma—they waited months at a time for a traveling cleric to administer the sacraments. His father was of Irish, English, and German stock, while his mother's maiden name, Brant, is English. She converted to Catholicism when she and her sister Alice attended an Indian mission school. If Kimes was 12 when he bumped along country roads in that 1925 Model T, he must have been born before 1913. However, most records list his birthday as November 16th of either 1916 or 1917.

Just as Oklahoma's dust storms and the country's Depression forced Sante's family to move West, Charles Kimes had to sell his farm for whatever he could get and take his wife and children to California's Monterey county. By then Kimes was in the 10th grade, but there would be no school for a while. His family joined thousands of others bent under the blazing sun all day, picking peas, lettuce, and other crops for hourly wages of only 15 cents, or a quarter, if they were lucky. When he made it big, Kimes would boast that he "could pick more melons than anyone in that field," said one of his attorneys, Gustav Bujkovsky. "They were itinerant pickers, the whole family. They would just travel from crop to crop up and down California."

Their father invested his savings into a few plots of residential land in Salinas. Kimes, and his older brother, Andrew, helped their father develop this land. Scraping together $300, Kenneth Kimes bought three of these residential lots for himself and scored his first profits as a developer. Working alongside a hired carpenter, Kimes nailed and plastered around-the-clock, building and selling the home in just three months, clearing $1,000. Hungry for more deals, he studied nights at Salinas High School for his contractor's license.

By the time Kimes passed the licensing test, the army drafted him in the spring of 1941. Luckily he was assigned to Fort Ord, only a few miles from Salinas, so he managed during leaves to finish houses under construction. Pearl Harbor then swept him and millions of others far from home. He trained in California's Mojave Desert with the 7th Division, 53rd Infantry, Company C, in preparation for fighting the Germans in North Africa. Instead, he and his comrades spent two-and-a-half long years in the deep freeze of Alaska and the Aleutian Islands.

The 7th Division was the only battle-ready command on the West Coast when the Allies decided to retake the Aleutians from the Japanese, who had managed the first successful invasion of American land since the War of 1812.

Kimes and his comrades had to adjust from 120-degree heat to frigid 100-mile-an-hour "williwaw" winds that batter the Aleutian Islands, usually when it's also raining or snowing or shrouded in fog. In the 19-day battle for the remote island of Attu, more than 500 Americans died, 3,330 were wounded, and nearly all 2,350 Japanese perished, either in combat or mass suicide, detonating hand grenades held to their chests. Kimes served with the campaign's backup forces that stayed behind to occupy the wind-swept treeless islands, so remote and nasty the climate drove soldiers to despair and sometimes madness. In a joke that rang with truth, Bob Hope said the Aleutians were the only place a soldier could "walk in mud up to his knees bucking a snowstorm that blew sand in his face, while being pelted (by hail) in the rear on a sunny day."

In a morale booster that put money in his pocket, Kimes got permission for a legal gambling hall for the men. Promoted by this time to mess sergeant, he had shown a head for deals by trading army supplies to the Eskimos for fresh fish and caribou that he served instead of tired rations. "As I think back, I don't know how he did it," said Frank Presse, a friend and soldier in Company C. "Feeding 210 men under the most difficult conditions you can imagine."

Playing banker in the army base casino he started, Kimes socked away a small fortune that sent him roaring back into the construction business just in time for the postwar boom. As the war was ending, he had married Charloette Taylor on February 24, 1945. She was a Texas girl he met while assigned to Camp Swift in Austin. His family members maintain she was the only wife he ever had. Together they worked to get Kimes Construction off the ground. Ever the shrewd investor, Kimes knew Disneyland was headed for Anaheim, so he bought up some of the orange groves in that area. His land eventually turned into the showcase of the Kimes Motel empire, the Mecca, on 1544 South Harbor Boulevard. An Arabian-inspired design with minarets, the hotel welcomed all those Mickey Mouse lovers on their own pilgrimage to Disneyland, just across the street. The Mecca was a cash cow, worth $3.5 million, according to 1985 court documents.

Outwardly he had the trappings of a happy successful life. The couple had two children, Linda Jane, born July 9, 1946, and Andrew Keith, born June 6, 1949. Settling first in Salinas, Kenneth joined the Knights of Columbus, the Chamber of Commerce, and the Rotary Club. The family worshiped at Sacred Heart Church, where, in a special ceremony, Kimes and Linda were baptized, he at the age of 50 and she at five years old. Not able to find his baptismal record, Kimes wanted to be sure he had the sacrament. For his family, he designed a custom-built dream house in Santa Ana at 2215 Victoria Drive, which had four bedrooms, six baths, and a swimming pool.

Yet his family life only looked good. After 18 years of marriage, Charloette filed for divorce in June 1963 on grounds of cruelty, launching a nasty battle over money, their reputations, and the two children. It dragged on for two years. In her version, Kimes caroused with other women for the last half of their marriage. She begged him to stay home, while he said he wasn't taking orders from any woman and could come and go as he pleased. She consulted with their parish priest, who suggested marriage counseling, but Kimes refused. He dragged the two kids into the mess, waging "a campaign" to win them away from their mother, overruling her discipline and buying them off with expensive gifts, like a Cadillac for Linda.

In Kimes' divorce papers, he portrayed Charloette as an hysterical woman who threatened to shoot him and commit suicide "on numerous occasions." To soothe her, he tried to come home every night even if that meant driving 200 miles round-trip to Santa Ana from Palm Springs, where he was building a hotel. He also said he tried to seek help from their priest, but his wife refused to see a marriage counselor. As for the children, both wanted to live with him. He submitted affidavits from 16-year-old Linda and 14-year-old Andrew that criticized Charloette as being unreasonable, while portraying their father as the one trying to hold the family together. He countercharged that his wife was cheating, however, the court file showed no evidence of this.

Both sides lobbed bombshells, but Kimes had more resources. He hired private detectives to follow Charloette after the court ordered her to vacate the Santa Ana dream home. He had the money to hire a top-gun law firm from Los Angeles, which basically protected his fortune, by then spanning 10 motels, a restaurant, and land throughout California. In a final divorce judgment on September 20, 1965, the court sided with Kimes on child custody; he got to keep the house. From an estimated $1,010,000 in community property, Charloette was awarded only $200,000 and had to pay off credit card debts and $35,000 in lawyers' fees. The courts even ruled against her when Kimes filed a joint tax return in 1965, making her liable for $25,200 in taxes even though the couple had separated and she didn't share in any of his income that year.

Flexing his muscle in court, winning most rounds in his divorce, Kimes was free with his money intact. Expanding his empire, Kimes spent more time in Palm Springs overseeing construction of a 150-room hotel, which featured two restaurants and two lounges.

A local magazine wrote a profile about the millionaire, which caught Sante's eye. She had a girlfriend who knew Kimes' sister and angled an introduction. The two began dating, and Kimes quickly realized he was being pursued, but seemed flattered.

"As I recall, I was introduced to Sante Walker in Palm Springs," Kenneth said. "Within the next year we saw each other four or five times. My schedule required me to return to Newport Beach, as I was building two motels in La Jolla. After leaving Palm Springs, Sante rented an apartment in Orange

County. It became obvious that almost every place I went, she was close by."

Kenneth also knew about Sante's criminal history. As he had during his divorce, he hired a private detective to spy on his woman. His hired gun unearthed her apparent kleptomania as well as information about her active social life in Palm Springs. None of these reports scared off Kimes, who saw her as a charming stunner, a solicitous helpmate, a single parent trying to support her son. Any darker picture was just gossip or jealous bad-mouthing. His family looked at her beehive wigs, black eye shadow, and low cut blouses and saw a gold digger with no class. "They seemed to like Sante at first; however, as time passed, they developed a positive dislike for her," Kimes said about his family. "I believe they felt that she was not sincere about my welfare, but was more concerned about her own."

Eager to impress him, Sante latched onto his idea to promote the upcoming American Bicentennial in July 1976, and make money, by marketing posters of state and country flags. Sante talked up her experience in promotions and sales and became his public-relations adviser. She wrote his press releases and speeches, scheduling him to fire up local PTAs and veteran groups with his patriotic message. He formed Kiosk Inc. on April 26, 1972, to market his "Forum of Man" posters for $10 a piece and set Sante up with a secretary and an office in Irvine, California. He hoped to get support from a well-known charity like the Rockefeller or Ford Foundation to underwrite the cost of putting the posters in 250,000 classrooms nationwide. With such ambitious goals, Sante started networking in high places. On a trip to New York City, the couple presented a full-color photo montage of the flags of the United Nations member states to Indian diplomat C.V. Narasimhan, then Undersecretary General at the United Nations. That was the first

THEY CALL THEM GRIFTERS

and last time the diplomat saw the Kimeses, although they kept using his name in their projects, he said.

At first, the American Revolution Bicentennial Commission in Washington, D.C., embraced the ideas of the California millionaire and his exotic escort. Duke Zeller ran public relations for the ARBC back then and remembered how striking the Kimeses were. "He's kind of a wholesome Jimmy Stewart-type, who loves his country and wants to, you know, show it and prove it, and she's kind of an exotic Far Eastern princess morphed with the Auntie Mame," Zeller said. "I remember Kimes as having presented himself as quote, 'a friend of Richard Nixon.'"

The commission's acting director Hugh Hall posed with Kimes and his posters for ARBC's newsletter. They printed this glowing blurb: "His extensive travels and outspoken enthusiasm for the goals and opportunities of our country's 200th anniversary have led Mr. Kimes to be widely known, although unofficially, as an Honorary Bicentennial Ambassador." As if giving a medal to a hero, Hall pinned a Bicentennial logo on Kimes' chest in a public ceremony in 1972. Kimes claimed it was Hall's idea to imprint the Commission's official logo on the Forum of Man posters. "They didn't ask me for any royalties," Kimes said. "They just thought the flags were tremendous. Hall asked if they could buy them for every one of our Bicentennial offices."

Kimes greeted New Year's Day 1974 from the speaker's podium at the Rose Bowl, exhorting the football fans with a rah-rah of his own for America. Under the Bicentennial letterhead of an American bald eagle with wings unfurled, perched atop Old Glory, Kimes issued this grandiose press release:

"Mr. Kenneth K. Kimes, Honorary Bicentennial Ambassador of the United States of America, will within the next three years plan, encourage, and develop the commemoration of our Countries [*sic*]

200th Birthday, and will encourage the observance and awareness of the American Bicentennial to all groups and activities throughout the Country.

"Chosen from private life, Mr. Kimes does not receive any compensation for his services, and is not to be considered an official Commission employee, but serves on an Honorary basis, and has dedicated himself to the observance and success of the American Bicentennial.

"Hailing from the Midwest, semi-retired from a career of hotel chains that became the base of his fortune and numerous philanthropies, Mr. Kimes has been recognized by heads of state and the United Nations and given recognition for his contributions among the world of schoolchildren.

"Within the next three years, Mr. Kimes will travel to various countries inviting Presidents and their people to participate in the American Bicentennial. He will place the gold star Bicentennial symbol pin on the world leaders in an invitation to the World to participate in the United States Bicentennial celebration. Already Miguel Aleman, former President of Mexico, has pledged construction [of a replica] of the oldest church in Mexico, Guadalupe, as a Birthday gift. The Undersecretary General of the United Nations, C. V. Narasimhan, also President of the India Temple Society, has begun preliminary plans for the construction of [a replica of] the Taj Mahal in New York City as a Bicentennial project.

"Early in May, Mr. Kimes leaves for India with the Secretary General to invite various leaders and their countries to participate in the Bicentennial of the United States.

"For further information, please write our United States of America Bicentennial plant office at 17835 Sky Park Circle Drive, Suite 'K,' Irvine, California 92707, or call (714) 557-1776, or write Chief of Publications, Edward P. Stafford, American Revolution Bicentennial, 736 Jackson Place, Washington, D.C. 20276, or call (202) 254-8007."

Riding high on their Bicentennial promotions, the couple went too far Tuesday evening, February 26, 1974, in Washington, D.C. Wearing a white fur hat, a turn-of-the-century-style white gown, diamonds— or (more likely) rhinestones—on her fingers with one pasted into her right ear, dark eyeliner, and bright pink lipstick, Sante looked like Zsa Zsa Gabor on a ski trip. For their night on the town, Kimes wore a subdued dark suit and polka-dot tie, but at six-foot-three he was a redwood with curly auburn hair and a mustache in a field of clean-shaven Republicans. The couple turned heads strolling into a diplomatic reception that night at the Blair House, hosted by Vice President Gerald Ford and his wife, Betty. Uninvited guests, the Kimeses joined the official receiving line, flashed wide smiles, and shook hands with the Fords as a photographer snapped their picture. Secret service agents, supposedly guarding the Vice President, let these party-crashers walk right up to Ford, explaining later that it would have been embarrassing to stop them. Trying to ease into the cocktail reception, Sante was surrounded by diplomat wives who asked who she was and why she had a diamond stuck into her ear. "My father is East Indian," Sante said. "It's customary." She told everyone her tall companion was an honorary Bicentennial ambassador, but ducked the question of who appointed him. "I don't know you," one guest said to her, "and I know everyone else here." Unflustered, Sante replied, "Oh, how nice, then I have a new friend." Kimes grabbed a drink and amicably told a reporter, "I'm self-employed, honey."

Next the pair crashed a black-tie dinner at the Renwick Gallery hosted by the dean of the Washington art world, Dillon Ripley, director of the Smithsonian Museum. The Kimeses weren't among guests invited to mark his 10th anniversary. "I was really shook up when I saw them," said Meredith Johnson, curator of special collections, who eased the strange couple out the door. Grabbing a taxi, they showed up next at the door of the German Embassy, where guests were toasting a diplomat on his way to Bulgaria. The ambassador's gracious wife asked the Kimeses if they were quite sure they wanted the German Embassy, and Sante quickly said no, they were actually headed to the Belgium Embassy. Believing them, Mrs. Von Staden instructed one of her staffers to drive the Kimeses to the Belgian Embassy, where the butler directed the couple to a private reception at the ambassador's home. Minister Andre Rahir admitted the strangers, mistaking them for his wife's guests. Discovering otherwise, he let them stay for cocktails but refused Sante's request to make a speech about the Bicentennial. When it came time to leave, the kind Belgians, knowing how hard it was to get a taxi at night, asked Danish Second Secretary Christopher Bo Bramsen and his wife to drop off the Kimeses at their hotel.

So in one night they met the Vice President and Mrs. Ford, crashed four A-list parties, and rode free in two diplomatic cars. Their excellent adventure also brought down a hailstorm of embarrassing headlines on their heads that triggered investigations by the FBI and the Justice Department. The *Washington Star* and the *Washington Post* ran five articles that portrayed their work for the Bicentennial as social-climbing self-promotion. "The Biggest Crash Since 1929," one headline blared. In another piece the caption "Kenneth Kimes (rhymes with 'climbs')" ran under a blowup of his face that caught him in a cat-ate-the-canary grin. Kimes had no right to use the title of honorary ambassador huffed Robert Miller, special assistant to the President for the Bicentennial, who said the Californian "hasn't been appointed anything. He has absolutely no official status and has not been designated anything by the President." As for inviting leaders of other countries to Bicentennial events, that's Nixon's job as head of state, the aide said.

Two investigative reporters for the *Washington Post* found apparent forgery on a White House letter Kimes flashed as proof he was an honorary ambassador. Signed by Richard Nixon, the short note on White House stationery thanked Kimes for sending flowers during the President's hospitalization for viral pneumonia in July 1973. Kimes flew round-trip to California to put the Nixon letter into the hands of doubting Thomas reporters. The White House checked the letter, dated August 16, 1973, and noted that the typeface for the salutation "Honorary Ambassador K. K. Kimes" differed from the script on the rest of the letter. "It was not the letter that went out of the White House," said Miller. "Somebody has obviously tampered with it."

Digging further, the reporters discovered that a memo setting up a visit between Kimes and First Lady Pat Nixon on April 18, 1973, also appeared phony. Communication director Herb Klein didn't remember writing a note asking for a date and time for Kimes and Sante to present the First Lady with the Forum of Man posters. Suspiciously, a phrase in the memo, "to kick off this noble undertaking," appeared verbatim in Sante's correspondence. The *Post* reported that the First Lady was uncomfortable meeting the Kimeses. "It was sort of a phony thing, and Mrs. Nixon realized it the very instant it happened. They tried to get Mrs. Nixon to give her blessing to the project of distributing flags in the schools. They needed a contact in HEW (Health Education and Welfare). Mrs. Nixon wanted nothing further to do with it."

Soon nobody at the official Bicentennial Commission wanted to hear Kenneth Kimes talk about a reception for world leaders or pie-in-the-sky plans for a Taj Majal in New York City. The American Revolution Bicentennial Commission chided the couple for using their phones, and threatened them with a Justice Department probe if they didn't remove the official Bicentennial logo from the flag posters. The FBI and Justice investigated the Kimeses for the gate-crashing, but didn't charge them with impersonation. His back against the wall, Kimes shrugged off the assault on his good name. "I'm going to proceed with these flags in exactly the same manner as I intended. No, I wouldn't destroy those with the Bicentennial logo. I'd give them away before I do that.

"I'm a fighter for Americanism, a fighter for the people. In every speech I've made I've never said one thing about these flags, only about the Bicentennial. I figured down the road later there'd be some place I'd recoup my investment.

"I'm a self-made man. Nobody ever gave me a dime. I used to send my money home by postal money order when I was stationed in the Aleutians. I saved it to buy land, to develop, and to build. I feel I can spend a little of my money now, but I cannot give away two million of these framed flags."

Sante told the *Washington Star* it was all a mistake. She said the Bicentennial people suggested they make the round of embassy parties, and she called ahead and got permission to attend the Belgian party. The Renwick Gallery was only supposed to be a brief stop to drop off a poster, but it was so close to the Blair House, they assumed the party-goers at Vice President Ford's party were actually the art crowd. "People were arriving for a party, and we thought this is the place," she said. "So we were sort of swept inside and warmly welcomed. The Fords were wonderful people. The Vice President talked to Mr. Kimes about the Bicentennial for three or four minutes." In the confusion she directed a taxi driver to the German Embassy, discovering her mistake, and then switched to the Belgian Embassy, where there was a party in the ambassador's private home. She defended Kimes and confirmed a personal interest in him. "Mr. Kimes is a Will Rogers type, a starter, a tiger. People ask me if I am involved with him. Well, I love him. I love his warmth.

"We're just confused about this," she said. "Mr. Kimes has only the interests of America at heart. We are not political people. We are not sophisticated. We just care about unity and getting rid of cynicism in the world."

CHAPTER 5

"She would con the shorts off you, if she could."

Home sweet home, domestic tranquility, peace and quiet—values that most folks hold dear appear alien to the life shared by Sante and Kenneth Kimes. Throughout their time together, almost a quarter century, she became the eye of storms born of everyday events. In court papers, she cast herself as the victim of contractors, lawyers, insurers, neighbors, and others who just didn't like her, of controversies that just seemed to dog her. However, her pattern suggests that while some ladies like to lunch, she gravitated to plots and schemes. Craving excitement, she created trouble, thinking that would amuse her millionaire or orchestrate her world. "I think I am a strong person," she once said about herself. "I do not think I am domineering. I certainly don't like to be out of control. So I guess you could say that I like to be in control, yes."

During the '70s and '80s, she piloted a staff of Spanish-speaking maids forced to scrub perfectly clean floors. Civil suits began mounting in those years; a merchant would insist the Kimeses owed him money, an insurance company would dispute a claim they had filed. Sante scattered angry lawyers in her wake. She hired attorneys; they later sued for nonpayment. She hired other lawyers, and the cycle began anew. And her arrests for taking things continued. While two months pregnant, she was charged with lifting an objet d'art from a store in Newport

Beach, California, on September 27, 1974. Pleading guilty to a lesser charge, she paid a $250 fine and was sentenced to two years probation.

She gave birth to her second child, Kenneth Karam Kimes, on March 24, 1975, but as with her older son, Kent, motherhood did not soften Sante. Law enforcement later nicknamed her "The Dragon Lady" for her personality as well as for fires that kept breaking out in her homes.

The Kimeses began spending a lot of time in their oceanfront villa in Hawaii, overlooking majestic Diamond Head. The wooden house had five bedrooms, a smaller cottage, a swimming pool, and a gazebo. Seeing flames shooting from the Kimeses' house, neighbors called the fire department at 1:03 A.M. on April 18, 1978. Their quick action allowed firefighters to contain the blaze, which appeared to be deliberately set with accelerants, according to the Honolulu Fire Department investigation report. Blazes burned in six separate areas over the master bedroom, living room, and dining room. Deemed "malicious," the fire caused an estimated $18,000 in damage, but no one was ever charged with arson.

The Kimeses wanted about $125,000 from their fire coverage, raising a red flag with Robert Grantham, vice president of claims with First Insurance Company of Hawaii. Without checking with Grantham, an adjuster with the firm, Don Hovieler, approved a $50,000 advance to the Kimeses; when he returned for another $75,000, Grantham balked, according to a deposition.

Wearing a full-length fur coat in tropical Hawaii, Sante arrived for negotiations at Grantham's office, accompanied by her latest lawyer. She got a second payment, but it was less than she wanted. At first polite and friendly, though "a little on the demanding side," Sante soon turned into a bully, said the executive. "As the controversy developed, and particularly on the telephone, she became, you know, almost abusive," Grantham said. "Like, you know, 'I'm tired of dealing with you, and I'm going to go to your superiors. And I'm going to talk to the insurance commissioner, and I'm going to get you straightened out because I don't like the way you're doing this, and you're very, very, you know, not a good person.' "

Making good on her threat to go to the top, Sante flew 6,000 miles to northern New Jersey, stepped from a limousine on a Sunday night, and knocked at the home of Continental Corporation's chairman of the board. It worked. That Monday he ordered his underlings in Hawaii to give this lady her third and final payment of $26,000. Hovieler was fired over the Kimeses' claim and later worked for Sante as caretaker on her Hawaii home until an arson fire destroyed the estate 12 years later, according to court records.

During this period, the executive vice president at First Insurance Company of Hawaii, Thomas Farrell, had committed suicide over problems unrelated to Sante Kimes. Returning from the funeral, Grantham found Sante in his office, wearing a flowing white muumuu and a gigantic diamond-looking ring. She shook the ring in his face and demanded her money. "And the discussion evolved into an argument, not a heated argument but an argument," he said in a deposition. "And the conclusion of the discussion was when she looked at me and told me that I was personally responsible for Mr. Farrell committing suicide. At that time I turned and walked away from her and left my office, asked her to leave, and had no further discussion with this person."

Sante even allegedly tried to bully the head of a federal agency when she lobbied in Washington, D.C., for a Southern California health care company, HMO Concepts, run by her doctor, Alfred Caruso. A wealthy physician in Orange, he bought flamboyant entertainer Liberace's $750,000 Lake Arrowhead home. Caruso had been unsuccessfully lobbying for federal certification, the gateway to government loans and grants. However, his company's financial structure troubled federal examiners, according to an exposé on Caruso and Sante published in the *Sacramento Bee* on January 16, 1979. Although nonprofit, HMO Concepts paid eight health supply firms owned by Caruso and his wife. Officials wanted to make sure that Caruso didn't reap huge profits through these subcontracts. This possibility led U.S. Senator Sam Nunn of Georgia to urge Hale Champion, U.S. Undersecretary of Health, Education and Welfare, not to certify HMO Concepts. HEW's William McLeod, director of the Office of HMO Qualification and Compliance, agreed.

A Washington insider advised Caruso he would fare better by hiring a lobbyist. Then, as he told the *Bee*, fate intervened in the shape of a new patient, Sante Kimes, who had been injured in a car accident. Gushing that he had saved her life, she offered to help him in Washington. Sante visited HEW's McLeod and proceeded to lambaste him as a "bad man," warning that in Washington, she had "very good friends who were very dear and very powerful."

In October 1977, Champion received a call purporting to be from C. V. Narasimhan, the United Nations Undersecretary General from India, whom the Kimeses met once when they had given him a flag poster. The caller wanted to talk with Champion about a new international school dubbed Freedom University that Kenneth Kimes was building in Hawaii. "She (Sante) got into this office on a ruse," Champion said. Sante talked about the school and then raised her real purpose for the visit beginning, "By the way, this HMO Concepts thing . . ." Champion referred her to the office of HEW Secretary, Joseph Califano.

Sante continued name-dropping in the capital, saying she was friends with *Washington Post* publisher Katherine Graham and that U.N. Secretary General Kurt Waldheim was her son Kenny's godfather. To another official, she named Califano as Kenny's godfather. She claimed to have a desk in California Senator Alan Cranston's office, but his staff never heard of her.

When HEW sent an auditing team to examine Caruso's books, and then approved a $437,000 federal loan, he attributed this victory to Sante. "I do not know what she did, but we started to get responses from the department." In gratitude, Caruso in February 1978 gave Sante a brand-new white Cadillac Eldorado worth $14,000 and an additional $15,000 to pay for travel expenses from Hawaii to Washington. Sante, however, wanted another car. On August 8, 1978, she returned to the McClean Cadillac showroom in downtown Santa Ana, where she got the Eldorado. She told the dealer that HMO Concepts was buying her a second car, a white $18,544 Biarritz, Cadillac's most expensive model. She gave the dealer $1,000 and showed him a letter on HMO Concepts stationery authorizing this second car. The letter bore Caruso's signature, but he later said he was in Spain and never signed it. Sante drove off in the new Biarritz, taking the authorization letter with her.

When McClean Cadillac tried to get HMO Concepts to pay the $17,544 balance, they refused. Sante told the *Bee* that Caruso owed her $80,000 for her eight months of work landing him the federal contract. He disputed both the debt and her rights to the Biarritz. His payments to Sante became part of a wide-ranging investigation into HMO Concepts' finances and cash-flow problems that ended with the firm losing a contract with the California Health Services Department and its federal certification in 1980. During the investigation, an unsolved arson fire burned Caruso's Orange County headquarters.

Sante was also tough on Kenneth Kimes' relatives, they said. Linda Kimes, Kenneth's daughter, idolized her father. At 16 she chose to live with him during his divorce and went on to work in his motel chain. Suddenly after Sante came into his life, Linda received a legal letter, ordering her to end contact with her dad.

Worried friends and relatives wondered what was overtaking Kimes. His daughter would say that Kimes seemed to be under the spell of his Cadillac-loving companion. "I'm not trying to paint a perfect picture of him, but on the other hand, he wasn't evil," Linda Kimes told friends. "She dedicated herself to figuring out his weaknesses, his need for sexual excitement, ego enhancement. She dedicated herself 100 percent to brainwashing the man and possessing the man and taking over his life. He had deep bonds to his family, so she really had to try hard to break those ties."

Kenneth Kimes even sued his own family. On May 7, 1979, Kimes and Sante demanded $100,000 each from his brother, sister, son, daughter, and son-in-law for emotional distress, invasion of privacy, and conspiracy. Filed in Orange County Superior Court, this lawsuit claimed the relatives sent cops hunting for the couple after falsely reporting them missing. According to the lawsuit, his kin falsely accused Kimes and Sante of insurance fraud over a lost tapestry. It also said the relatives bad-mouthed Sante by calling her a criminal who used aliases, stalked them, threatened their lives, held Kimes hostage, and wasn't legally married to him.

Different dates for their marriage appear in various documents. In a 1985 interview with a court-appointed psychiatrist, Sante claimed she had married Kimes in 1971. She said the same thing to a sentencing consultant in 1986, and in a deposition three years later. Kimes, in another deposition in 1989, guessed that they had wed in Las Vegas "around" 1979. "It could have been earlier, but I don't recall exactly," he said. A marriage certificate on file in Clark County, Nevada, said Kenneth K. Kimes wed Sante Singhrs at the World Famous Chapel of the Bells in Las Vegas on April 5, 1981. Linda Kimes doubted they ever married. In a probate petition to gain control of her father's estate, filed in the spring of 1999, she described Kimes as a divorced single man.

Lies by his relatives upset Kimes so much, said the Orange County suit, he suffered "recurring epigastric distress and eructations," elaborate descriptions for an upset stomach and belching. By 1981, the lawyer who filed this suit turned around and sued his clients Sante and Kimes for $12,407.40 in unpaid fees and $100,000 in damages. Attorney Charles Catterlin listed 21 aliases for Sante in his complaint. "She would con the shorts off you, if she could," Catterlin said. "The husband was quiet. She always said he was ill. He wasn't like her. She always used dirty language. She had big bosoms, and she wore low-cut dresses to show off everything she had." The Orange County Court dismissed the suit against the Kimes family on November 14, 1984, and Catterlin said he never got paid.

For such a litigious person, Sante seemed unable to calmly accept civil subpoenas and went to great lengths to avoid being served. She instructed maids and house sitters never to open the door to strangers or accept any papers. Once in the late 1970s, Sante telephoned a friend and neighbor in Hawaii, Beverly Bates, and wept over receiving legal papers from a contractor. Sante urged her friend to pretend she was the woman who had been served the papers, according to a 1987 affidavit. When Beverly balked, Sante begged, claiming she was going to lose her house.

Sante talked her friend into a wild scheme. She convinced Beverly to don a white muumuu, black wig, pancake makeup, and fake eyelashes. Now dressed like Sante, Beverly accompanied her to the sheriff's office. "She was very, very aggressive and domineering in a really warm way," said Beverly. "And she could really talk you into anything." The two women hoped to demonstrate to the sheriff how easy it was for the contractor to mistake Beverly for Sante, since they both looked so much alike. The sheriff saw through the ruse immediately and the scam fell apart.

"As soon as he confronted me, I realized that I could not go through with what Mrs. Kimes was asking me to do," Beverly said in an affidavit. "I acknowledged that I had not actually been served and that it was Mrs. Kimes who had received the legal documents. We then left the sheriff's office." There is no mention of the sheriff taking any action against Sante for her stunt.

By early 1980, she had been arrested nine times, but none of the criminal cases amounted to more than a slap on the wrist. All were essentially minor brushes with the law that never hit the papers. That changed when the Kimeses visited Washington, D.C., in February 1980, six years after the Beltway dailies had pilloried the couple as self-promoting party-crashers. The *Washington Star* had folded by this time, leaving the job of writing about Sante to the *Washington Post*.

Heavier now, her mountain of dark hair, huge rings, and heavy mascara still reminded people of Elizabeth Taylor. Like a star, she traveled with a personal maid, a tutor for Kenny, then 4, and an English butler. They were all staying at the Mayflower Hotel

on Connecticut Avenue, a 10-minute stroll from the
White House. When they arrived, Sante said she left
one of her fur coats with the hotel lobby coat check.
Then she and Kimes ordered drinks in the hotel's
Town and Country piano bar. Dressed in a bulky
floor-length white fox fur, Sante kept circling the bar
Monday evening, February 4, like a caged snow tiger.
At one point she returned to the lobby coat check
and began screaming and crying when they insisted
that she hadn't left any fur with them. Black mascara
cascading down her cheeks with her tears, she was
quite a sight. "Did you just see how I was treated?"
she said to guests staring at the scene. "Did you see
what the manager said to me?" She convinced five
Good Samaritan types to give her their names and
phone numbers as witnesses.

Returning to Kimes in the lounge, Sante spotted a
well-dressed group arrive at the bar and dump their
coats on nearby chairs. A fine dark brown ranch
mink lay on the pile. Worth about $6,000, the floor-
length mink had a custom lining by William Tsamisis
furriers in Greenwich, Connecticut, embroidered
with "KK" for its proud owner, Katherine Ann Kenworthy. She and her husband, Robert, owned a firm
that managed industrial trade shows, and they were
in Washington for a mass transit exhibition at the
Sheraton Hotel. They treated their staff to dinner at
the Gaslight Club, and the group proceeded to the
Mayflower's piano bar for a nightcap of Irish coffees.
The Kimeses moved to the table near the pile of
coats, and Kenenth Kimes struck up a brief conversation about former President Richard Nixon with Mr.
Kenworthy. Shrugging off her fox, Sante was wearing
a black velvet jacket over a white ruffled blouse.

With the Kenworthys just three feet away, Sante
leaned forward and slowly pulled the unattended
mink toward her. Staying in her seat, she put on the
mink without the Kenworthys noticing. In just a few

seconds right under their noses, Sante then slipped her own white fox fur on top of the other woman's coat. The trick was so risky, one wonders if she wanted to get caught. The stunt must have given her a thrill. The mink now hidden, she sauntered out of the bar with Kimes, but she didn't make a clean escape. Nursing their own drinks, two out-of-towners had a clear view of Sante's fur-over-fur trick from a table about 10 feet away. Thinking it was so brazen and weird, they just sat there stunned.

"Look at that," said Charles Crane, a Hewlett-Packard manager, to drinking companion, Rena Cusma, an Oregon government official.

"I thought, 'Am I really seeing what I'm seeing?'" Cusma said to herself. "Did we really see what I think we did?" she asked Crane.

"I think we did," he replied.

At first they didn't say anything to the Kenworthys. The witnesses grew even more confused when Sante sashayed back to the bar, wearing her white fox fur, approached the Kenworthys, and talked to a man in their party. "I couldn't believe that I hadn't misunderstood what I had seen," Cusma said. "I mean, I can't believe somebody would come back into the room and sit down and strike up a conversation with them if they had just stolen the people's coat." All doubts evaporated when, after last call, the lounge lights came up bright and Mrs. Kenworthy burst into tears. "My coat is gone," she cried. "Where's my coat?" Although Sante had returned to her hotel room by this time, she was easy to find. Two cops were already in the bar, summoned to quell a fight when one patron broke into a loud chorus of "It's a Long Way to Tipperary," annoying another equally inebriated man. "It was a large woman in a white coat that looked like a bad Elizabeth Taylor," Cusma told the cops.

Just as her eye for that I. Magnin fur coat in Palm

Springs caused problems in 1972, it was the same story eight years later in Washington, D.C. Finding Kenworthy's coat lining thrown onto a roof five floors below Kimes' hotel window, a detective arrested Sante on February 5, 1980. For the first time, Kenneth Kimes was also hauled away in handcuffs. Police charged them both with grand larceny, a felony. The *Washington Post* headline writers dubbed the caper "Minky Business," and the accompanying story resurrected the couple's prior gate-crashing. When arrested, according to the police report, Sante shaved 12 years off her age, claiming she was born in 1946, and spelled her first name "Shante." She talked to the *Post*, saying it was all a mistake and that her mink was the one stolen. "It's an outrage," she said, the rhinestones on her glasses catching the light, "to think that I would need to steal someone's fur."

Arrested at 2:00 A.M., the millionaires stayed in jail until late the following afternoon over Kimes' protests that he was missing an appointment with President Jimmy Carter. In fact, Kimes just had tickets to the standard VIP tour of the White House. "It was awful," Sante said upon their release, "they handcuffed us, frisked us, and then put us in these little green-barred closets that had a toilet with no seat."

Kimes moved the family to a five-bedroom home bordering a golf course in Las Vegas, the adult Disneyland where Sante's over-the-top glitz fit right in. However, she managed to immediately create a tempest on their block of lawyers, doctors, and bankers. She asked the next-door neighbors if she could please use their phone until hers was installed, and of course they said yes. Next thing the man noticed was that his Bulova watch that had been on the kitchen counter was not there anymore. She ordered a $1,450 Advent projector television from Desert TV & Appliance, then only paid the store $500, according to a lawsuit they filed. It seems she was back to amusing herself with small-time scams. However, she was poised to go too far again. The next time she got arrested, it would eclipse all the embarrassing headlines from the past and drag Kimes down with her.

CHAPTER 6

Mrs. Clean.

"Take off your pants," Sante ordered her maid. "Take off all your clothes."

Maribel Ramirez Cruz stopped ironing, twisted her hands together in a nervous reflex, and turned toward her boss, Sante. "Somehow, she knows," the 19-year-old maid said to herself, all the while trying to look nonchalant and stay calm. Inside her bra, Maribel had tucked a slip of paper with the home telephone number and address of another Kimes maid taken from her family 10 months ago. Maribel wanted to call that girl's family and free her from Sante's grasp, but now it looked like that good deed was about to detonate in her face.

Maribel pitied the other maid, Adela Sanchez Guzman, a field hand's daughter raised in a three-room shack in Mexico who once believed America promised a better life. Leaving her village, Adela couldn't find a job to support herself in nearby Puebla or Mexico City, so the 16-year-old crossed the border in early 1984 and went to live with her aunt, a hotel maid in Costa Mesa, California. Her aunt knew Sante as a hotel guest who needed a baby-sitter, and Adela applied. Four-feet-eleven, with short black hair and small dark brown eyes that darted around, she looked like a kid herself. "Call me Mama," Sante said, promising the girl a job close to her aunt, but taking her 250 miles away to Las Vegas in February

1984 and then an ocean away to a million-dollar home on a beach in Hawaii.

There, on one of Oahu's most expensive streets, orchids thrived in the front garden at Sante's home, while out back a floor-to-ceiling picture window framed the ocean and Diamond Head in the distance. Adela's view began at the handle of a mop. She scrubbed the toilets, washed the clothes, made the beds, cleaned the dishes, polished the brass and silver, organized the closets, fluffed the pillows, wiped the windows, vacuumed the cars, watered the plants, tended the garden, and hosed down the patios. Morning until night she worked without wages or days off. Sante forbade her to use the phone, locked the gates on the estate's six-foot iron fence, and warned the girl that the Immigration and Naturalization Service would be waiting to arrest her if she tried to escape. When Adela begged to go home to Costa Mesa, Sante called her a "bad girl" and slapped the tears off her face. "You are going to be here forever with me," she told Adela. "Here you have your new family." Her real family in California couldn't reach Adela at the fake address and phone Sante had provided, so they filed a missing-person's report with the Santa Ana Police Department.

An illegal alien like Adela, Maribel had emigrated from El Salvador a few months before meeting Sante outside a California employment agency in the summer of 1984. She was thin, barely five-feet-two, and her short hair made her look young. She needed money to send to her mother in El Salvador. *La señora* promised her $120 a week to clean in Newport Beach, close to her family. Days later, the Kimeses whisked Maribel off to 271 A, Portlock Road, in Hawaii Kai, pretending, as they had with Adela, that they were staying in Oahu for just a few days. Instead the beachfront home became an unlikely prison for Adela and Maribel, where silence was among the many rules. Three months passed before the two maids dared speak to each other. "You have no business talking with her," Sante told Adela the day Maribel arrived in late July 1984. "I'll hit you if you talk to her. You each have work to do."

She gave Maribel the same warning and the same schedule. Up at six every morning, Maribel cleaned until sunset. She painted the four-bedroom house and the two-car garage and also did Sante's manicures, ironed her clothes, and crocheted her sweaters. The nights she had to wash the cars, she worked until 10 o'clock.

After summer passed into fall, Maribel finally broke the silence. While both maids cleaned the kitchen, she whispered to the younger girl, "Have you seen your family?" Frantic to see her aunt, Adela complained about *la señora* slapping her around and screaming "hurry up" about the housework. Adela was so unhappy and isolated, she didn't even know she was in Hawaii. The two maids spoke for just two minutes, but someone overheard. Adela guessed that Kenny Kimes, then nine years old, passed by the room and reported them to his mother, while Maribel assumed one of the child's home tutors spied on them. Or it could have been Sante, secretary of her high school Spanish club, who knew what they were saying.

La señora made good on her threat, smacking Maribel's face a few times and unleashing a fury on Adela. Closing a bedroom door behind them, Sante immediately started slapping Adela's head. Grabbing some wooden clothes hangers from the closet, she smashed them on Adela's feet with such force they broke. Then she dragged wire hangers on the girl's legs until her skin turned red and blotchy.

Eyes cast down and silent, Adela now moved like a robot through her chores. By late November, Sante decided to uproot Maribel to Las Vegas, but before they left, the maid tucked Adela's home phone number and address into her bra, vowing to help the broken girl. The night they reached the Kimeses' five-bedroom home at 2121 Geronimo Way, sandwiched between the first and second holes of the Sahara Golf Course, Sante somehow sensed Maribel was up to something. She ordered the maid to begin ironing. Then about 10 P.M. November 24, 1984, Sante confronted Maribel, triggering a chain of events that led the FBI to dust off old antislavery laws dating before the Civil War.

Maribel refused the order to strip.

"My own mother wasn't able to get me to undress, so how are you going to do it when you aren't even my relative," she told Sante.

"Take off your clothes, or I'll rip them off," Sante said.

Lunging at Maribel, Sante threw her against the ironing board, which brought both of them crashing to the floor. Sante grabbed the hot iron and advanced toward Maribel's face. Protecting her face with her hands, Maribel shrieked as the iron seared the flesh on her left wrist, opening a two-inch welt.

"I'm going to kill you," Sante yelled, and struck her in the mouth.

Hearing their screams, Kenneth Kimes ran inside the room and separated the women. Her mouth bleeding, Maribel clung to his waist and wailed, "I'm going to leave here any minute because she's crazy."

That night, Sante locked Maribel in the closet of the master bedroom. At five a.m., November 25, she woke her up, ordered the entire house cleaned, and threatened her. "I'm going to call the police or bring some friends of mine over here," Sante said. "They'll put you away for good."

"Call the police," Maribel said.

Somehow she cleaned that day, nauseous over her stinging hand, and managed to unlock a back door without Sante noticing. At one a.m. on November 26, 1984, taking only pajamas, an ill-fitting pair of pants, and some old shorts, Maribel walked into the chill of the desert night, free after 82 days with the Kimeses. Left alone in Hawaii, Adela eventually made her break December 16, 1984, finding sanctuary in a nearby church. She had been held for 339 days— 11 long months.

In Las Vegas, FBI Special Agent Tom Nicodemus tried to assure the maid with the burned hand sitting in his office that nobody was going to hurt her again. "Maribel was nervous, you could see fear in her eyes, she was scared to even have to talk to us," he said. Her tale of slavery in the lap of luxury sounded bizarre, but the names, places, and circumstances she gave checked out. Nicodemus believed her; he just had to find a law to cover the evil she described. The Las Vegas police passed on her complaint because the crimes spanned at least three states, which moved the case beyond local jurisdiction. Nicodemus went to the law manuals and found a possible place for her tale of assault, fraud, conspiracy, transportation of illegal aliens, and forced labor under statutes dating before the Civil War. Termed involuntary servitude under Title 18, United States Code, section 1584, the laws date from 1818, even before Abraham Lincoln engineered passage of the 13th Amendment, which in 1865 abolished slavery. The statutes were expanded twice around the turn of the century because they originally concerned only blacks, "mulattoes, or persons of color." It was only the second time in nearly 40 years that authorities west of the Mississippi had seen a case like this.

The case Maribel brought was a first for the FBI in Las Vegas. Yet it was not the first time the FBI had heard about Sante and her maids. Beginning in 1982, other special agents in California and Mexico found themselves listening to frightened young women who had escaped from Sante's other homes and wanted the government to stop her. It took Maribel's complaint for the agency to investigate in earnest, gather all the earlier FBI files on the Kimeses, and build a comprehensive case.

Two years before Maribel surfaced, a former tutor for Kenny Kimes reported Sante to an FBI agent in Fremont, California, on November 18, 1982. Fresh out of Indiana University with a bachelor's degree in elementary education, Teresa Richards, 22, had just returned that July from a program in Europe. The summer is too late to start looking for most teaching jobs, so Teresa searched the listings at IU's placement office, where at first Sante's name was gold. She was the soft voice on the phone promising a life of chauffeured limousines and tropical beaches for the graduates who agreed to home tutor her son Kenny. "She sounded wonderful," said Naomi Lee, the assistant placement director. "She said, 'We're a fabulously wealthy family, and this would be a dream job. They would have everything they needed. They wouldn't need a salary.' She said because of their great wealth, they didn't want Kenny going to public school."

When Naomi placed a highly recommended graduate with the Kimeses in early 1982, Sante sent flowers and seven-year-old Kenny wrote a thank-you note in neat block letters on lined composition paper. The placement even made the newsletter of IU's School of Education in Spring 1982 under the headline "Unusual request demonstrates school's wide reputation," so proud they were that a jet-setter like Sante looked to IU for qualified teachers. "The family, which is associated with a lengthy chain of hotels, was simply pausing between return from Switzerland and departure for Hawaii," said the newsletter. "The new teacher should be ready to leave with them in one week. Mobility apparently is a hallmark of the pattern of their lives."

After six months, Sante called again looking for another teacher. She claimed the first one preached religion so much that Kenny began saying, " 'It is too bad you are going to hell, Papa, for drinking,' " Naomi wrote in a 1982 report. Not hearing from the teacher, Naomi believed Sante and sent her a replacement: Teresa Richards. Sante painted the same glamorous picture for Teresa during a phone interview, and she signed on for one year, believing that her first job out of college that summer of 1982 would be a wonderful adventure.

"I was really naïve; I trusted everybody before all this," Teresa said.

At the bar of the El Camino Real Hotel in Puerto Vallarta, Mexico, Teresa met the busty Elizabeth Taylor look-alike who was her new boss, the ruddy-faced husband who always seemed to have a drink in his hand, and their chatterbox little boy. Sante told Teresa that Kenneth Kimes was worth $388 million, owned half of Disney World, and had been ambassador to two countries. Sante added that her own résumé included eight years at the United Nations, and that Bob Hope and a French ambassador were Kenny's godfathers. She even pulled out the 1974 newspaper clipping showing her and Kimes meeting Vice President Gerald Ford and his wife, Betty. It all sounded exciting to Teresa, who grew up in a small Indiana town, where her dad managed an Osco pharmacy.

Along with the name-dropping, Sante also tried to charm the young Midwesterner, a green-eyed brunette who stood model tall and thin at five-feet-eight and 125 pounds. In the mornings, they shared the same mirror, where Sante offered makeup tips, like rubbing pink lipstick into her cheeks as rouge. She fixed her gaze and listened intently to the tutor's ideas about teaching Kenny, even telling the young woman "to think of me as your sister." Then there

were the gifts. Teresa received a "welcome" sundress, a belated birthday sundress, a "rainy day
Tuesday" dress when bad weather ruined one day,
a new bathing suit, a gold heart pendant, yet another
sundress, and a short outfit in white, Sante's favorite
color. "He (Mr. Kimes) bought her a 22-karat diamond engagement ring," Teresa gushed in a letter
home to her folks. "I've never seen such a rock! It
goes great with her big black bouffant wig, size 50
bust (?)! and never-fail white lacy ruffled tops! Seriously, her whole wardrobe is white!! and see-
through. It is a scream! Only she can get away with
it. People do stare at her, for the wrong reasons, but
she loves it. She really is a sight!! I was embarrassed
at first, but I've gotten used to it. $ talks, and she
doesn't care what she says, how loud or what!"

Palm trees ringed Casa Conchita, their beachfront
rental in Puerto Vallarta, located just 30 feet from the
ocean. From the patio, Teresa looked past a garden
full of papayas, bananas, and coconuts to a nearly
empty beach and ocean dotted with an occasional
sailboat. Above, pelicans kept diving into the water
for fish, and the sky blazed orange and red every
evening as the sun began its descent seemingly
inches from the house right down into the ocean.

This paradise had a dark side, as Teresa slowly
discovered when she met the pregnant maid and
heard Sante recite the rules of the house. Settling into
her private room and bath in Casa Conchita the first
day, Teresa was alone only a few minutes. Sante had
ordered Gloria the maid to give the new tutor a pedicure, a beauty parlor staple Teresa never had experienced before. Eight months pregnant with her ankles
swollen, Gloria sank to her knees and applied bright
pink polish to Teresa's toenails. At that moment
Sante decided to tell Teresa that some people were
just better than others were.

"She told me that we were around different

classes, and that the maids had to understand that, that they were to do what I told them to do," Teresa said. "She told me to watch Gloria. She was never to use the telephone. She said, 'She's a sneaky bitch.'

"She told me to watch her, she was never to leave home without myself or a member of the family. And that I was not to lift a finger. She said they're supposed to do everything." The next day the Kimeses left for Las Vegas, and Teresa was alone with Kenny and Gloria for five days. She watched as Gloria cleaned and ironed under the hot Mexican sun from 7:00 A.M. until 10:00 P.M., with only two 15-minute rest periods and a short lunch break. With Sante gone, Teresa told the poor woman to rest, and she began confiding in the new tutor, claiming Sante hit her, hadn't taken her once to the doctor during her pregnancy, and never paid her. She also suspected Sante of stealing her Salvadoran passport.

Alarm bells rang in Teresa's head, but she didn't quit her job. She wanted to think things through, and when the Kimeses returned, she asked for a day off and poured her doubts into a diary while sunning herself on a large rock about 50 feet offshore. She swam out holding aloft a big satchel jammed with a lifetime of keepsakes, like photos from her European trip, her address book, wallet, passport, Kenny's passport, even her First Holy Communion rosary. As she wrote, she looked up and saw Sante in the distance, staring at her from the balcony of Casa Conchita.

As evening drew near, she swam back, tossed her bag on her bed, and hurried to the kitchen, where Sante was calling for her to help peel potatoes. When she returned to her room, the bag and all her momentos were gone. Out of fear or denial, she didn't want to believe what she suspected, that Sante had taken her bag. She never confronted Sante and followed her instructions not to report her passport stolen, since that was too much of a hassle; besides Sante claimed she had a duplicate one for Kenny. In the days to follow, Sante's conversation echoed with passages from the missing diary. Teresa had speculated in the diary that the Kimeses could be a Mafia family. Suddenly, Sante brought up the subject of mob influence in Las Vegas as the reason she didn't like going there.

Even more unsettling was the last time she saw Gloria. Uncharacteristically, Sante invited the maid out to a restaurant with the family, Teresa said. Before the meal arrived, Sante grabbed Gloria by the arm and took her outside, saying she was putting her on a plane home to El Salvador to have her baby, even though her family was in Santa Ana. Carrying only a paper bag, Gloria was whisked away and Sante returned 15 minutes later, too quick, Teresa thought, to get to the airport and back. At Casa Conchita, Gloria's clothes were still in the closet with her beloved Bible. The FBI never found her when it began tracking down the maids to build its slavery case against Sante.

Teresa spent two months and two days working for the Kimeses. She hung on for weeks after Gloria left, saying years later that she foolishly was acting like a Nancy Drew trying to conduct her own investigation. She also secretly rebelled. Left alone for a moment with a potential replacement for Gloria, Teresa whispered, "Don't take the job," to the young Mexican girl. She also helped another maid escape.

By this time, unbeknownst to Teresa, Sante had already called Naomi Lee at Indiana University asking for another tutor, complaining that Teresa had taken Kenny boating without permission. She also wouldn't let Teresa near any more prospective maids.

In late August, the family flew to Guadalajara and stayed in the Malibu Hotel, where under the palm trees in the courtyard, Sante interviewed for more maids and a baby-sitter. One applicant had brought along her 14-year-old kid sister, a pixie with short black hair and dark eyes who looked easy to boss around.

"Mrs. Kimes said that I could work better with her because I was younger than my sister and I could play with Kenny because I was a child," said Dolores Vasquez Salgado.

Sante assured the girl's parents that 14-year-old Dolores would have a wonderful life full of new clothes and travel. In Guadalajara, the Salgado family of two adults and 10 children lived in a two-bedroom house. Dolores had already dropped out of school after the sixth grade and worked in a sewing factory for two months before meeting the Kimeses. Sante said Dolores would keep in touch with letters, and the family would get $200 by mail each month if they let Dolores go to the States. The talk of money seduced Dolores, who dreamed of a fancy dress and big party for her 15th birthday, the traditional coming-of-age celebration for Latinas.

Sante's promises worked, so by early September, Dolores and another teenager from Puerto Vallarta had joined the Kimeses. When the group arrived in Tijuana, Sante informed Teresa it was her job to get herself and Dolores through Customs. "She told me to get her across, use my imagination and walk her through, make up a story," said Teresa. Instructing Dolores not to say a word, Teresa told Customs that she was a teacher who had lost her passport in Mexico and that the 14-year-old Mexican girl was her deaf-mute student. When that lie failed, Sante put Teresa and the two maids into a cab and sent them to the border, telling them to meet the family at a Holiday Inn in San Diego.

Stubbornly, Teresa stayed in the cab, her fighting spirit and anger at Sante greater than the fear of

THEY CALL THEM GRIFTERS

smuggling two illegal aliens across the border. "At this point I thought, you bitch. I'm going to beat you at this game. I'm going to get to San Diego. You are going to see me in that hotel," Teresa said.

The cab dropped them at a deserted beach on the border outside of Tijuana. For an hour they walked along the beach. All of a sudden 100 feet of ocean loomed between them and the American shore. Teresa told the two Mexican girls to sit down on the beach and wait, while she waded across the chin-high water. It was high tide. A man on the American side ran over to Teresa, screaming that she was foolish. Rough currents had washed many people out to sea from that inlet. Waiting for the tide to pass, she and the man then pulled the two girls across the inlet to the American side, keeping their heads above water.

Soaked, exhausted, and broke, Teresa piled the girls into a cab for the 45-mile ride to downtown San Diego, not knowing at which of several Holiday Inns Sante was staying. By chance, they pulled up to one just as the Kimeses were getting into a van to take them to the airport for the flight back to Las Vegas. They weren't waiting for Teresa anymore, it seemed. "The look on her face was, 'Oh, My God, you weren't supposed to make it,'" said Teresa.

Teresa stayed just two weeks longer.

She saw Sante slap Dolores in the face when she broke a lamp while dusting in the Las Vegas living room. Scared for the girl, she advised her to think of a safe escape. Teresa said she was also frightened for herself, worried about breaking her one-year contract. "I was to the point that, at this time, after two months, I was delirious," she said. "I was scared, I was brainwashed.

"I think we had such a fear instilled in us, we were so intimidated, we didn't—the look just—it's hard to explain the eyes, the look in Sante's eyes," Teresa remembered years later. "You know, and the fear that she can instill in you, just with a glare. I didn't know what would happen if I tried to go, what would happen to me and what would happen to the maids.

"I look back on it myself, and I think, how could I have, why didn't I just up and leave?" she added. "And it goes back to, at that time, it was just a total— I felt like our minds were in chaos and not knowing what was truly right, what was truly wrong."

When she finally took a plane to her sister in San Francisco, she told Naomi Lee not to send any more graduates to Sante. One last IU girl had already been dispatched as Teresa's replacement, but she lasted just a month after Sante pulled a gun on her, according to a claim made in a civil suit settled before it went to trial. Naomi typed out a long report to her university about Sante and arranged for the FBI to interview Teresa.

Still with the Kimeses, Dolores said she also thought about leaving. "But the lady would tell me if I would get out on the street, she would call the police, and I was going to be taken to jail." At first she submitted to the routine of cooking, laundry, ironing, and housework, even though Sante had promised her a baby-sitting job. The other maid sewed all day long, and Sante forbade the two domestics from talking to each other. Instead of the new clothes she was promised, Dolores wore cast-offs.

Slowly the pixie began to stand tall. Letters she had written to her parents were thrown under a car seat, where Dolores found them weeks later while cleaning. She confronted *la señora*, who had promised to mail the letters to Mexico. "Stupid," Sante replied, slapping her in the face. During a two-day trip to Miami, Dolores accidentally burned a hamburger bun in a hotel room, and Sante threw boiling water on her back in the bathtub. That was it for the daughter of Jesus Vasquez and Concepcion Salgado. "I have a very strong personality, and I told her the next time she beat me up, I was going to return it all to her," Dolores said.

Of all the maids, Dolores was the only one who hit back at Sante, prosecutors said. Although it happened just once, *la señora* went into a frenzy, following Dolores all over the house, pushing and slapping her. Then in November, toward the end of her stay, Sante pulled a gun on her little rebel. "I was lying down," said Dolores. "She came with a gun on that day she got mad at me, and she put it in my stomach, and she said, 'You're going to be sorry, stupid.' "

Sante decided it was better to switch maids than keep fighting with Dolores. She took the spunky 14-year-old to the border near Tijuana and gave her $32 for the 36-hour bus ride back to Guadalajara, where a few days later, in December 1982, Dolores told her story to an FBI agent at the American consulate.

When tutor Cynthia Montano left the Kimeses after two months in the spring of 1984, she also made a beeline for the FBI. A month after graduating from the University of New Mexico, Cynthia answered a want ad in the early winter of 1984 for a job tutoring a third-grader that promised "travel, excitement, and excellent opportunities." Following phone interviews with a secretary of Sante's, Cynthia, who spoke Spanish fluently, was hired after sending a letter to the Kimeses about why she was right for the job. She met the couple for the first time at the Las Vegas airport on February 27, 1984, and heard the same promises given to Teresa Richards: world travel, free time, being part of a loving family, an "opportunity of a lifetime." A month later Cynthia said her passport, birth and teaching certificate were missing and she found herself walking the slums of Mexico City during Easter Week, recruiting new maids for Sante.

"She wanted me to go to a rural part of Mexico to

look for young girls under the age of 18 who didn't seem very well educated and who had a subservient-type personality and attitude. I was to make sure they weren't wearing makeup or jewelry or had their fingernails painted," said Cynthia. "Someone that she said that I thought would be very pleasant, that would be someone who wouldn't put up a fuss about having to take orders.

"She would tell me to just tell them that they would be paid very well, and that it would be an excellent opportunity·for the girls, and that we would be offering them a better way of living. And that's what I told the parents."

At turns cajoling and forceful, Sante conned Cynthia into smuggling two teenaged Mexican girls past Customs in Tijuana by hiding them in the trunk of a rental car charged to the tutor's own credit card. Inch by inch, Sante pushed Cynthia into this predicament by orchestrating crises that seemingly left no other way to cross the border. Claiming she couldn't get airline reservations for everybody, Sante put Cynthia and the maids on a bus to Tijuana from Mexico City while the Kimeses flew.

After the 30-hour bus ride, Cynthia called Sante's answering service expecting to meet her in Tijuana but found that *la señora* had flown on to Newport Beach, California, because, she said, Kenny fell sick. Relax and stay the night, she told Cynthia, promising to fly down the next day, and "we'll all come back together." Tomorrow came, and Sante said she was planning to take the afternoon flight out and they could all go shopping together in Tijuana, but first they needed a rental car and could Cynthia go get one? "And I told her that I didn't have enough money," Cynthia said, "because they had only given me enough for meals and lodging for the night. And then she told me, 'Well, don't you have a credit card?' And I said, yes, I do. And she goes, 'Well, use that.' And I was real reluctant, and I said I didn't really want to. And she said, 'Well, that's nonsense. We'll give you the money when you get back.' "

So Cynthia rented a car, using her own credit card. Next Sante called, announcing that she had changed her mind again and wasn't coming down after all because Kenny felt sicker. "You're going to have to come back yourself," Sante told Cynthia, outlining the breezy way she expected the tutor to break the law and smuggle in the two maids.

"Well, how am I supposed to do that when I don't even have any identification for the girls?" Cynthia asked. "I don't even have my own passport or anything to get across. She just laughed and said, 'Well, it's really very easy. You're just going to have to put the girls in the trunk and come back across by yourself. If you just laugh about it, it's really very easy. There's nothing to it. People do it, millions of people do it all the time.' "

Cynthia said she was frightened. " 'Nothing will happen to you if you get caught,' " Sante assured her. " 'Now, stop acting like a little girl. It's time for you to grow up now. Don't you care about Kenny? You see, I can't leave him alone. You'll have to be a big girl now and grow up and do this by yourself.' "

After some more arguing, Cynthia gave in, figuring she had no choice and smuggled the girls through just the way Sante had apparently planned all along. Those two Mexican girls ran away after only a week in Newport Beach, when Sante slapped one of them. Then *la señora* told Cynthia she had to return to Mexico and find more maids, actually suggesting that the smuggling benefited mankind.

" 'Can't you see that it would be better to bring them over here,' " Sante told Cynthia. " 'And you're supposed to be a grown-up lady now, and you claim that you're a Christian and you love people. Can't

you see that giving them a home here with us would
be giving them a better life?' "

Sante told Cynthia to bring back six or seven
maids; with her Spanish she could manage that
many. On the way to the airport, Kenneth Kimes
secretly told Cynthia to scale back the operation.

" 'Now, if you tell Sante that we had this conversation, I'll deny it,' " Kimes told Cynthia. " 'And you'll
be the one in trouble. But for our own good and
your own safety don't bring back that many. That's
ridiculous, we don't even need that many. If you can,
bring back one or two. One is even plenty.' "

This time, the ruse failed. Mexican officials found
two maids in Cynthia's car trunk, detained the tutor,
and confiscated the rental car, forcing her to walk
alone across the border at one a.m. When she called
Sante from San Diego, she heard no sympathy for
her ordeal, just an order to go back and get more
maids again.

"She threatened me at one point, she said, 'Well,
you're not coming back without a maid. And if I
have to go and sit there in the hotel room while you
go out and find these girls, that's what I'm going
to do.' "

Finally Cynthia called a friend for a little perspec-
tive and quit her job. Like Teresa before her, she
found Sante's alleged influence frightening. "I was
so scared because of the money they had, and the
power that she told me that they had," Cynthia said.
"I was just afraid that they would try and threaten
my family, jeopardize any future possibilities of my
employment. I was just scared."

Written threats were as common as newspapers
in the Kimes' household, filling dozens of pages of
instructions for the maids and tutors. Sante's propa-
ganda read like "Mama Knows Best" meets "Brave
New World." She presented rules like never using
the telephone or never venturing outside as crucial

to the safety and health of everyone in the home. In boldface type, she promised certain disaster for breaking the rules in these notes, translated into Spanish, that she told the maids to learn by heart.

"If you don't have your papers, BE VERY CAREFUL. IT IS VERY DANGEROUS!! Many times in the past the family has had beautiful women working for them, but they DID NOT PAY ATTENTION, AND SOME BAD, ENVIOUS AMERICANS called the police and the immigration, and they told them that the girls were illegal. THE GIRLS WERE VERY STUPID AND TALKED WITH THESE PEOPLE AND THEY ANSWERED THE DOOR AND THE POLICE CAME AND THEY TOOK THEM TO JAIL. IT WAS VERY TERRIBLE, AND NO ONE COULD HELP THEM.

"IT IS VERY IMPORTANT THAT YOU DON'T SPEAK WITH ANYBODY WHO IS A STRANGER. IT DOES NOT MATTER IF THEY CAN SPEAK SPANISH. DO NOT SPEAK TO THEM! That is how it was with these girls, they talked to them only because the Americans knew Spanish, and they took them to prison for many years. STAY IN THE HOUSE, OR THEY CAN TAKE YOU AND PUT YOU IN PRISON, where it is like a hell, where they treat you very ugly, they hardly give you anything to eat, they beat you, they molest you and everything!!

"IF YOU PAY ATTENTION TO THE FAMILY AND YOU DON'T GO TO THE DOOR AND YOU DON'T ANSWER THE TELEPHONE FOR ANY REASON, DON'T DO THESE THINGS, then everything is going to go very beautiful and you are going to have a very happy life. IF YOU DON'T PAY ATTENTION, IT IS GOING TO BE A HELL, HELL FOR YOU.

"THIS IS VERY IMPORTANT! NEVER go to the door or answer the phone. NEVER SPEAK WITH SOMEONE IF THE FAMILY IS NOT THERE TO

PROTECT YOU!!! Try to be very happy because you are going to be here permanently, and you are going to continue a very happy life with your family. Find yourself with a lot of LOYALTY for the family and work hard, and thank GOD THAT YOU HAVE A GOOD LIFE. Only treat with loyalty and love your family and PAY ATTENTION TO WHAT THEY TELL YOU, IF NOT, YOU ARE GOING TO LIVE WITH WOE AND HELL FOR MANY YEARS. ONLY PAY ATTENTION TO EVERYTHING THE FAMILY TELLS YOU AND EVERYTHING WILL GO WELL!! Go with God!!"

Family here meant the Kimeses. Sante's writing extolled the cult of her family as a God-fearing group who fed, clothed, and thought for the maids and thus deserved their devotion. She wanted the maids to call her Mama or Mother and referred to Kimes as Papa or Father. In a questionnaire translated into Spanish for prospective maids, she promised "you will become like part of my family. You will be like my little sister, and I will teach you how to do many things." Questions 21 and 22 bluntly asked, "Are you ready to work hard and become part of my family? Are you ready to spend the rest of your life with my family?"

This family was a matriarchy. "Treat Mother like a QUEEN, AND SHE WILL TREAT YOU VERY WELL." Sante scripted home life—from the prune juice and tea taken with half a spoon of cream and imitation sugar that Mother wanted in the morning to turned down beds and soft lights that Mother wanted at night. Sewing instructions, which said "sewing is very fun," marched on for 42 pages, giving techniques for woven fabrics, knits, lace, leather, vinyl, interfacing, nap materials, threading, hems, plain seams, French seams, gathering, darts, patterns, ironing, creasing pants, and starch. "The starch should be used liberally, but only where each individual likes it. It should be used on Papa's collars and cuffs. His shirts should look perfect, or we will get furious. Mama likes starch on her ruffles. Kenny's shirts should be ironed just like Papa's, PERFECTLY!"

For the tutors and house sitters, Sante also wrote detailed instructions about keeping the maids as busy as traffic cops at rush hour. "4. Maid: CONTROL! CONTROL! CONTROL! CONTROL! CONTROL! CONTROL! CONTROL! CONTROL!" Under this heading she listed eight tasks like cleaning the closets ("wax everything"), organizing, dusting, "sew, sew, and sew some more!!!" No. 8 was "begin again and have her redo things if run out!!!" In another note, she told the staff, "We are very kind to our maids, but if needed we can become Dracula" and listed rules that turned the teachers and house sitters into jailers: Don't let them be idle, don't be their friend, don't let them talk to visitors or maintenance people, don't accept or give them mail, lock the doors and hide the phone when out of the house. Always she had excuses for such measures, like process servers bearing subpoenas or long-distance telephone bills if the maids called Mexico.

In the nine months the FBI investigated the Kimeses, agents weren't able to pinpoint the exact number of maids tricked into slavery, but evidence suggested that Sante had been turning her posh homes into sweatshops as far back as 1978. They never found that original slave, but learned of her through the Kimeses' former friend and neighbor in Hawaii, Beverly Bates, the woman Sante convinced to impersonate her once.

In the fall of 1978, Sante extracted another huge favor. Beverly planned to fly to Los Angeles on business, and Sante asked her to pick up a maid she had hired there through an employment agency. Explaining she had argued with the agency's owner,

Sante wanted Beverly to use her own name to pick up the young Mexican girl. The night before Beverly left, Kenneth Kimes telephoned in a drunken rage. "He didn't want me to bring back another Mexican maid," said Beverly. "He was sick of them. And they were the ruination of his life. That his child couldn't even speak English." In the past Sante had joked to Beverly that the maids were her slaves, and her friend took the comment as jest. Next morning, an apologetic Kenneth Kimes called Beverly back and sweet-talked her into picking up the maid in Los Angeles and escorting her back to Honolulu.

At the employment agency, Beverly found a young woman in her 20s wearing raggedy clothes and carrying a small satchel. To Beverly, she seemed to be a sweet person unsure about traveling so far away. She spoke almost no English, so Beverly used a Spanish dictionary. They managed some basic conversation, although she had since forgotten the woman's name. Beverly said she began to feel responsible for the woman and pointed out her own house on Portlock Road before dropping the maid off at Sante's. She asked Sante if she could visit the woman, and her friend said no, explaining that maids work better without social contacts.

That excuse didn't sit right with Beverly, so when Sante was out of the house, she checked on the young maid a few weeks later during the winter holidays. "The minute she saw me, she broke out in hysterical crying and was begging me to help her," Beverly said. A long narrow burn ran along one arm, and Beverly wanted to take the woman away immediately but she was watching Kenny, then three years old. Beverly collected the woman's clothes and told her to walk down the beach to her house later. When the maid arrived at dawn, she crawled into Beverly's closet, where she stayed most of the day, shaking and crying. That evening Sante and Kenneth went to

Beverly's house looking for the maid, still cowering in the closet. Beverly made up a story that a Mexican friend had rescued her, and Sante and Kenneth left on the trail of that person. Beverly bought a return airline ticket for the woman and put her on the next plane to Los Angeles. Some time afterward, Beverly noticed that the Kimeses had erected a wrought-iron fence in the back of their property, blocking off the beach where the maid had walked to freedom.

CHAPTER 7

"I was diagnosed critical. I am now medically unable to protect myself."

Walls began to close in on Sante and Kenneth Kimes from both ends of the country during the summer of 1985. The FBI raided their Las Vegas home on July 12, 1985, freeing a 17-year-old maid who in Mexico had barely completed the second grade. Naïve and scared, she had been held captive for 226 days. The same day the FBI hunted for the Kimeses in Nevada, Sante faced a jury in Washington, D.C., on the fur theft case. The Mayflower Hotel caper unfolded past midnight on Tuesday, February 5, 1980, during a damp evening when ladies needed their furs. However, the case only made it to trial five years and six months later in the heat of July. Over those years, the Kimeses had requested 21 postponements and submitted a barrage of doctors' letters from Hawaii and Mexico claiming all sorts of dire illnesses. Prosecutors who later checked the claims found them full of holes. For example, the docket sheet indicated that Sante spent a year in a Hawaiian hospital precisely when tutor Teresa Richards saw her boss larger than life in Mexico, flouncing around in see-through white outfits. By riding a merry-go-round of 20 different attorneys, the Kimeses postponed the fur trial even longer as each change of counsel produced another delay. "It is virtually inconceivable that a defendant of lesser wealth and position would have escaped or delayed the law's processes as the defendant has done in this case," said exasperated prosecutors.

Delay is like rust on the wheels of justice. So much time had passed that prosecutors were forced to drop a petit larceny charge against the couple when one of the complainants died. Besides the purloined fur, the Kimeses had swiped a man's herringbone topcoat and cashmere scarf from the Rogues Manor bar in the Capitol Hilton on February 3, 1980, police said. The coat owner had died Christmas Day, 1982, and because he couldn't testify in person, the rules against hearsay evidence meant the charge also died. The fate of Kenneth Kimes also improved with the passage of time. In the five-year-long docket sheet, neither the judge, nor the prosecutor, nor the 20th defense lawyer could decipher what their predecessors on the case had decided about the millionaire. Although an original codefendant, he was the invisible man at the Washington, D.C., courthouse that July 12 morning when the jury heard opening arguments. When the judge asked where Kenneth Kimes was, Sante's defense counsel said Mexico while the prosecutor said Hawaii. Both sides referred to the paper trail of health problems and the notion he was too ill to travel to Washington, D.C. Wishing to avoid yet another postponement, Judge Sylvia Bacon allowed Sante's trial to proceed without her partner, scheduling an umpteenth hearing on his status for September 5, 1985.

However, Kenneth Kimes was not on his sickbed 6,000 miles away under the Hawaii sun. He was just across the Potomac River in Arlington, Virginia, at an apartment that the Kimeses had rented for the duration of Sante's trial. The couple's nerve didn't end there. Defendant Sante wore turbans and flowing ensembles to court each day that were cleaned and pressed by yet another Mexican maid, slaving away near the capital of freedom.

''The lady would change sometimes three to four times a day, the blouse and the pants because she would only use white clothes, and I had to wash that every day, every day," said Maria de Rosario Vasquez Camacho. Just three months before, Maria, 21, had kissed her four-year-old daughter good-bye, left her with relatives in Acapulco and crossed the border in hopes of finding a better job than selling pints in a liquor store. She found Sante, who promised $250 a week when they met in Santa Ana, California. *La señora* whisked her to Kimes' Motel Mecca in Anaheim then on to the rental in Arlington, where Maria stayed glued to a sewing machine late into the night. "I would sew in the afternoon her clothes or hats," Maria said. "She liked wearing hats a lot, and she used to tell me to put on laces or things like that." Maria was so exhausted that Kenneth Kimes even told her, "Go to sleep. Mama is very crazy."

Sante spun a dramatic tale on the stand of being naked "for a good 15 minutes" and screaming as 8 to 10 strange men burst into her Mayflower Hotel room, several pinning her down on the bed as they turned suite 742 upside down looking for the stolen fur. Testifying in a failed bid to suppress evidence found in her hotel room, Sante also introduced herself with a flourish: "The spelling of my first name is *S-h-a-n-t-e*, with a little thing over the *e*." Awakened from her sleep, she said the men in her hotel room "grabbed me, pulled me out of the bed with no clothing on. I didn't know who they were. They knocked over the lamp. . . . They attacked me. I was trying to get away from them to get to the phone to call for help. I was literally held down to stop from reaching the phone."

The men, who turned out to be police officers and a hotel security guard, let her get dressed only after they had handcuffed her arms behind her back, she said. It's quite a feat to get dressed with your hands in manacles, so prosecutor Kenneth Carroll quickly asked, "You had to put the clothing on with the handcuffs on?"

"No," she said refining her story. "They took off the handcuffs because I couldn't get them on."

Hotel security guard Alvin Dozier testified that Sante was wearing a negligee when he and three cops knocked at her door and she let them in. Washington, D.C., Detective Thomas Grace said Sante "sounded a little intoxicated" when officers arrived. "Her speech was messed up. It could have been the door. I couldn't tell. But, it—she just kept saying, 'I can't see it. I can't see what you're talking about,' when I held up my I.D. card. I believe I held up my badge also."

Dressed in his underwear, Kenneth Kimes was more accommodating saying, " 'Come on in, we have nothing to hide,' " Grace testified. Grace was skeptical at first that a crime had been committed. "At that time, I felt that it could have been a mistake. The lady might have been intoxicated. She may have picked up the coat as a joke. It just didn't seem right that somebody would steal a coat like that."

In the Kimeses' room, cops found three other garments, including the white fox coat and a short champagne-colored mink, which were missing their labels. However, Katherine Kenworthy's stolen mink was not in the room. Noticing a broken lock on their hotel window, Detective Thomas Grace looked out and saw a garment on the lobby roof five floors below. It was the torn custom-made monogrammed lining from Kenworthy's coat. On the windowsill, Grace noticed a small piece of material that turned out to be lining tape from the stolen fur. Grace found the lining tape on the rooftop the next day and guessed that it fluttered to the ground when he had opened the window. Two weeks later a hotel maintenance man discovered the Kenworthy fur coat balled up and stuffed behind the ice machine near the seventh-floor elevator.

Defense witness Jose Duran was one of five Good Samaritan types who gave Sante their names and phone numbers during her yelling match with the Mayflower checkroom over one of her coats. Four of these passersby testified in her defense at the trial. A Bolivian immigrant, who ran a cleaning company in Arlington, Duran said he stepped forward that day as Sante was screaming for the police to help her with the coat check dust up, "because I was really sorry for her. She was crying and she was very, very nervous and—I mean she was treated rotten too, that lady." Duran then walked into the Town and Country lounge with a friend and stayed at the bar until closing. Sante was sitting 15 feet away from him. He testified that Sante wore only her white fox fur and never returned once she left with Kenneth Kimes. Given the prior scene in the lobby, Duran noticed her at the bar and she waved good-bye to him when she left. Another witness to Sante's hysterics at the coat check testified that she did nothing strange in the piano bar. Peggy Brown, a word processor at a trade union office, said she had a clear view of Sante in the lounge and was watching her because of her big white fur and glitzy costume jewelry. She swore Sante wore only her own fox in the bar.

Prosecutor Carroll had trouble giving the jury a logical reason why Sante would take another woman's coat. His case was based on the two eyewitnesses in the bar, who saw the fur-over-fur trick, and the items recovered from the Kimeses' room and hotel rooftop. Carroll theorized that Sante was upset over the coat check allegedly losing her fur and after a few drinks, "maybe she thinks, 'maybe this looks like my coat, maybe I'll take it. Or maybe I'll get back at the hotel because the other woman (Mrs. Kenworthy) will get on them about it, and maybe they'll do something about that.' " Carroll also suggested that Sante got a thrill from stealing. "Or maybe it's just like when you're a teenager, sometimes when you go in the drugstore—kids have done it, you all know it, you'll take something just to see if you can get away with it. Or maybe she has a problem."

Defense attorney Gary Kohlman pointed out the absurdity of the stunt to argue that it couldn't be true. "Did that lady, as two government witnesses say, go through a charade there in the lounge and put one fur coat on and then put another on, after having made all this disturbance in the hotel? Did that happen? Or, are four other witnesses more correct, that that lady had a dispute with the hotel management, that she was in tears, that she had asked for the police to come, that she had gone and had some drinks with her husband. Then she said goodbye to the people who had helped her and very conspicuously, because that's the way she is, she walked out of there wearing that full-length coat that she always had and never took off, not carrying anybody else's coat out of there?"

During all of this, Maria the maid, ironing at the Arlington rental, was growing ever more homesick for California. Nearly every day she wrote a letter back home, but Sante only mailed the first two. When she asked when they were returning, Sante praised her work and counseled patience. Sante never hit her, but Maria claimed that 10-year-old Kenny became the enforcer in his mother's absence. She said he wouldn't let her pick up a phone, saying, " 'No, no, Maria, my mommy is going to get angry.' " She also claimed that the boy kicked her legs, pulled her hair, and barged in on her in the shower during his bad days. Maria's liberation was just two short weeks away, set in motion by Sante's bizarre disappearance just as the Washington, D.C., jury convicted her.

After five days of testimony, the jury got the case at 11:20 A.M. on July 18, 1985. At 12:17 P.M., Judge Bacon gave them a lunch break until 1:20 P.M. and specifically instructed Sante to be back in the courtroom by 1:30. After lunch, Sante was nowhere to be seen. She missed getting butterflies in her stomach when the jury sent a note at 2:37 P.M., saying, "We have reach(ed) a verdict," followed four minutes later by another message reading, "Please disregard the last note." The verdict was in by 3:55 P.M., but Sante still was not. Her lawyer Gary Kohlman requested a delay, which the judge refused because several jurors had already completed their service. The panel voted to convict Sante of grand larceny. Immediately after hearing the verdict, Judge Bacon issued a bench warrant for Sante's arrest. She was now officially a fugitive from justice.

At the moment she was expected in court, Sante claimed to be walking across North Fairfax Drive in Arlington just as the driver of a Fiat was making a right turn onto that street. The driver allegedly struck her, then drove away. According to doctor's notes from Arlington Hospital, "report of the EMT (emergency medical technician) is that the pedestrian and a car were both stopped and both started moving at the same time and she was brushed by the auto. She does not recall the accident. She complains of pain in head, neck, chest, abdomen, and legs, and complains of nausea."

On the accident report filed in the appeal of the fur-theft conviction, the hit-and-run driver was listed as Jose Duran, a janitor living in Arlington. Inexplicably, this name, occupation, and city matched the Jose Duran who took the stand in Sante's defense. Neither the court records nor several defense lawyers on this case could clarify whether the driver Duran was the witness Duran. Emergency room doctors described Sante as shaken, with some amnesia surrounding the accident but "oriented as to month, year, name, and place." X rays found no evidence of head trauma or broken bones, still she didn't call her lawyer or the court. Instead, against medical advice, she yanked out her IV tubes and checked herself out at 8:30 P.M. that evening. Prosecutors suggested she was faking: "Even a cursory review of the medical records demonstrates that the bases for her hospitalization all appear to be subjective, i.e. her own complaints, rather than objective evidence of broken bones, internal injuries, or the like."

On the run from the verdict in D.C., and from the FBI in Vegas, she went underground with Kenneth Kimes, Kenny, and the last of her Mexican maids, Maria. After taking the train to New Jersey, they flew to Las Vegas the next day, checking into the Ambassador Inn, since the FBI was watching their Geronimo Way home. On July 21, Sante telegrammed her attorney, Gary Kohlman, and Judge Bacon, saying the car accident knocked her unconscious, rendering her "unable to return to court or advise the court of my dilemma." She claimed she was only in Arlington to get her lawyer money to prepare an appeal and said someone stole her wallet, money, and personal papers during the car accident. "I left the medical facility against the orders of medical personnel," she said. "My condition became worse, and I was forced to obtain additional emergency medical assistance. I was diagnosed critical. I am now medically unable to protect myself. Please protect my interests and advise me what to do as my attorney. And what has happened in my proceedings."

While in hiding, Kenneth Kimes wore sunglasses and a hat, constantly looking over his shoulder. The Kimeses stayed in three more Las Vegas hotels, drove a van to San Diego, then to La Jolla, where they rented a $1,700 a month condo at 8203 Villa Mayorca Street under the aliases Kenneth and Sandra Louise

Estrada. Left alone when the others went grocery shopping in early August, Maria finally got her hands on a phone and called her sister in Santa Ana, giving her the telephone number of the La Jolla condo. Maria slipped and told Sante about the call, and *la señora* yelled, " 'Why did you call? Be happy. Be happy here. We are your family, we are your family.' "

Tracing the phone number, the FBI showed up on Saturday, August 3, 1985, and arrested Sante and Kenneth Kimes for slavery. Perhaps feeling guilty or wanting to look good in front of the agents, Kenneth Kimes handed Maria two $100 bills from the wad of $5,000 in his wallet. A federal prosecutor later did the math, adding the $32 bus fare Sante had given 14-year-old Dolores Salgado in 1992 to argue that the millionaires paid just $232 for all their maids.

CHAPTER 8

"Clinically speaking, this is a person who 'snaps' from time to time."

The government accused Sante and Kenneth Kimes of using "false promises" to trick eight "young naïve Spanish-speaking alien females" into slavery, holding them "by force, threats of force, intimidation, threats of deportation and arrest." A federal indictment portrayed Sante as a cruel Scarlett O'Hara who made slaves jump with harsh words, quick fists, and hot irons. Threats of violence, actual beatings, and stories that the police rape Latina women weighed like chains on the maids, for no shackles held them down.

Kenneth Kimes appeared as an aloof partner who didn't hit the help yet failed to stop his wife's violence and shuttled the maids among the couple's luxury houses. Unable to bolt every door or window, the couple turned their American tutors and house sitters into sentries who made sure the domestics stayed inside. "The defendants instructed their other employees not to allow the maids to answer the door, to use the telephone, or to be seen by visitors or guests. The maids were to be kept busy all of the time. The maids were never paid and were allowed no contact with their families."

Charged with 17 counts, including conspiracy, involuntary servitude, and transporting illegal aliens, Sante, if convicted, faced five years in prison per count for a maximum term of 85 years, if the sentences ran consecutively. Her husband, described as "aiding and abetting" in the scheme, was charged

with 15 counts, which carried a worst-case sentence
of 75 years.

The story of a wealthy couple enslaving the help
made the news in San Diego, Los Angeles, Las Vegas,
and Washington, D.C. It was a story that on the surface defied reason because the Kimeses could afford
live-in maids. Why would millionaires risk arrest,
jail, public shame, and civil lawsuits just to save a
few hundred dollars a month in wages? Their friends
and acquaintances were baffled.

"I can't even imagine, not even in my wildest
dreams, them being guilty of that," said Marvin Par-
ker, manager of Kimes' Mecca Motel in Anaheim,
across the street from Disneyland. "They are the
exact opposite of that—quiet, soft-spoken, very
wealthy. Why would they want to do something like
that?" Sante's lawyer at the time, Bert Sheela, Jr., told
the *Los Angeles Times*, "I know the Kimeses are very
upset. They are amazed that anyone would do this
to them. Both Mr. and Mrs. Kimes deny the charges."

Possible motives for their bizarre behavior surfaced
as court hearings began. Six days after their arrest in
August 1985, federal prosecutors suggested the couple were alcoholics. "Almost every witness that has
been contacted in connection with this investigation
indicates to us that both Mr. and Mrs. Kimes use
alcohol extensively and that they begin bingeing first
thing in the morning and continue drinking all day
long," prosecutor Susan King said. Friends said Kenneth Kimes appeared to retreat into his cups to avoid
conflict with his flamboyant wife. Kenneth Kimes at
times downed Jack Daniel's despite suffering a heart
attack. Sometimes the drink emboldened him to op-
pose Sante, as he did when he telephoned Hawaii
neighbor Beverly Bates and asked her not to pick up
a maid in Los Angeles. Mostly, he seemed to have
settled into his own haze and let his wife run the
household. Alcohol gave free rein to their worst

sides. "Sante can be very pleasant and fun loving, but I think she is a very neurotic, emotional person," said John Mitchell, a retired Marine Corps colonel who knew the couple in Hawaii. "They both drink too much, and this doesn't help. They're both suspicious people, they can change their minds real fast. They are always real careful about being seen. You've got some real characters there, they both have problems, emotional problems."

Federal prosecutor King, dubbed the "slave queen of the Potomac" for trying seven involuntary servitude cases, believed that Sante thrived on chaos. "There is some part of her that needs that charge, like an adrenaline rush," said King. "So if there's no excitement happening, she creates it, if she has no danger around, she creates it. Sure, it would have been cheaper to pay for the maids, but that wasn't as exciting." King also indicated that she believed consequences didn't matter to Sante, because her will was so strong. During the FBI investigation several months before the indictment, King got a phone call at her Washington, D.C., home from a woman, claiming to be a paralegal from Las Vegas, who began pumping her about the Kimes case. "I knew from the kinds of questions, I knew it was her," King said. "I called the FBI immediately. That's what I mean about her, she is just very gutsy." Prosecutors felt that Sante was the force behind the scheme and pushed her husband around. "Obviously, he had some kind of business acumen, but when it came to picking soul mates, I don't know," said King. "You've got to wonder."

While Kenneth Kimes let Sante lead at home, in court, his lawyer forged a separate path for him. Emphasizing that the 66-year-old millionaire did not strike any of the maids and had no prior convictions, his lawyer succeeded in getting him released on $100,000 bail. First Kenneth Kimes had to swear that prosecutors were wrong in saying he had assets in Mexico and Switzerland. In an affidavit, Kimes listed the $3.5 million Mecca Motel across the street from Disneyland as his major property. Running that motel was his primary business, he claimed, and he had no other financial dealings outside the United States. Among other significant assets, he listed the $800,000 Hawaii home and $250,000 Las Vegas house. Sante in her affidavit claimed her husband was the sole owner of his properties and that she was worth just $1,400.

Sante's track record ensured that bail would remain a fantasy. Her rap sheet began in 1961, spanning 10 arrests and four convictions for theft. Even worse, Sante's disappearing act during the fur trial in Washington, D.C., provided a fresh example of her "flight risk," so she awaited trial at the Clark County Detention Center in downtown Las Vegas. Inmate number 660599-9D-06 griped like a crank about aches and pains, logging 30 medical complaints in just 25 days. She claimed a laundry list of ills: cancer, pancreatic problems, headaches, dizziness, abdominal distention, tumors, high blood pressure, pain, no vision, dry skin, dry scalp, vitamin deficiency, feet swelling, inability to digest meat, vomiting, nausea, body swelling, vaginal itching, a broken toe, foot pain, bad body odor, weak feeling, aching teeth, bad hearing, multiple head injuries, confusion, memory loss, numbness in her right eye, sleep deprivation, and visions of "funny little sparkly lights."

Noting that doctors already gave her new shoes, eyeglasses, and medicine, jail official Joseph Evers hinted that her problems were mental not physical. "I am hard-pressed to understand the range of your complaints and suggest that as a result of the high incident of complaints, you contact the staff psychologist to discuss your present emotional state," he wrote in August 1985.

Prosecutors suggested Sante faked her illnesses. Jail physician Dr. Maurice Gregory found no evidence Sante had cancer, her most serious complaint, but didn't label her a con woman either. "I think malingering is out, but I do think that she has another psychiatric problem." Weeping during her exam with Gregory on August 27, she flitted like a hummingbird from topic to topic, unable to stay focused. He diagnosed her headaches, anxiety, hypertension, and confusion as post-concussion syndrome, which dovetailed with her story of being struck by a hit-and-run car the month before in Arlington, Virginia. "There is confusion, short attention span . . . distorted appreciation of what is really going on, where she was, and what was available to her there at the jail," Dr. Gregory said. "All of those taken together gave me the impression that she both had suffered some injury that may have caused her to become confused, plus I think she had a certain amount of confusion all the time." Like a lost person "coming out of the mountains," she was improving from the head injury and suffered "minimally" from the post-concussion syndrome, Gregory said. Under cross-examination by prosecutors, the doctor admitted Sante had no observable signs of a head injury and her symptoms could be hypertension she had suffered before the car accident.

Sante's mental illness was another possible motive for her behavior. Defense attorney Dominic Gentile suggested in a court document that Sante might be mentally ill. "There is reasonable cause to believe the defendant may be presently insane," he petitioned the court on September 6, 1985, to order psychiatric tests. "The defendant exhibits and relates an unusual amount of fear directed toward certain persons. Such fears may indicate paranoia unless there is a sufficient basis for such fears."

A court-appointed psychiatrist examined Sante on

September 18 and 19, 1985, and, while judging her competent to stand trial, he found she had a personality disorder. "The record indicates a basic, moderately severe character disorder of a mixed type," wrote Dr. William O'Gorman. During a three-hour-and-10-minute exam over two days, O'Gorman found her insight poor and her judgments impulsive. "She is a person who is very sensitive, shows rapid changes of mood, much grievance gathering, is moody, and is greatly concerned regarding her physical well-being. She did state that she had some grievances while in the detention center in view of the fact that she was not allowed to use the phone. She admits that she has been quite desperate while incarcerated and hopes that she will be released."

Asked to describe herself, Sante told the psychiatrist that she was stubborn, sensitive but not moody. She said she didn't like giving up, worried a lot, wanted people to like her, and enjoyed classical music, walks on the beach, socializing, and parties. She said she drank only an occasional glass of wine, switching to vodka and orange juice on weekends. "She states that she is a loving and warm person, loves children, is a romantic. 'I'm a one-man woman.'" Despite this vow of fidelity, she also told O'Gorman that while married to her second husband, she had an affair with a businessman and bore him a son.

Her early life, as related to O'Gorman, was a sad tale of being caught as a hungry 9-year-old stealing cheese. At age 18, she said she stole lipstick because she had no money and admitted using her adoptive father's credit cards four different times. As for Army National Guard Colonel Edwin Chambers, the adoptive father who saved her from a life on the streets of Los Angeles, Sante branded him a rapist who had sex with her from the time she was 11 until she turned 18. He had already died of a stroke by the time Sante made these accusations. In giving her family history, Sante was selective, omitting her first husband, whom she met and married while a journalism student at the University of California at Santa Barbara. With Kenneth Kimes, she claimed she had another baby after Kenny but gave this infant, named Kenian, to a family in Mexico because her husband didn't want any more children after his heart attack. "She regrets this action very much," O'Gorman wrote.

In a preview of her defense against the slavery charges, she blamed her troubles on the "Creeps"—her husband's adult son and daughter by his first marriage, his brother, a dentist, and his sister. She told the psychiatrist that the federal indictment was the latest in a string of hassles masterminded by the Creeps whom she claimed resented her marriage to millionaire Kenneth Kimes. "The patient stated that since she married her husband, the husband's relatives have constantly harassed her and have 'set us up.' " She said they put rattlesnakes in her car, broke into her homes in Newport Beach, Palm Springs, and Hawaii, poisoned her drink in 1970, told police in Hawaii she had kidnapped her mother-in-law when the lady was only visiting, and tried to kidnap her son Kenny. Their alleged antics have made her "frequently suspicious."

Describing her arrest in Washington, D.C., for stealing a fur coat, Sante again used the phrase "someone set me up," telling O'Gorman she later learned the real thief was a 52-year-old business associate who "was not a nice person."

While O'Gorman had some doubts about her sob story, her delivery was convincing enough that he didn't dismiss her tale outright. "The facts as presented to this examiner appear bizarre, but may not be without some truth," O'Gorman wrote, adding, "it is important, in the opinion of this examiner, to define delusion as a fixed false belief, unamenable to reason. It was recommended that these facts be checked to verify and substantiate her statements."

Sante's quirks and obsessions had been obvious for years. Like a Mack Truck on a two-lane highway, she dominated her surroundings. Ever since her high school days, people said she liked to control anyone and anything in her path. Appearances meant the world to her, from her fake eyelashes and white gowns to the neatly embroidered pillows in her spotless homes. Dirt and messiness were forbidden, perhaps explaining why she felt the need to acquire and boss so many maids.

"She has always had a very obsessive personality," said her second husband, Ed Walker, in court papers. "She's very preoccupied with cleanliness. The house had to be a showplace every day, and she was always dressed like she was getting ready to go pose for modeling pictures. She didn't even like me to lounge around in Levi's or informal clothes. She wanted me to be completely neat at all times. You couldn't relax around her, we had no home life."

"Mom has no midpoint on anything," said her oldest son, Kent Walker, in court papers. "Everything is to the extreme. She is very extreme emotionally. I've always thought she needed more leveling. She was just overly strict and very preoccupied with neatness. She would go on cleaning sprees where we would have to soak down the patios and scrub them with disinfectant. She needs to be more tolerant and even in her approach to life. The house just has to be immaculate, she's fanatical. Everything she does is with good intentions, though. It's just that her methods are questionable."

Sante later bristled as this portrait of her as a fanatical Mrs. Clean whose bad side overwhelms her good intentions. "I think all of me wants to be nice. I think I am just like anyone else," she said in 1989. Asserting that "cleanliness is next to godliness, I guess," Sante denied going on scrubbing binges. "The house is clean. I think a kid, a young man, might think it is too clean. . . . All kids sometimes think their parents are maybe too clean or too harsh or too dedicated."

While preparing for trial during the fall of 1985, Sante agreed again to be seen by mental health-care experts. Dr. Robert Sadoff examined Sante and agreed with O'Gorman that she had an underlying personality disorder. He also found that mental problems caused by the hit-and-run accident clouded her mind after the fur trial. "In my opinion, it is the concussion that Mrs. Kimes sustained that accounts for her erratic behavior and her impaired judgment in leaving the Washington area during the weekend when she was on trial for the theft of the fur coat." Finding that she was recovering gradually from the concussion, Sadoff was still concerned over her complaints of double vision and recommended she go to a hospital for a complete eye exam and special neurological tests, including an electroencephalogram (EEG) and a CAT scan. He suggested extensive testing of her to assess any long-term effects of the head injury and of her mental state to gather a better picture of her "underlying personality configuration and to detect the presence of paranoid configurations."

Sante's defense team paid psychologist Verdun Trione $2,000 for an evaluation on December 20, 1985, that found she suffered from brief reactive psychotic episodes. "There is a history of disabling conflict, aggressive preoccupations, borderline, seemingly deranged behaviors," Trione wrote. "Clinically speaking, this is a person who 'snaps' from time to time, because of environmental conditions, as levels of frustration increase; hostility increases, hysterical lack of control are apparent. The clinical picture, overtly, is one of repressed anger, rage reactions resulting in conflicting disorganized social judgments."

Unlike the medical doctors, Trione saw her character disorder as second to an overwhelming depression, anger, and hysteria, which "demobilized her to a point of panic." He found that she was not psychotic, understood the consequences of her actions, knew the difference between right and wrong and had "a potentially superior intelligence." Yet he stopped short of saying that she was fully competent to stand trial, describing her clear moments as irregular, unpredictable interludes.

He diagnosed her as suffering "intermittently" from Ganser Syndrome, which makes people lose touch with reality and act illogically. This disorder also can make someone fake symptoms or believe they are ill, as prison doctors would later say about Sante. Trione found her to be immature, manipulative, and full of "paranoid ideas that people were out to get her, although she seemed to have no substantial evidence, at least in my judgment." She scored high on tests for narcissism, histrionics, and anxiety, while her hysteria made her overreact to circumstances that wouldn't faze normal people. Grilled by prosecutors, Trione rejected the idea that Sante had fooled him, Sadoff, and the other experts by pretending to be hysterical and was actually a "manipulative sociopath," as prison medical records indicated.

Acting on her stream of medical complaints and recommendations from her doctors, Clark County jail officials let Sante go to Southern Nevada Memorial Hospital the day after Christmas, on December 26, 1985. Still technically in the custody of U.S. marshals, she was now a hospital patient under the less seasoned eyes of minimum-wage security guards. She escaped after four days. While in a wheelchair headed for the EEG brain tests that Dr. Sadoff had recommended, Sante made her break. Her nervous guard, barely three weeks on the job, told different stories about how Sante became Houdini, first claiming she asked for her leg irons to be removed so she could visit the bathroom and then saying she vanished on the way to a hospital pay phone. Later Sante would offer her own versions of the great escape, first saying that the guard felt sorry for her and let her go and then claiming the guard released her in a blackmail attempt. The guard quit the next day. All FBI Agent Tom Nicodemus knew was that the con lady had manipulated things her way again, despite the warnings he had given the marshals. "They were too embarrassed to look me in the face," he said.

She escaped on Monday, December 30, 1985, at 5:45 P.M., and by the next day, New Year's Eve, was soaking in a hot bath at her friend's apartment, around the corner from a Las Vegas bar. Her friend tended bar at the Huddle Lounge where the Kimeses were steady customers for two years. "She was very, very terrified and just said that she had been through a lot and had been hiding out," said barmaid Sheila Bishop. "I told her she looked terrible. She had lost a lot of weight, and we talked about that."

While on the run, she had to climb over fences and hide behind bushes, bruising and cutting her hands and legs. Sheila contacted Kenneth Kimes, who left $100 for Sante at the bar on New Year's Day 1986. The barmaid moved the fugitive to an empty apartment. Sante told a Chinese woman next door that she was Taj Kime from California, divorcing her husband who had chased her with a pistol.

"I asked her what happened to her hands and with her leg," said the neighbor. "She told me she had been horseback riding, the horse ran away, and she fell on the ground, and she will never ride again on a horse."

While on the lam, Sante telephoned another friend,

vowing never to return to jail. "She said she would die rather than go back," said piano bar singer Kay Frigiano. Sante claimed to be in Los Angeles, bleeding and in pain after a Doberman pinscher attacked her. "She was hysterical," said Kay, who urged her to surrender. "Please give yourself up, because you're only hurting yourself. That's when she said, 'But they're so bad to me. I'm so scared.'" She denied escaping from the hospital, Frigiano recalled. "She said that one of the guards opened the door and told her, 'Go ahead out, because you'll never make it otherwise' and pushed her out the door."

By January 2, 1986, Sante had pored over maps, telling Sheila she had arranged for a car and $5,000. That's when Nicodemus and the marshals arrived at the Huddle Lounge and told Sheila she could spend five years in jail for harboring a fugitive if she didn't help them catch Sante. "It was me or her," Sheila said of her chat with the FBI. "And I agreed to do it their way."

So when the women were set to meet at the Elbow Room bar at 1590 East Flamingo Road on Friday January 3, 1986, FBI agents and U.S. marshals were waiting in the parking lot. Wearing a gray wig, baggy pants, and flowing scarves that made her look like an Arab, Sante had been posing as a homeless woman in the skid row part of town. She surrendered without a fuss at 4:45 P.M. "She's the best female con I've ever seen," Nicodemus said.

Her stunt added two counts to the slavery indictment—one against her for escaping and another charging Kimes as an accessory for giving her money.

CHAPTER 9

"These are lies. It's all lies. They just want money."

Tissue box squarely in front of her on the defense table, Sante Kimes, 51, faced her jury of five women and seven men on February 10, 1986, in the box-like Foley Federal Building, heart of the no-nonsense section of Las Vegas dotted with law offices and municipal courts. She was the lone defendant. Papa Kimes had struck a plea bargain sparing him from jail by admitting he knew about the slavery but failed to stop it.

In opening statements, prosecutor Steven Clark described Sante as a willful rich woman who could afford to pay the maids but instead treated them like doormats. She kept them isolated behind locked doors, hid the phone, their lifeline to their families, didn't mail their letters home, and threatened or hit them if they complained. "This case involves greed, arrogance, and cruelty," Clark said. "It involves the intentional abuse and use of human beings as so much household furniture. It involves cold and calculated deception of young women, vulnerable and little able to defend themselves."

At first, Sante tried to intimidate her accusers, shooting withering glances toward the prosecution table and witness box. "Bitch," she whispered as tutor Teresa Richards passed by after testifying. Seven months behind bars had stressed Sante so much; she had shrunk several sizes from her muu-muu-wearing days. Her face was drawn, and she looked older. Gone were her trademark turbans, white pantsuits, and floor-length ensembles. During this trial, she wore conservative dresses in neutral grays and blues.

Early in the 11-day trial, she changed her demeanor in an apparent bid for sympathy. Grabbing for the tissues in front of her, she cried when maid Adela Sanchez Guzman described her beating in Hawaii. "She was lying," said Sante a few years later, explaining her tears, "and I felt very badly for her, that she could tell those kind of lies to make money, because I thought she had been a very nice girl and I felt badly." The defendant wept when a U.S. marshal testified about her escape from Southern Nevada Memorial Hospital. She cried often, as 14 former maids, tutors, and house sitters testified against her. They told of 62 instances where she had threatened, bullied, or hit the household help. One maid had to get down on her hands and knees and beg God's forgiveness for saying she was unhappy. In a public humiliation of another maid accused of being a slacker, Sante pulled the girl's hair and slapped her face in front of two tutors.

"At first, Sante would try and stare everybody down during the trial," said FBI Agent Tom Nicodemus. "Then she went for a look of lost innocence. Kind of like, 'I don't know what I'm doing here.' A blank look."

Maid Maribel Ramirez Cruz with her burned hand was the most compelling victim, and prosecutors chose her as the first of their 37 witnesses. Maribel and Adela Sanchez Guzman, the younger maid she tried to help, had by this time become comfortable enough with their new country that they took advantage of that most American of remedies—the lawsuit. They were filing a $24 million civil suit against Sante Kimes as the criminal trial against her unfolded. Lawyers for the maids even roamed the hallway of the Foley Building as the trial began, recruiting more witnesses for the civil action as they left the criminal proceeding. Federal Justice Howard D. McKibben, who was presiding over Sante's trial, quickly threw out the "ambulance chasers" as Sante's defense lawyer called them in court.

Defense attorney Dominic Gentile used this multi-million dollar civil suit as a rhetorical sword to slash at the maids' credibility and accuse them of lying from greed. "You know, you got 24 million reasons to disbelieve or to at least question the veracity of both Adela Sanchez and Maribel Cruz," he told the jury. "And you have to." He dismissed the women as illegal aliens "willing to stretch and bend and torture the truth to be able to stay here for a little while longer." While conceding the maids weren't paid, they enjoyed perks like travel to expensive resorts. They ate the same food and wore clothing made of the same cloth as Sante. "If they were paid money, in terms of what they were worth on an hourly basis, they couldn't have done as well."

Sante did not take the stand in her own defense, presumably wary of answering questions about her criminal record under cross-examination. However, she managed to broadcast her low opinion of the maids. Quietly seething as prosecutor Karla Dobinski described how Maribel shrieked as the steaming hot iron neared her face, Sante erupted. "These are lies," she shouted in the courtroom. "It's all lies. They just want money." Justice McKibben immediately called for a recess and gently scolded Sante once the jury left.

"I would like to admonish you, Mrs. Kimes," he said. "I ask that you do the best that you can to not have any further outbursts like this in front of the jury."

"I'm sorry," she said.

"I know it's an emotional thing for you," said the

judge, "but, in fairness to everyone, we have to have you try to compose yourself. Do you feel that you're ready now to have the jury come back in?"

"Yes, sir," she said. "I'm sorry."

The defense tried to soften Sante, portraying her as a victim who needed to take extreme security measures to safeguard her house. The rules about not answering the door and hiding the phone were not to enslave the help but to protect Sante against her evil in-laws, said Gentile. "Sante Kimes for all of her life, from the time that she was a destitute woman growing up without a mother on the streets of California and having to steal to eat, has lived in fear," Gentile said. "As a young woman she was very poor, she was sexually abused, and that's where her fears began. That's the genesis of her fears." Partner to millionaire Kenneth Kimes, she grew fearful of his relatives, the lawyer told the jury. "The Creeps are those members of Ken Kimes' family who so deeply hate his wife. And this woman, Sante Kimes has good reason to believe from the conduct of the Creeps over the years that they are out to harm her and harm her family and most particularly her 10-year-old boy, Kenny."

Nasty pranks that seemed the stuff of witchcraft dogged Sante when she was pregnant with Kenny, said defense witness Sandra Spears, her former secretary. Spears was a marine officer's wife who worked part-time for Sante in California on Bicentennial promotions from winter 1974 until April 1976. With her husband away in Vietnam, Spears had to raise her two young sons alone and Sante acted more like a friend than the boss. If Spears worked overtime, Sante gave her money to buy dinner for her boys, saying it was too late to cook. Some afternoons, the two women went shopping, and if Sante liked something, she also bought an outfit for Spears.

Spears testified that one day she saw graffiti that

looked like blood scrawled all over a wall inside
Sante's house in Laguna Beach. Sante blamed the
Creeps. "It was a threat, but I don't remember what
specifically it said," Spears testified. "And then the
picture of like a person hanging with a noose. And
it just terrified her. She just knew that it was her,
that they were after her and they were going to hurt
her baby." Another time, Spears said Sante burst into
the office as if the Furies were at her heels.

"She was like a ghost. She was white. Just absolutely drained. She was frightened out of her wits.
She was just—her eyes were like saucers and she was
just hysterical. She said someone had put rattlesnakes
in her car, live rattlesnakes." Spears said Sante told
her about the snakes right after it happened, but the
secretary didn't see them herself.

A graphics artist who worked on Bicentennial posters for the Kimeses offered another example of
Sante's fears of "the Creeps." With Sante at the bar of
the Anaheim Hyatt in 1977, commercial artist Wayne
Hendricks said Linda Kimes suddenly appeared. She
wore a long coat with her hand jammed inside a
pocket, as if hiding something, he said. "I glanced
back at Sante, who looked at me and then looked
past me and went white," Hendricks testified. To escape, Sante flung herself over the bar. "She was
climbing the bar, and this woman started screaming
obscenities at her. She told me that Linda had a vast
hatred for her, and because of her intrusion between
Ken and herself would do anything to get rid of her."
Under cross-examination, Hendricks said he didn't
know that at Sante's behest, Linda had received a
letter from a lawyer, ordering her to sever ties with
her father. In her statement to authorities, Linda said
she never screamed, just asked in a soft voice if they
could talk.

Former FBI agent Grant Christopherson, a Kimes
family friend, said Sante blamed the Creeps for set-

ting fire to her Hawaii home in 1978 and trying to kidnap Kenny off the beach. He said Sante told him of these events after the fact. "There was one incident where somebody on the beach in Honolulu or where their house is on Port Lock tried to grab her son and run off with him," he testified. "And there was an altercation on the beach, and she was able to rescue her son."

Spears and Christopherson were among 17 character witnesses who had been inside Sante's homes through the years and saw none of the maids mistreated. Some were friends, like Kenny's playmates, ages 10 and 12, and a retired Marine Corps colonel from Hawaii. Others—like a TV repairman, a sewing machine repairwoman, a travel agent, and a landscaper—visited the Kimeses' homes on business. Several of these witnesses said they spoke Spanish, and that if the maids were in trouble, they could have easily told them. Grant Christopherson's wife, Patricia, said that during a two-week stay in 1978 with the Kimeses in Hawaii, their maid looked happy. "On one occasion, I had been out on the patio and I came in. Mrs. Kimes was getting ready. We were going out someplace, and there was some article of clothing; I don't remember what it was, but she didn't want it. It didn't fit or something. She gave it to [the maid]. She called her in and gave it to her, and it was a beautiful piece of clothing."

"Did the maid appear to be well fed?" Gentile asked.

"Yes," said Christopherson.

"Did she appear to be abused in any way?"

"No."

"Did she appear to be free to leave if she wanted to?"

"Yes. The doors were open. [The maid] was there with Kenny when we were touring the islands."

On cross-examination, Christopherson said she

didn't know that the maid had run away from the Kimeses later that year.

Lounge singer Kay Frigiano disputed the notion the maids were captives, saying they came over to her Las Vegas home with Sante for homemade spaghetti. On a 10-day visit to Hawaii in 1984, Kay said her friend was polite with the maids. "I couldn't see any evidence of any kind of mistreatment or anything. It was always, 'Por favor, would you do this.' Or, you know, there was kindness that I could see. I thought it was great."

Witness Haroldine Simer, owner of the All-Oahu Sewing Machine Service, was so convinced that Sante was innocent, she sent a three-page, single-spaced letter to Judge McKibben describing three repair visits to the Kimeses' Hawaii home in 1984. She described a happy home. "On my second visit the tutor and Mrs. Kimes had to do all the translating for the two maids, whom I was instructing how to use the machine. They were laughing at times, and I would look puzzled, and Mrs. Kimes would be laughing and tell me their [sic] only joking. I spent an hour that time, and had refreshments. Mrs. Kimes invited me to see her home. We talked, she was very jolly and warm." Simer added, "Here's this woman above my means being so nice to me, and her warmth was sincere, not a put-on act. Even my son commented about her attitude. She wore a lot of makeup, but her heart showed her sincerity."

As for the incriminating lists of written rules for controlling the maids, the defense called a Kimes attorney who said she reviewed completely different household lists. Attorney Susan Ann Moraga said she saw only one-line instructions for turning out lights, watering the lawn, and safety measures like not using glass around the pool. She said she never saw the document describing the boss as capable of turning into Dracula if the help misbehaved. Moraga had done legal work for the Kimeses in Anaheim for three months in 1985 and had never been to their homes in Las Vegas or Hawaii. Sante had a strong work ethic but also knew how to have fun, Moraga said. "There was a term that she used very frequently that 'We work hard and we play hard' and she was basically looking for people who wanted to work hard and play hard, people that she enjoyed being around. Personalities were important to her."

All these employees and friends who weren't present every day saw a sanitized view of Sante, argued prosecutor Dobinski in her closing arguments to the jury. "Sante Kimes was smart enough not to let on to them the dark side of her household. The beatings were behind closed doors: the threats, the thefts of personal papers. Of course, she's not going to tell a television repairman about that."

Dobinski said the civil suit filed by Maribel Ramirez Cruz and Adela Sanchez Guzman arose after the maids told their stories to the FBI. And she said Sante couldn't blame all her actions on her fear of the Creeps. "Where were Kenneth Kimes' relatives when Sante Kimes is beating these women behind closed doors? Did the Creeps make her do that? Did these relatives of her husband tear up the letters, burn the personal papers, hide the mail of the victims? Did the Creeps tell these victims they'd never see their families again; they were going to be with the Kimeses permanently. The fact is the Creeps, whoever they are, have nothing to do with this case."

In his closing, Dominic Gentile candidly suggested his client was not the most likable woman. "Even if you think Sante Kimes is a bitch, if you follow the law you can't do anything but acquit," he said. In a dramatic flourish, he seized upon the leg irons that became a court exhibit during the testimony about Sante's hospital escape. Waving them around, Gentile said these literally mean bondage and slavery—not what may have happened to the maids. "Retaliation is a badge of slavery. Incarcerate. Incarceration is a badge of slavery. Find me an incarceration in this case. Find me retaliation in this case. Everybody left. And you know when they left? They left when they didn't want to work anymore."

He said the entire case might be a wage or battery dispute that belonged in civil court. "Did she lose her temper a couple of times? Probably. Probably. Did she pull somebody's hair? Maybe. Did she burn them with an iron? No.

"You know, maybe it isn't easy to be rich. I'd kind of like to know what it's like, but maybe it isn't easy to be rich. Maybe there's . . . Maribels and Adelas who start out happy and satisfied, but then when they see how well you're doing, they get unhappy and they want more. Maybe that's what it's about. If they're entitled to money, let them go to a civil court and let them get a money judgment and we'll pay for it."

The jury got the case at 2:45 P.M. on February 27, 1986. By the following afternoon, after nine hours of deliberation, they convicted Sante on 14 of 18 felony counts, including involuntary servitude, conspiracy, transporting illegal aliens, and escape from prison. The charges the jury discarded concerned three maids who worked for her less than five days. After all the hysterics she displayed in her trial, Sante showed no emotion at the end. In contrast, the prosecutors "broke out in grins," said the front-page account of the verdict in the *Las Vegas Sun*, whose banner headline blared: KIMES GUILTY IN SLAVE CASE.

Desperate to avoid a jail sentence, Sante threw herself into one last legal battle to convince Judge McKibben that she needed psychiatric treatment. Again, she paid for experts to produce reports. Family physician Abraham Rudnick weighed in on April 3, 1986, saying that Sante's mental health plummeted during the eight months she already spent behind bars. "She has become more nervous and high-strung. This prolonged separation from her husband and children have [*sic*] contributed to mental symptoms of desperation feelings, erratic behavior, and mood swings. She requires some kind of psychologic support system or antistress management program."

Psychologist Verdun Trione said Sante's manipulative, self-centered, impulsive behavior was so serious, she needed to see a psychologist three to five times a week or be committed to a mental institution for six months. Only after two years of steady therapy would any significant change begin, he said. He recommended probation and then either inpatient or outpatient therapy. "She has to be treated," Dr. Trione said. "If she goes to prison, there is no doubt in my mind that she will become psychotic. Just the time she has already spent in custody has caused significant deterioration."

She hired a San Diego consulting firm, Alternative Sentencing Resources, to produce a 31-page "This is Your Life" about her problems. They interviewed 18 people from her best friend in high school to her son Kent Walker to Dr. Trione to Sante herself. The report traced the roots of her emotional disorder, including her claims that her natural mother turned to prostitution to support the family and that her adoptive father raped her. An irrational fear of poverty dogged her still, despite marriage to a wealthy man. The consultants even analyzed her letters, noting that she wrote in rambling non sequiturs and squeezed in double the amount of script between each single line of her notepaper. "Her involvement with the criminal justice system appears to be an expression of her emotional problems," the report said. "In this regard she does not show the narrowly focused self-aggrandizing motives normally associated with classic criminal behavior. This is further shown by the fact that, while her past contacts with the law have all been theft-related, invariably she has had the money to purchase what was taken.

"Contrary to what might be one's first impression of Mrs. Kimes, she is not a spoiled rich woman but a troubled, emotionally disturbed individual whose early background of deprivation and sexual abuse undoubtably [sic] sowed the seeds of the unreasonable, even bizarre, conduct which brings her before the court today."

Prosecutors argued that Sante was crafty, not crazy. "She is a selfish, calculating, and manipulative woman, fully aware of the consequences of her actions," they said in a sentencing memorandum. "Sante Kimes' attempt in this case, to blame her conduct on others, (the Creeps), or some ephemeral 'fears' or insecurities, is but another in her unending and unlimited efforts (which this court observed before and during trial) to do or say whatever she believes is necessary to avoid taking responsibility for her actions when she is caught."

Dr. William O'Gorman, the court-appointed psychiatrist who had evaluated Sante the previous summer, did another review for the prosecution. While praising Dr. Trione's treatment plan, O'Gorman said Sante didn't deserve probation because she had escaped from authorities twice before. "Until this patient has been trained to recognize consequences of behavior before action, not after action, antisocial behavior will continue. My only conclusion, based on the history of this patient, is incarceration in a controlled setting, with possible professional guidance put on simple terms that are practical.

"The prognosis in the future is guarded," he concluded, "until this patient has accepted simple restraints of action, in the light of what is constructive living and behavior."

In sentencing her on May 15, 1986, Judge McKibben followed O'Gorman's lead. "You have some fairly deep-seated emotional and psychological problems," he said, adding that she could receive available therapy and counseling——but from behind bars. The judge said her "fairly substantial emotional disturbances" must not obscure the "reprehensible acts" she committed.

For each of the 14 counts, the judge sentenced her to the maximum five years in prison with the terms to run concurrently. She also had to pay a $300 fine.

It was the first time in a criminal history stretching back to the Kennedy Administration that Sante Kimes got sent to jail. In the past she either paid a fine or was sentenced to probation. As per his plea bargain, Kenneth Kimes ducked jail completely. In a letter to Judge McKibben, he blamed business affairs for the blind eye he turned toward the maid saga in his own home. He also suggested Sante was the root of the trouble with his family, an extraordinary admission given the Creeps defense she mounted at trial. "As I look back and analyze the situation, my feeling is that Sante, with her motives, was trying to separate me from my family, mainly because she never had a family. She developed resentment toward them, because of their closeness and love for each other. I'm sure our relationship would not have survived, except for our 10-year-old son, Kenny."

His friends wondered why he didn't leave Sante during this mess. To one relative, Kenneth Kimes suggested he had no alternative but to stick by her after so many years. "I can't get away from her," he said. "I've gone too far and stayed too long."

The judge called his crime "one of omission not commission" but insisted, "I can't condone your activities. I think the message sent out by this court is that it will not tolerate this kind of conduct." McKibben gave him a suspended three-year prison term, two years of probation, and ordered him to pay

$70,000 in fines and undergo 60 days of alcoholic treatment.

Sante still had to face another sentencing that year for the mink-coat theft in Washington, D.C. Her maneuvering to get rid of the trial judge appeared to backfire. The day before sentencing, Sante's attorneys accused Judge Sylvia Bacon of erratic behavior and acting impaired on the bench and asked the judge to remove herself from the case. A week later in a front-page story, the *Washington Post* reported that Judge Bacon was in treatment for alcohol abuse. However, she rejected Sante's motion without comment and threw the book at her on July 24, 1986. It was the first time Judge Bacon saw Sante since she vanished the summer before as the jury convicted her of stealing Mrs. Kenworthy's coat. Now Sante stood before the D.C. judge as a convicted slave keeper.

In asking for probation for stealing the mink instead of jail, defense attorney Samuel Buffone said Sante was a victim of her personality disorder.

"I can understand how it would appear to the U.S. Attorney's Office and perhaps to this Court that what we have here is a cunning, crafty, manipulative person," he said. "All I'm trying to say, to this Court, is we have a person who is in need of help, a person who manifests that behavior, not out of any cunning premeditation to avoid the system, rather out of fairly deep-seated psychiatric problems, and an inability to deal with reality in any other way."

Prosecutor Kenneth Carroll called Sante a repeat offender with an "alarming" number of past arrests who always managed to play the system and avoid jail and now deserved the maximum 15 years in jail, preferably to begin after serving her five years for slavery. "Mrs. Kimes on occasion feels the need to do this, (commit crimes) perhaps for excitement, perhaps just to see if she can still get away with it."

In an impassioned 10-minute plea for mercy, Sante

began by saying she was "very, very sorry and very remorseful about the problems I've caused" and was finally getting needed psychiatric help. Yet she still blamed others for some troubles. Believing she had permission to use her adoptive father's credit cards, she said she was arrested at her mother's behest because of "sexual problems"—an apparent reference to her claim that her father had raped her. The Creeps have scared her, she said. Papa Kimes allegedly forced her to give up her youngest son for adoption. At one point, Sante's words sounded like the pivotal scene from her favorite movie, *Gone with the Wind*, where Scarlett O'Hara vowed "As God as my witness, I'll never be hungry again."

Sante told Judge Bacon, "I'm not trying to excuse myself, Your Honor, but I'm telling you that with God as my witness, I believe my life is in the hands of God and having used God on this earth, I have changed. And, I'm dedicated and committed, trying everything I can do—what expert people are telling me I should do. I didn't know I needed any help. All my life, all I've ever known is fear. I've come closer to God than I've ever had, because that's all I've had."

Judge Bacon didn't buy any of it. She sentenced Sante to three to nine years behind bars, to be served only after she finished her five years in federal prison.

CHAPTER 10

"I also swear to you that in the future I will never disobey another law for as long as I live."

A woman who said she'd die rather than stay in jail was never going to accept a 14-year prison sentence. With parole for good behavior, Sante actually faced about five years behind bars. Losing even one day of freedom just galled this jet-setter, accustomed to bossing around maids and frolicking on tropical beaches. Professing her innocence with the zeal of a storefront preacher, she threw every ounce of her considerable will and every dollar she could pry from Kimes into hiring lawyers and filing appeals to overturn her convictions. The couple also needed other lawyers to fight the multimillion dollar civil suit filed by the maids. Shrewdly, the Kimeses dragged their insurance companies into this mess, figuring that their homeowner's policy covered maids in their home. The insurance companies naturally objected to paying the consequences of slavery and countersued.

Her letters, motions and depositions in these years exploded with wild, bogus claims and sexual allegations. In a bold move she said her lawyers didn't know about, she begged Judge Howard McKibben for early release in an impassioned nine-page letter. She deserved mercy because a money-hungry lawyer in Hawaii drummed up the slavery charges so he could win millions for the maids in a civil suit, she wrote the judge on September 22, 1987. Dumping even more dirt on this attorney's reputation, she claimed he made child pornography films. There was no evidence to support any of these claims against this lawyer, considered to be among the most prominent members of the Hawaiian bar.

She often tried to use sexual allegations to besmirch the maids and tutors who had testified against her. During a deposition that dragged on for four days, she called one maid a whiskey-guzzling "prostitute" who had sex with two gardeners in Hawaii and an "elderly gentleman" in Las Vegas. She said another maid had a lesbian affair with a tutor, while yet another tutor was fired for making porno flicks with the money-hungry lawyer. In another deposition, she told Hawaii civil attorney Fernando Cosio that Latina women start having sex when they are children. "Well, most Spanish women are much older than their years," she said. "You know, you are Spanish, you know that an eight-or-nine-year-old Spanish girl is the equivalent of an 18-year-old woman, or a 16-year-old woman in this country. They are very sophisticated, and they are very—you know, they are having sex usually by the time they are nine or ten. I am sure you know what I mean."

Sante admitted to the judge that she hired illegal aliens, but swore she never enslaved or beat them. Then she made a vow that would ring with irony, considering the trouble that lay ahead. "But I swear to you, Your Honor, on my children, I did not ever physically abuse my help or hold them against their will. They were free to leave at any time, and did. I also swear to you that in the future I will never disobey another law for as long as I live."

In a bid for sympathy, Sante told the judge that she ached for her children, including the toddler, Kenian, she allegedly gave birth to at age 49 and gave up for adoption in Mexico. His existence has never been confirmed.

One benefit of jail, she told the judge, was discovering her love for the law. Working as an assistant law librarian at Pleasanton, a federal correctional facility for women in California, Sante said she cracked the law books every day: "I find it absolutely fascinating and find I am becoming addicted to it." Then she proved herself a true jailhouse lawyer by writing her own motion to reduce her sentence. Complete with required citations to legal precedents, the 38-page motion also included Sante's harrowing view of prison life. "I have been attacked and beaten, scorned because I was thought crazy, lived in fear of my life every moment, witnessed the most terrifying and obscene acts possible, one of which was a brutal attack on a young girl by a homosexual inmate with a bloody plunger, who beat her into silence. I have had my hair ripped and cut off trying to help a pregnant inmate who was being mercilessly beaten and kicked in the stomach. I have crouched in freezing cells with rats and varmints crawling, too sick and terrified to know what to do. Because of my race and background, I have been hated and ridiculed. And this horror has not gone on for weeks, or months, it has gone on for years.

"I have cried out to God to give me strength to survive this nightmare and let it make me stronger so that I may go to my children and raise them and protect the future they deserve. I WILL NOT LET MY CHILDREN DOWN, AND EVERY SECOND OF MY LIFE IN THIS HORROR, I WILL DO EVERYTHING HUMANELY POSSIBLE to prove to the Court that I am constantly endeavoring to rehabilitate myself and return to society as a contributing mother and citizen."

Sante swept away inconsistencies or seemingly illogical behavior by blaming an alleged concussion, from the hit-and-run accident in Virginia, with clouding her mind. Attacking her own attorney, she claimed her head injury made her putty in the hands of lawyer Dominic Gentile. Sante alleged he only grudgingly defended her when she refused to plead guilty. Gentile, who had vigorously waved around the leg irons in a rousing closing, was "so totally unprepared to defend me," Sante wrote. She claimed he screamed at her and physically shook her to force a plea.

Her mental fog also kept her from immediately recognizing that a juror turned out to be a neighbor who didn't like her, she claimed. Then when she complained to Gentile, he said it was too late to get rid of this juror, she said. Sante alleged that before the trial, she found this neighbor in her home several times talking with the maids and had clashed with the woman in a minor parking dispute. This juror, Rhonda Shonkwiler, swore she had never met Sante before seeing her in the courtroom. Rhonda was a busy 27-year-old, planning a wedding and honeymoon, when she moved to Geronimo Way in December 1984. A producer of television commercials for a local advertising firm, Rhonda worked from seven in the morning to eight at night and then freelanced. Mostly her contact with neighbors was a polite wave as she zoomed by in her car. Although she lived just a house away from the Kimeses, Rhonda said she had never personally met Sante, had never talked to her, never been in her house, never chatted with her maids, and didn't speak Spanish.

Claiming this juror hated her while her own lawyer and mind failed her, Sante won an appeal hearing. A 1988 Supreme Court decision overturning a slavery conviction in Michigan provided more ammunition. In that case, United States v. Kozminski, the high court ruled that just psychological coercion, or "brainwashing," wasn't enough to prove slavery. Dairy farmers Ike and Margarethe Kozminski had been convicted in 1984 of brainwashing and enslav-

ing two mentally retarded men for 11 years. The Kozminski reversal gave Sante grounds to challenge the
instruction to her jury to convict if she caused the
maids to believe they had no choice but to serve her.

At an evidentiary hearing on October 20, 1988,
Sante admitted that during jury selection she and
Gentile passed notes back and forth. She detailed
how frightened she felt of her own lawyer, how he
allegedly demanded $50,000 more in fees, how he
brushed aside her concerns when she finally recognized Rhonda on the jury.

"You distinctly remember all of those things, do
you not?" Judge McKibben asked.

"Yes, now," Sante said.

"Do you understand why I might have some diffi-
culty understanding how you could clearly understand all of those events, but you are also telling me
at the same time that you remember nothing that
happened in the courtroom?" the judge asked.

"I remember some things that happened in the
courtroom, your Honor," she said.

He replied, "You just don't remember anything
about the jurors. Is that correct?"

"No," she said. "When I got my gla (glasses)—
like right now, when I'm looking at you, you are a
fuzz. If I would have seen that juror and I——when——
the moment I saw that juror, I told you the truth. I
would never, ever, not tell you. Because the juror
was——we did not like each other. And there were
problems."

Seeking to prove that Sante faked her illnesses,
prosecutors called her treating physician at the Federal Correctional Institution at Pleasanton, Dr. Sonya
Cabrera. She considered Sante a "challenging patient" who was "unreliable medically." After her hit-
and-run accident, Sante flew to California, was arrested, escaped from the hospital, was captured, and
went on trial for slavery. However, she told doctors

at Pleasanton that the car accident left her hospitalized in a coma for several months. Cabrera said medical tests found no cause for Sante's complaints of
chest pain and vertigo. Neurological exams were in-
conclusive. Doctors could never confirm Sante's
claim that cancer forced the removal of her uterus
instead of a routine hysterectomy. Once, Cabrera
said, they tried a simple exam for vertigo on Sante
called the Romberg test, where patients stand up,
close their eyes, and extend both hands in front of
them. Vertigo sufferers tend to lose their balance and
move their hands. "She would sway at those times,"
said Cabrera, "but it's very subjective. She did not
have the drift in the hands that we normally, also,
expect. And we, also, try to see if we can make it
more objective by pushing one way or the other and
seeing if they really do lose their balance. And that
was always—I never could conclusively say that she
had a positive Romberg. And she never did have
any drift."

  Under oath, Sante insisted that she was ill during
her trial. "I was very sick. I suffered from intense
headache pain. I could not see. My—I had a film
falling over my eyes, and my ears were weeping. I
suffered from dizziness. I found it many times hard
to concentrate. I was very dejected. I felt generally,
overall, terribly ill." Her lawyer asked if she believed
that mental problems affected her condition. "No, I
do not," she said. "I think all my injuries were because of my—a brain concussion, injuries that now
continue with vision and hearing. I think that after
the accident that my—all of my medical, as far as
my real problems, were the accident, the hit-and-run
accident and the trauma to my head."

Sante's credibility suffered an embarrassing set-
back when her friend Kay Frigiano, the lounge
singer, denied writing a six-and-a-half page letter to
Judge McKibben pleading for mercy. A sketch of a

single rose in a vase adorned the left side of the lined notepaper filled with a flowing script. The writer of this January 16, 1988, letter described Kenny Kimes thumbing through a photo album of family pictures then bursting into tears and begging Frigiano to help free his mother. The letter was signed, "Respectfully, Kay Frigiani."

"No, it's not my signature," said Kay Frigiano. "And my name ends with an *o*. I did not write this letter."

"Do you recognize that handwriting?" asked Judge McKibben.

"Not really, Judge," said Kay. "But it is not my handwriting."

"Well, when you say 'not really,' do you believe you recognize the handwriting?"

"I can't say that I do truthfully," said Kay. "Just that this name I know is not my name."

"I understand that," said the judge. "I'm just asking you if you recognize the handwriting? If you don't, you don't,"

"I don't," she said.

Sante lost her appeal to overturn the slavery conviction. The district court believed Dominic Gentile's testimony that the defense considered juror Rhonda Shonkwiler potentially favorable and wanted her on the panel. Gentile testified he was so optimistic that Shonkwiler would be a friendly juror he "died and went to heaven" after learning she was on the panel. He did a background check, discovered she was the wife of a colleague, and "liked what he heard." McKibben also found that Sante, during voir dire, was mentally competent to agree to this juror.

Sante appealed to the United States Court of Appeals for the Ninth Circuit, and they also discounted any problems with jury selection or misconduct on Rhonda's part. As for the brainwashing issue from Kozminski, Sante lost again. "All the evidence at

Kimes' trial was designed to demonstrate that she engaged in physical or legal coercion to keep the victims in her service. Thus, regardless of the instruction concerning the relevance of what the victims believed, the jury could not have convicted Kimes unless it believed that she had engaged in compulsion of services by the use or threatened use of physical or legal coercion." Sante appealed to the United States Supreme Court, but the nine justices declined to take the case.

Sante fared better in her quest to whittle down her three-to-nine-year sentence for taking Mrs. Kenworthy's mink. Getting hit by that car in Arlington was the best thing that ever happened to her in a legal sense. Her absence from the courtroom when the jury decided her fate gave Sante legal grounds to overturn her felony conviction. The Sixth Amendment grants defendants the right to confront their accusers, including facing the jury come judgment hour. The District of Columbia Court of Appeals gave Sante a Halloween present on October 31, 1989, ruling that the trial court failed to determine if her absence for the verdict was voluntary or not. The appeals judges ordered the nine-year-long saga back to the lower court for a hearing. Rather than waste any more time or resources, both sides agreed to let her plea bargain down to a misdemeanor petit larceny charge. Exactly ten years to the day that police arrested her at the Mayflower hotel, Sante on February 5, 1990, essentially got away with taking the coat. Sentenced to a year in jail, she was given credit for time already spent behind bars. She did have to pay a $10 fine.

Buoyed by this victory, Sante seemed like a fountain of charm, enthusiasm, and charisma to a Washington, D.C., area real estate agent. She had contacted realtor Charles Gallagher to find her an apartment while she served time in a Washington, D.C., halfway house. "We just automatically became friends," Gallagher said. "She was just the most—it's not something I can put into words. This woman is power itself, literally. You have to meet her to know, to see her in action. This woman could rule the universe single-handedly. She has a power that is unbelievable. I've never met anyone like her in my life. I've met presidents and royalty and corporation executives, and they were children compared to this woman." After renting her a $2,400 a month apartment in Georgetown, Gallagher stayed in touch. Sometimes he would drive her back at night to the halfway house on Langston Place, in a rough part of town. Sante was full of big plans at that time.

In Washington, she worked on her appeals as well as the civil suits filed by the maids. She was a demanding legal client. Unhappy with the efforts of an appeals lawyer, Sante waited until dark, went to his office, called security, and convinced them to let her wheel out all her boxes, Gallagher said. Returning to her schoolgirl love of writing, she talked about starting her autobiography. Gallagher, an Irishman presumably good with words, would be coauthor, she declared. When she moved back to Las Vegas, she invited Gallagher to visit. She enjoyed her freedom at the blackjack tables, he said. "After she had a few drinks, she would go up against anybody," Gallagher said. "The rich Arabs. I watched her at the black jack tables, the bets were in the thousands."

The Kimeses still had millions of dollars in possible civil judgments hanging over their heads with the maid lawsuits. They hired Las Vegas lawyers from established firms but also liked to keep someone on retainer as "house counsel." In the summer of 1990, the Kimeses placed a want ad for this kind of lawyer in the *Las Vegas Review Journal*. Elmer Ambrose Holmgren answered in mid July. The Kimeses were offering $500 a week, no chance for more, and Elmer, down on his luck, accepted. It would be the end of the line for this 59-year-old Chicago native, son of a judge and aide to a billionaire whose own grab for the brass ring always fell short. He began his career following in the footsteps of his father, Elmer Napoleon Holmgren, a Republican from the South Side of Chicago elected to the Illinois General Assembly in the 1920s. In a close race, he ran for Superior Court judge in heavily Democratic Cook County and won. "Reporters came the day after to my parents' home, and they didn't know my dad had been elected," said Elmer's only sibling, Judy Weidlich. "When they went to bed that night, it didn't look like he would be."

Born May 31, 1931, Elmer was raised in a two-story red brick house at 54-17 South May Street by his parents, Elmer and Helen Ambrose Holmgren. Ambitious even as a child, Elmer grew up hearing his relatives predict riches in his future. At the age of 27, he was already married and the father of three children. An executive by day with the First National Bank of Chicago, he was a law school student at night. When he was admitted to the Illinois bar on May 21, 1959, with the other law school graduates, it was his father Judge Holmgren who made the formal motion to the Illinois Supreme Court to accept the 180 shiny new faces. The *Chicago Daily Tribune* ran pictures of both Holmgrens smiling on the big day. The bank promoted him to the legal department, but after a few years he wanted more and started his own practice. "We thought he was kind of foolish to give up the security of the bank," said his sister, Judy. "He probably would have become a vice president and had a good retirement. I think he was interested in getting ahead. Making money was important to him."

Nothing seemed to work. His first marriage failed when he fell in love with the secretary in his new law firm and later made her his second wife. Trying his hand at business and real estate, his deals fell through. In the late 60s, Elmer invested in the Continental Professional Football League and became one of the owners of the Chicago Owls. The league tanked. Hoping for better luck in Florida, Elmer moved there and hooked up with a man he thought would turn his life around, eccentric billionaire John D. MacArthur, the insurance and real estate magnate. The names of MacArthur and his late wife live on in the John D. and Catherine T. MacArthur Foundation, one of America's biggest charities. An eccentric loner tight with a dollar, MacArthur spent his last days living in a modest Palm Beach hotel overlooking a parking lot. Hardly a guide to easy street, Elmer's job for the old man was basically keeping him out of trouble. When MacArthur died in 1978 at age 80, Elmer was left on his own and fell onto hard times. "After MacArthur died, my dad pretty much jumped from deal to deal, many of which didn't pan out," said his son, Ken Holmgren. "He had borrowed money from friends of mine and many other people to maintain his lifestyle." By this time his second marriage failed, and he returned to Chicago with his third wife, whom he had met in Florida. He drove a cab to make ends meet.

By 1985, he had failed to register with the Illinois Attorney Registration and Disciplinary Commission, so was unable to practice law in his home state. Desperate to make money, he fell in with a broker allegedly selling unregistered real estate securities. This venture eventually landed them both in hot water with the state Attorney General, who charged them in 1990 with consumer fraud. While lecturing in the fall of 1988 at a seven-week adult education course called "How to Buy Real Estate Wholesale," Holmgren and the broker enticed students to invest in property deals, the AG charged. Holmgren and his partner allegedly promised the students at Oakton

College in Park Ridge quick windfalls if they invested in unregistered firms that would buy, renovate, and resell property. The complaint charged that the ventures failed to return a profit or give an accounting to investors. The AG eventually won a judgment ordering the broker to pay the students back $49,512.93.

Discredited at home, Elmer looked to Las Vegas, the booming metropolis in the desert, as the place for another shot at the big time. He followed his third wife there in January 1989, but failed to make money with "fast grass," a lawn-growing venture for the desert climate. His marriage ended. "In hindsight, I would have to say my dad was always one who wanted a little more than what he had," said his son, Dan Holmgren. "In his career, he would swing for the fences rather than opt for security." Instead, fate seemed to deliver him to Sante and Kenneth Kimes. Sensing his desperation, Sante picked him for a dangerous mission barely a month after meeting him. According to his family, Elmer confessed to Alcohol Tobacco and Firearms agents that Sante asked him in August 1990 to torch her Hawaii estate. She claimed to want the house destroyed so Papa Kimes would spend more time on the mainland. In failing health, he shouldn't be hopping airplanes across the Pacific anymore, she said. Her first offer was $2,000 to set the place on fire, but Elmer, desperate for money, negotiated for another thousand dollars. She promised it would burn quickly, since the house was 41 years old and made of wood.

At that time, a mountain of litigation was crushing the value of the Kimeses' Hawaii home with its terrific view of Diamond Head. They agreed to sell their home for $1.8 million on January 18, 1989, to a buyer from Honolulu only to discover just two weeks later that the United Pacific Insurance Company had placed a $905,000 lien on the property. This lien represented the judgment four insurance companies won in their battle against covering the costs of civil suits from the enslaved maids. The Kimeses appealed that award, but they also quickly backed out of the original deal for their Hawaii estate, now demanding $1.975 million to sell. The buyer accepted the higher price but then sued, claiming the sale was taking too long. The Kimeses countersued in federal court alleging fraud. Scores of files for this and all the other lawsuits jammed that house when it went up in flames at 1:00 A.M. on Sunday, September 16, 1990. A Kimes lawyer later used the loss of these papers to request extensive delays in cases.

Elmer confessed that Sante wanted the fire set at the end of August but postponed the mission until early September because of an unexpected houseguest. She bought Elmer's plane ticket, but made him pay for his hotel and rental car. Arriving in Hawaii on Saturday, September 15, he watched TV in his hotel room to calm his nerves then accidentally fell asleep. Bolting up around 11:30 that night, he quickly dressed and drove to the Kimes estate.

It was after midnight, the waves hitting the beach the only sound he heard when he slipped into the silent house through an unlocked door and headed for the master bedroom. His hands shaking like an old man, he could barely hold his cigarette lighter steady after spreading accelerant around the house. Flicking the lighter, he finally pressed the flame against some drapes and then moved onto another room. Scared by the wall of fire now around him, he ran outside and flew back to Las Vegas that Sunday September 16.

A neighbor awoke to the sound of breaking glass and spotted flames shooting from the kitchen straight up to the roof. The main house collapsed into rubble. Only the concrete floors remained. No walls were left standing. It took three fire companies four hours and five minutes to battle the blaze, and they managed to save the cottage. Flames were so intense glass shattered, ceramic tiles cracked, and the furniture melted down to the metal frames. The charring and burn patterns bore the classic mark of an arsonist who had liberally poured liquid accelerant around and then ignited the drenched areas, said the fire investigation report, which ruled the blaze "malicious in nature."

When Elmer next spoke to Sante, she acted surprised that her house had burned. Elmer figured she thought her phone was tapped. In person, she assured him he would be paid in a day or two. Sure enough, Sante instructed him to go to her Las Vegas house and look under the front seat of a parked car, where he found his $3,000.

In the following weeks, Elmer continued to represent the Kimeses as their negotiator and wrote long letters to the insurance carriers about the maids' suit. He both prodded and cajoled them into making a settlement. "But over and beyond all of the foregoing is the fact that litigation on these issues will be prolonged and very expensive to all parties," he wrote on October 23, 1990. "And the ultimate costs of litigation alone to the insurance companies could greatly exceed the amounts for which the Kimes are ready to settle all of these cases."

Nearly every day during this time, Elmer visited Las Vegas attorney Douglas Crawford, who was also working for the Kimeses. Just starting out in his own practice, Crawford considered the $10,000 the Kimeses gave him in 1989 a "huge retainer." For months Sante told him of this unsupported conspiracy against her by the lawyer in Hawaii who represented the maids. She claimed this prominent attorney was hooked up with the mob and would stop at nothing to get his way. All these claims were utterly unsupported.

Elmer reinforced this alleged conspiracy. "He came

to me one time with bruises and a black eye," Crawford said. "He told me he was at so-and-so bar and some guys jumped him in his car and said, 'You're getting too close, this is a message. Next time we'll take you out to the desert and kill you.' " Sante also began warning Crawford that he could be in danger saying, " 'Listen, they are going to do something to you,' " or " 'when you get close enough to the truth, they are going to stop you.' "

On October 24, 1990, Sante and Kenneth called Crawford and asked for a last-minute meeting that evening at his new office at 526 S. Seventh Street, a one-story beige stucco building, once a private home. The couple then invited him to dinner at Lillie Langtry's, a Chinese and steak place at the Golden Nugget casino. When they left for the restaurant around 6:25 P.M., he set the burglar alarm on his modest office. As dinner ended, he said Sante kept cajoling him to stay longer and have one more drink. Finally departing after two-and-a-half hours, Crawford said his car phone rang like high-noon chimes when he arrived at the valet parking. It was bad news. Half of his office had burned down to the dirt in a suspicious fire that broke out at 7:54 P.M.

In an affidavit dated two days after the fire at Crawford's, Elmer Holmgren listed this blaze as well as the one he secretly set in Hawaii among the reasons why he believed the Kimeses were in danger from the Hawaiian lawyer. "Affiant believes that with conditions such as they are in the above cases, there is a real threat to the Kimes and all involved parties in the said cases, and that the lives of the Kimes and others and myself are in jeopardy."

Still, Elmer's stint as an arsonist must have gnawed at his conscience. Drinking one night, he confided in a Linda Tripp-like friend at a Las Vegas bar. His friend went to authorities, got fitted with a wire and then secretly recorded Elmer's confession in mid-January 1991 while the two were out drinking again. When ATF agents arrived at Elmer's home at 3770 Swenson Street, he told them everything, agreed to secretly become an informant against Sante and record her talking about the arson. Elmer planned to wear the wire in early February but had to cancel when the Kimeses suddenly asked him to accompany them to Santa Barbara. In one of the last letters he wrote for the Kimeses, dated February 4, 1991, Elmer defended their honor and integrity as he pushed Chubb & Son, the insurance company, to process the claim on the burned Hawaii home. "As lead counsel of all Kimes' legal matters, I again assure you that the Kimeses have not only suffered a terrible loss of their home, but they are totally innocent of any innuendoes and derogatory statements made. Their home burned down on September 16, 1990, through no fault of their own, and they have tried to cooperate with you in every possible way to resolve this matter."

On February 8, 1991, Elmer called the ATF office in Honolulu from Santa Barbara and in a hushed voice whispered that the Kimeses were in the next room and the sting would have to wait. That was the last the agents ever heard from Elmer. A few days later, an unidentified woman, whom the agents suspect was Sante, dialed the same ATF number wanting to know what office it was. She might have found a telephone bill and tried to figure out what Honolulu number Elmer had called, agents believe.

Soon afterward, in mid-February 1991, Elmer vanished. A few days before he dropped from sight forever, Elmer had confided in his son Ken that he was informing on his employers but he didn't name them. He instructed Ken Holmgren to call the ATF if he hadn't heard from him in a few days and mentioned that he would be going with his bosses to the Dominican Republic and Antigua. No one knows if he ever made it there. "I knew my father was involved in something in Honolulu," said Ken. "I talked with him a couple of days before he disappeared. He didn't want me to know their names, thought there might be reprisals against the family. He said he had turned federal witness and that he was scheduled to testify against The Dragon Lady and that if I didn't hear from him by a certain date that I was to call the ATF."

Bombshell statements in legal papers dated after Elmer vanished indicate the Kimeses knew he was informing against them. In an affidavit dated March 19, 1991, their attorney said, "Kenneth Kimes was told by a third person that Elmer Holmgren had, while employed by the Kimes interests, made statements damaging to Kimes Construction and Kenneth Kimes, including accusations of commissions of serious crimes." The affidavit went on to accuse Elmer of being a liar and a thief. "Mr. Holmgren appears to have used his position of trust and confidence to make false and criminal accusations against his clients while still purporting to be their counsel. Mr. Holmgren appears to have solicited payoffs or bribes for untrue information adverse to his clients. Mr. Holmgren has stolen and secreted records and documents of the Kimes." A memorandum asking for a delay in the maid civil proceeding stated, "Holmgren has either approached or been approached by adverse persons for the purpose of betraying the Kimes interests for his own personal gain." It accused Elmer of a "monstrous fraud," since he claimed to be an attorney but was not licensed to practice "in any jurisdiction."

On March 8, 1991, a subpoena was issued for Elmer to testify about these matters, but he failed to appear for the deposition three days later in Las Vegas. His family and friends have not seen or heard from him either. They doubt he is hiding from the arson case, since the statute of limitations on that crime expired in 1995 and he could not be tried for it even with his confession. Authorities have not charged Sante with arson, after their secret informant and key witness vanished. The Illinois Attorney General also dropped their consumer fraud case against Elmer on August 15, 1997, basically because he had never shown up for any hearings. "I don't think he's alive," said his son, Dan. At the time, there was no criminal investigation into Elmer's disappearance. His ATF handlers felt their informant probably dropped out of sight to avoid getting squeezed by both law enforcement and the Kimeses. Today the agency refuses to talk publicly about Elmer or the arson case.

After Elmer vanished, Sante pressed on with her quest to collect insurance money on the fire he had secretly confessed to setting at the Hawaii estate. Their insurance carrier was Federal, part of Chubb & Son Inc., and also among the companies madly battling the Kimeses over paying for the enslaved maids' civil suits. Worn down by all the litigation, the insurance carriers ultimately opted to settle out of court on the maids' case, offering an undisclosed sum. On the major civil suit filed by the maids, the Kimeses went through 19 attorneys. At least a half dozen lawyers they had hired for this suit and other actions turned around and sued the couple for nonpayment of fees.

Despite this history, the Kimeses were able to get fire insurance coverage from Federal on their Hawaii home just two months before the arson fire in September 1990. Their application failed to list the prior coverage and apparently without checking, Federal approved policy number 1081-91-68-01 for the Hawaii estate in July 1990. However, by the fall of 1991, Federal and the head office of Chubb & Son in Warren, New Jersey, realized who the Kimeses were, learned that the Hawaii fire was arson, and refused to pay anything. The policy required homeowners to be examined under oath, but at the risk of having the claim rejected, Sante and Kimes skipped these depositions three times. Sante decided to go straight to the top, the same tactic she successfully used in 1978 with the first fire at the Hawaii home. Now 13 years later, she again showed up unannounced at the home of an insurance big shot in suburban New Jersey. This time she went one step further and made home visits to both the company's chairman and president.

Her efforts only succeeded in terrorizing the two executives. Affidavits they filed to obtain a restraining order against Sante suggest that she would do or say anything to get her way. The following account is given by Chubb witnesses in that court case. She arrived in the exclusive suburb of Far Hills, New Jersey, bearing white lilies on a Saturday afternoon November 9, 1991. As she walked up the driveway of Chubb chairman and chief executive officer Dean O'Hare, he thought the stranger with the flowers was soliciting for charity. He continued with his yard work and let his wife answer the door. "Hello, I'm Sante Kimes and I have an appointment with Mr. Dean O'Hare," said the visitor. Kathleen O'Hare coolly lied and said her husband was out of town, knowing full well that insurance customers never arrived uninvited at the chairman's home on a Saturday afternoon. Still, she was kind enough to drive Sante to the train station after learning that the surprise visitor had planned to take the bus back home without realizing the nearest stop was miles away. On the way to the station, the two women talked about their children and Mrs. O'Hare unwittingly told Sante the ages of her two sons.

Sante didn't take the train home. She made a beeline for Symor Drive in Convent Station, New Jersey, home of Chubb's president, Richard Smith. His wife had organized a surprise birthday party and guests jammed their living room when Sante, now calling herself Elvira, rang the doorbell. "I have a message for Richard Smith, president of Chubb," she said, then asked to come inside because it was cold. She froze when she saw the birthday party in full swing and promised to return the next day. When Elvira rang the bell before noon on Sunday, the Smiths didn't open the door. Twice that day a woman identifying herself as Sandra Chambers telephoned Smith, but his wife and daughter intercepted the calls. A few days later at 4:00 A.M. on Thursday November 14, the jangling of a hotel phone woke up O'Hare. He was in San Francisco's Fairmont Hotel on business, but Sante had tracked him down. She wanted to talk about her insurance claim and O'Hare said it was too early and hung up the phone. Two hours later at 6:00 A.M., she called him again, and this time he asked for her name and claim number. She insisted on sending him a package, and he directed her to the next stop on his West Coast business trip, the Jonathan Club in Los Angeles. When he arrived at the club and was handed a package, the nervous executive called for the police to examine it. Before the cops arrived, the package mysteriously vanished.

At his home that Thursday, his wife received a strange phone call from a woman claiming to be from the TV show, *All My Children*. The caller wanted to film the exterior of the O'Hare home for a segment, a request Mrs. O'Hare turned down upon hearing that the crew would need to get inside the house. The next day, a package from "ABC" in Los Angeles addressed to Mr. O'Hare arrived, but the "ABC" referred to the American Hotel Business Center not the TV network. Inside was a letter saying that the K.K. Kimes Construction Company had hired them to deliver a package that didn't get to Mr. O'Hare at the

Jonathan Club. Freaked out by all this, Mrs. O'Hare called the Far Hills police to open the package, which was full of papers about Kimes' fire insurance claim. Both O'Hare and Smith then hired private security guards to patrol their houses.

Next Sante picked Friday the 13th of December, 1991, to show up unexpectedly at Chubb headquarters in Warren, New Jersey. She arrived with a secretary who claimed to own a recording company called, "Cloak and Dagger." Kenneth Kimes joined her there later that day. Not wishing to provoke Sante, O'Hare and Smith agreed to meet with her.

"A woman always has the right to be unpredictable," Sante told the insurance executives. She insisted on speaking with O'Hare alone and confessed to him that the Hawaiian syndicate had torched her home. Moving closer to O'Hare, Sante stared him in the eye and spoke about a friend's 17-year-old son whose body was chopped up and sent home in pieces. Another friend's 12-year-old son dropped out of sight forever. This was the punishment for those who upset the Hawaiian syndicate, she warned him. O'Hare had two sons, ages 17 and 12, and remembered that his wife had innocently told Sante about the boys on that ride to the train station.

Sante then asked to speak privately with William Falsone, the vice president and national manager of Chubb's property claims. He heard the conspiracy theory, spouted to everyone from Judge McKibben to attorney Doug Crawford, that the Hawaii lawyer handling the maid claims was mob connected, according to Falsone's affidavit. Now she accused the attorney of engineering the arson fire. In a version of the child-torture story she told O'Hare, Sante said that the 17-year-old son of a friend who tried to fight the mob was found in little pieces scattered in a sugarcane field. Falsone thought Sante's dramatic visit was designed to shake down the company for money. "I interpret Sante Kimes' unannounced visit to Chubb's headquarters as a calculated attempt to find out as much about our operation as possible and to catch the company off guard to the point where Chubb would react by reaching a settlement with them," he said in court papers. "I believe the Kimes surprise visit was an attempt to intimidate Chubb by demonstrating to Chubb that they had easy access to our operations."

The Friday the 13th atmosphere continued. At 3:30 A.M. on December 16, 1991, the security guards saw a strange car arrive at the O'Hare home driveway. The driver shut off the lights, immediately backed down the driveway, and sped away. As the sun rose, the guard spotted something under Mrs. O'Hare's car, which had been parked at the top of the driveway. It was a large dead crow.

CHAPTER 11

"Don't you ever speak morals with my son again. There is a time to lie and a time not to lie, and I will be the one to teach him that."

Kenny Kimes was just seven years old when he blurted out his anguish over his mother. In those days, his sandy brown hair shimmered with blond highlights, thanks to the Mexican and Hawaiian sun, and he looked at the world through big blue-green eyes. The cute little boy loved crawling into his papa's lap and cuddling. He could also be a charmer around other adults, impressing them with big words or simply by saying "please" and "thank you." Other children made him antsy, perhaps because he was rarely around his peers. Sante isolated him from regular contact with kids his own age by keeping him out of school and hiring private tutors who traveled with the family. She also made sure that no one teacher ever held sway over her boy. By the time he turned 10, his mother had lost count of how many tutors she had hired and fired since he was seven, guessing there were about a dozen. "It's not good to have a child have just one kind of teacher like that for too long a period, because what happens is that they get too family oriented and they stop teaching," Sante said in a 1989 deposition. "And they can't become kind of like brother and sister. It is not a teacher relationship. It is much better to have kind of a professional relationship with a student if you can. It is very difficult to do."

Kenny's tutors had to submit written progress reports to the host school in his home district, which in Hawaii was the Cocohead Elementary School in Honolulu. Sante made sure the reports were glowing, reading them over and approving the final copy. For the first quarterly report in 1982, when Kenny had just turned seven, tutor Gail Kriegbaum was only required to send the school district one paragraph about the boy. She submitted six typed pages.

"To summarize Kenny's progress in this quarter, a short paragraph would not do him justice," it began. "His increasing knowledge in phonics has enabled him to continue to read at an advanced comprehensive level. He is gaining a beautiful singing voice and has no problems retaining many memorized songs and poems. Kenny is charming with adults, performing well in front of audiences, yet at the same time he can easily mingle and play with children of his own age. He loves to travel, and continues to be interested in the changing world around him. It is encouraging to see Kenny handle a situation as the individual he is, but most people would unthinkingly follow the status quo. He contains an abundance of energy, which he uses in schoolwork or social play as a very caring and loving child."

This dream child was not the boy tutor Teresa Richards met on July 13, 1982, in Puerto Vallarta, Mexico. She found a complex little kid who was smart, but unable to focus on his lessons. Sweet and affectionate at times, he grabbed onto her hand and curled up in her lap. He was also the brat who laughed as he yanked down her bathing suit top, Teresa remembered. Sante brushed off her son's behavior as natural curiosity. Naomi Lee, the Indiana University placement official, recounted Teresa's version of the incident in a November 23, 1982, letter warning Ohio State not to send Sante tutors. "One of the teachers (Teresa) objected when Kenny pulled down her bathing suit, to her waist. Mrs. Kimes said that that was all part of life and they wanted to know that Kenny knew all about life."

Teresa said Sante warned her not to feel inhibited if she saw Kenny shower with his mother. She never did see that, but said the boy spied on her once while she showered in their Las Vegas home. As a teacher, Teresa was more alarmed when she discovered Kenny telling several white lies. He also whined when he didn't want to study. Sante herself realized her son sometimes weaseled his way out of homework. "Don't let him con!" she wrote about Kenny in a list of instructions for the tutors when she and her husband were away. "Expect same performance (or better), but be sensitive since parents aren't near to talk to."

In a July 23, 1982, letter to her parents, Teresa described her new pupil as a handful: "And now for that adorable, lovable, spoiled-rotten, bratty Kenny. Sometimes I love him to death, and other times I despise him. He really is mature and big for a seven-year-old. Has always had anything he's ever wanted! He thinks he's boss, can do whatever he wants, etc. I'm showing him a thing or two! He has a very short attention span, hates to do schoolwork, and is easily distracted—so I'm facing a huge challenge. It's been real tough so far, but I'm determined to conquer this one. I've told Sante everything I've observed in him, etc. She agrees with me and said she'd help and back me up in any way—but it is difficult when she thinks he is the greatest thing on earth!"

Almost by accident, Kenny revealed a deep shame about his mother. He opened up when he and Teresa were alone at the beachfront rental in Puerto Vallarta, after Sante and Kimes traveled to Las Vegas. As the boy walked along the shore with his new teacher, they spotted a small paddleboat lodged in the sand,

Teresa said in a 1990 deposition and again in a recent interview.

"I can't wait for Papa to get home because we're going to steal a boat and go fishing," he said.

"Kenny, I don't think you mean steal. You and Papa will probably buy a boat or rent a boat," Teresa said.

When the boy insisted they would steal the boat, Teresa sat him down on the beach for an impromptu lesson about the evils of stealing. He grew quiet, frowned as his mind struggled with the concept, then suddenly burst into tears.

"My mama is a bad lady," he cried, and Teresa thought, "Oh, God, what Pandora's box is opening now?" The boy described being in a jewelry store with his mother, watching her distract the clerk and slip a pair of diamond earrings into her purse.

"He was crying, and I felt bad and said Mama didn't mean to take them, and he said, 'No, I saw her take them.' "

To curb his appetite for lying, Teresa also taught him Aesop's fable about the boy who cried wolf so often that nobody believed him when the animal really came to eat him. When his parents returned, Kenny rushed to them all excited over his lessons, vowing never to lie or steal. "He was so proud of himself," Teresa said. Sante on the other hand was enraged, Teresa said. Grabbing the tutor by the arm, she led her to a room downstairs, pushed her on a bed, and shook a finger in her face. "Don't you ever speak morals with my son again," Teresa remembered her saying. "There is a time to lie and a time not to lie, and I will be the one to teach him that."

Born at 8:19 A.M. on March 24, 1975, at Cedars of Lebanon Hospital in Los Angeles, the birth record for Kenneth Karam Kimes lists his mother's age as 30 when she was actually 40. His father's name is also wrong, given as Keith Kenneth Kimes, reversing his middle and first names. Sante told a dramatic story about Kenny's birth to tutor Gail Kriegbaum in 1982, claiming he had two birthdays because he was born dead with a "hyaline membrane," a lung disorder, but doctors were able to revive him.

This story comes as news to Sandra Spears, who worked as a secretary for Sante while she was pregnant. Spears remembered Kenny's birth as routine, though during her pregnancy, Sante was bounced around in a cab that crashed into another car. Hospital tests pronounced her fit. As an expectant mother, Sante was excited and happy, Spears said. However, Sante didn't want Kimes' relatives to know she was pregnant, Spears said, and described the type of loose clothing Sante wore to hide her shape.

Sante's paranoia, demands for secrecy, security, and control shaped Kenny's world from the start. A jet-setter from his infancy, Kenny traveled between his family's lavish homes in California, Hawaii, Mexico, and Nevada. Yet all his movement landed him behind locked doors and high fences erected by a suspicious, domineering mother. And it seems like he didn't have much carefree fun. Just as she pushed her first son, Kent Walker, to be a Harvard-educated attorney, a path he didn't take, she pressured Kenny to excel academically. "She believes what she is doing is good, but she just gets carried away," Walker said in court papers, when Kenny was 11. "She wanted me to study excessively. I never had any tutors, but she wanted me to study three hours a day, even when I was in the third or fourth grade. She would talk to my teachers weekly. I know now she wants weekly reports from tutors on my brother Kenny's progress. At times, he was being tutored seven or eight hours every day. She and the tutors would have arguments because they thought she was too demanding of them and of Kenny."

According to several tutors and maids who

worked for the Kimeses, the young boy also seemed to have inherited his mother's cruelty toward the household help. "He was weird," said Ann Dumke, the tutor succeeding Teresa Richards. "He didn't learn very well, and he also didn't focus on what he was doing. He just seemed like he knew he had it easy or had it made, and he didn't really have to do the work. I considered him a brat . . . and around the maids, he treated them horribly. He was real snippy with them."

Maid Dolores Vasquez Salgado, who was 14 when she worked for Sante in 1982, claimed seven-year-old Kenny had a nasty temper and kicked her feet, stomach, legs, and shins at least 20 times.

"Why would he kick you?" she was asked while giving a deposition in 1988.

"Because he didn't want to do—he wanted to do whatever he wanted to do, his whims."

Dolores said Sante just replied "because you are stupid," when she complained about the boy. He was careful only to kick her when his mother wasn't around, the maid said. In the two months she worked for Sante, she never saw other children come to the Las Vegas house to play with the boy. "Kenny didn't have any friends," Dolores said.

By the time Kenny was eight, Sante allowed him to play with a boy his own age, Andy Miller, the son of a navy lieutenant commander stationed in Hawaii. The boys met at Star of the Sea school, where Kenny took some classes while in between tutors. Testifying at the slavery trial, Andy described playing hide-and-seek with Kenny and the maids in the backyard of their beachfront home. Once, he said, maid Adela Sanchez Guzman and he played a joke on Kenny, hiding his clothes when he was in the shower. Mrs. Kimes lost her patience and "told me not to do it again," Andy said.

Adela testified to nastier pranks, like the time

Kenny allegedly mixed Tabasco sauce, vinegar, milk, and booze together and then tried to force her to drink it. Other maids said he kept them from using the phone or going outside, and one said he taught her obscene words. However, at least one time, Kenny apparently tried to intervene and help one of the maids. According to court papers, Kenny wrote a note to a tutor, saying his mother took maid Maribel Cruz's Salvadoran identification papers. Sante found his note under a seat cushion and apparently spanked the boy.

The last of the Latina maids had the worst memory of Kenny, who was 10 years old when she knew him. Maid Maria de Rosario Vasquez said the kid acted like a sexual predator, but wasn't strong enough to overpower her.

"He would kick me, and he would pull my hair, and sometimes I was taking a bath or a shower, he would come and open the door, even if it was locked, and then he would tell me, he would [try and] force me to make love to him," she said in a 1988 deposition. "I didn't want to speak too much because I thought that the lady was going to get angry with me. And sometimes while cleaning up the house, he would tell me, go take your clothes off. Like he would start kicking me, let's make love. That would make me unhappy, make me sad."

Maria tried scolding Kenny into behaving and in frustration once even told Sante, who promised to speak to the boy. Sante, years later, denied ever hearing a word about this. "Excuse me while I vomit," she responded when a lawyer read Maria's statements. Kenny was "a very frail little boy" she said, and while the maids complained at times that he was difficult and didn't want to go to sleep, they never said he kicked them. Then she added, "He wasn't frail, he was a poor eater." She said her boy was incapable of hurting the maids. "I wouldn't have believed it, because they were so much bigger than he and so much more sophisticated. And he was a very sweet kid, a beautiful kid, and kind and very gentle." As she had during her criminal trial, she accused the maids of lying for money. "There is no truth to that," she said. "I think if you check Maria's original FBI statement you will see that she never said anything like that, and that she is embellishing, obviously being told to embellish and lie for monetary gain."

When he was 14, Kenny had to respond to Maria's charges under oath, while being deposed on October 11, 1989, in the civil suit filled by Sante's maids.

"Okay," began attorney Fernando Cosio. "The next question may be a bit embarrassing, but nevertheless it's my job to ask you. Realize that it's nothing personal."

"Okay," said Kenny.

"Okay, Maria Vasquez claims that you barged in on her while she was showering and asked her to make love with you. Is that—is there any truth to that?"

"None," said Kenny.

"That's something that you wouldn't do?"

"I couldn't do," he said.

"You couldn't?" the lawyer asked.

"And wouldn't," he replied.

He also denied kicking any of the maids, keeping them inside and away from the phone, or forcing them to drink anything.

Only when scared Latina girls no longer toiled in his homes, and Sante went to prison for enslaving them, did Kenny get a chance at a more conventional childhood. Away from his mother for the first time, the boy bonded even more closely with his beloved Papa. Already semiretired, Kimes sold off the Mecca Motel in Anaheim to spend more time with his son.

"Kenny's closeness with his father is apparently not a consequence of his mother's arrest," said a correctional consultant in a 1987 report urging that Kimes not be send away to alcohol treatment. "Kenneth Kimes stated, and both Kenny and Mrs. Gager (a neighbor) confirm, that Kenny has always been closer to his father. Apparently Sante Kimes, who has been described as 'flamboyant, outgoing, and generous,' is also regarded as volatile and unpredictable. As a contrast, Kenneth Kimes is rather subdued and consistent. As a result, Kenny has been much closer to his father throughout the child's entire life."

By the time of Sante's arrest in August 1985, Kenny was performing at or above grade level, thanks to home tutoring. For the first time, he got a chance to be in school with other kids. Based in Las Vegas now, Kimes enrolled his son in a Lutheran school, First Good Shepherd, but then switched him to Ruby Thomas, a public school, because it was closer to their house on Geronimo Way. In the sixth grade at Ruby Thomas, Kenny earned high grades: an A in reading, B in oral and written skills, B in math and E in social growth, science, and social studies.

Dan Etter, a neighborhood kid a year older than Kenny, began hanging out with him around the time the slavery case hit the news. The notoriety embarrassed Kenny. "I remember the conviction was on the front page of the newspaper and him saying, 'My parents are on the front page' and what a disgrace it was," Dan said. When he was 12, the correctional consultant interviewed Kenny and found him "somewhat troubled" despite progress in school. "He still exhibits anger and resentment toward his mother, primarily because she behaved in such a way that she was taken from him . . . Upon interviewing Kenny, one is struck with how 'adultlike' he behaves. He uses sophisticated language for a 12-year-old and responds to questions and converses in a very clear and appropriate manner. When he doesn't believe he is being observed, however, the insecurity and neediness are apparent."

By the time of this report, he had just started the fall term at a new school, St. Viator, considered the best Catholic grammar school in Las Vegas. About one mile from Kenny's house, the pink stucco school had a large statue of St. Viator in front. Every Friday the entire student body of 360 kids, from kindergarten through eighth grade, trooped to church for a communion mass. For a kid used to living under house rules for practically every hour of the day, Catholic school probably didn't seem so strict. His father eased up on Kenny during these years. He indulged him with Nintendo games, vacations with his friends, new CDs, even a 1960 vintage pink Cadillac to go tooling around the neighborhood when he was old enough to drive, just as he had treated his daughter Linda to a car during his divorce.

"His dad was a really easygoing guy," said Dan Etter. "One of his main purposes was for Kenny to be happy. He was still his father, but basically if Kenny wanted to do something very badly, he would find a way to please him."

Paul Huffey, father of Kenny's classmate Neil Huffey, remembers the elder Kimes as a caring man who attended many St. Viator functions. Like the mess sergeant he once was, Kimes cooked all his son's meals at home and often drove him on the five-minute trip to school. Kenny impressed Paul Huffey with his adult manner during a trip to an antique auto show. As they passed by priceless Bentleys, Rolls Royces, and Packards, the kid paid attention and asked good questions.

"Kenny thanked me profusely for taking them to the car show," said Paul Huffey. "He was a nice young man, a little more vocal than the average kids, more conversational with adults. He would strike up a conversation and keep it going, rather than the typical 13-year-old. I think it was obvious, his father was old enough to be his grandfather, and I'm sure he included the boy in his circle of friends."

Kimes also made sure Kenny had fun with kids his own age. The indulgent father treated Kenny, Dan, and Tory Raho, a St. Viator classmate who lived a block away, to a weekend at a Beverly Hills hotel, where they ate breakfast in bed and window-shopped on Rodeo Drive. Kenny often carried $20 to $40 and sometimes $200 if he was going shopping. He insisted on treating his pals to pizzas or subs when they hung out at the local shopping center on Maryland Parkway. If they weren't at the mall, the trio descended on Kenny's house after school. There they jumped on the backyard trampoline, threw the plastic fruit centerpiece at each other, bounced on the many couches, and blasted their favorite music at the time, the rib-cracking beat of the dance-rock band INXS. "I remember going over there a lot, having free rein," said Neil Huffey, Kenny's classmate. "That's why it was fun going over there, it was such a crazy house, always very dark, it seemed like no doors. You would walk into a room, and there would be so many cleaning services in and out of the place, and it still seemed dirty, cluttered."

At school, Kenny was the jokester who made people laugh with pratfalls as well as quick wit. His pale complexion betrayed him, and he turned deep red when he blushed. Yet Kenny was not shy about hurling himself into the swirl of hallway recesses or playing clown during lesson breaks. "He was charming, he always got away with it," said Neil Huffey. "It was always tongue-in-cheek stuff."

A picture of Kenny and 10 pals in his eighth-grade yearbook captures that carefree time. Decked out in the school's uniform of white polo shirts and navy blue pants, most of the boys stand straight with arms folded in a mock tough-guy stance. Not Kenny.

Wearing a wide grin, his eyes closed, he is splayed out on the ground in front of his friends. On his side, his legs bent as if in mid-kick, both hands cup his joyful face.

Below the surface, he felt a jumble of emotions for his mother, his friends said. He loved her out of loyalty, but the public mess with the maids deeply embarrassed him, and he rarely spoke his heart about it when she was away in prison. His father would take him once or twice each month to visit Sante at the Federal Correctional Institution in Pleasanton, California, one of only three federal jails at the time that housed women.

"He'd make light of it," Neil Huffey said. "Obviously he was ashamed about it, and he knew what the situation was. I think his really close friends knew, and I knew too, but it was no big deal to us. He would say, tongue in cheek, that she's away at the hospital getting better."

Kenny was dragged into his mother's efforts to overturn her slavery conviction. He took the witness stand in federal court barely a month into his fall term in the eighth grade at St. Viator, backing up his mother's claim about her feud with juror Rhonda Shonkwiler. He testified in front of Justice Howard McKibben during an evidentiary hearing on October 19, 1988, that Rhonda had spoken with the maids and argued with his mother over the Kimes family dog, a mischievous wire-haired terrier. It would run all over the neighborhood, and Rhonda personally brought the dog back to the Kimeses "approximately about seven times herself," Kenny said. Under cross-examination, the 13-year-old Kenny couldn't explain how he arrived at the figure of seven times and backtracked madly, saying he remembered seeing Rhonda return the dog "more than once." Then prosecutor Karla Dobinski bore down and tried to get Kenny to admit that his mother coached his testimony. Dobinski almost succeeded. Kenny grew nervous and confused, switching his answers around like someone who didn't study hard enough for finals.

"You and she have talked about the problem with the Shonkwilers. Is that correct?" Dobinski asked.

"No," said Kenny.

"You never have?"

"Well, in the past, about—far past. But—"

"When is—" Dobinski began.

"Go ahead," Kenny interrupted her. "I'm sorry."

"—when is the far past?"

"I don't remember," said the boy.

"A year ago? Two years ago?"

"Well," Kenny began, "it would probably be about—if we discussed it, it would probably be about three to four months ago, but I don't think we ever discussed the Shonkwilers. I just—I would probably think that we would discuss it, because we're—I'm on the case now, so I might be confusing the thought."

"Please explain," said Dobinski.

"Because I have my mind on the Shonkwilers, I might be confusing what I'm thinking about with what me and my mother have been talking about."

Dobinski shot back, "You're not certain what you've talked about with your mother?"

"Well, things like, 'I love you,' and like that," Kenny said.

"But also you may have talked with her about the Shonkwilers?"

"If we had," Kenny said wearily, "it wouldn't be recently."

"Okay," said the prosecutor, not letting him go. "It might have been as long ago as three or four months?"

"Yes," Kenny said.

"And you would have been sharing what you remember about the situation?"

"No, she'd tell me—well, I'm not sure. I'm not sure what she'd say. It was a long period of time ago, so I don't remember."

"What time of day did these incidents occur with—the seven incidents of Rhonda Shonkwiler returning a dog?" Dobinski coolly asked.

"I don't remember," said Kenny.

"Could it have been any time of day, or night or what?"

"I don't remember," he repeated.

"How many times did you see Rhonda Shonkwiler speaking to the maids?" Dobinski asked.

"I don't remember," Kenny said again.

"Which maids?" the prosecutor asked.

"I don't remember. I don't remember," he said yet again.

"You just said, 'I don't remember,' and I didn't ask a question," said Dobinski.

"I was repeating myself because I blurred," he said.

Mercifully, she then let him get off the stand.

At the end of that school year, his last at St. Viator, he paid tribute to his father in the school's yearbook. For the person he most admired, Kenny picked "My Dad." The kindly millionaire indulged him, and unlike his mother, never put him in tough spots. As for future plans, Kenny's rough time on the witness stand seemed to have left an impression. His yearbook listing said he wanted "to become a lawyer and an actor."

CHAPTER 12

"Ken only does things when he won't get caught. He is very good at not getting caught."

After graduating from St. Viator, Kenny headed to the pride of the Catholic education system in Las Vegas, Bishop Gorman High School, where 90 percent of the seniors advance to college. For graduation, families buy full-page photo spreads in the school yearbook, displaying their child's progress from baby snapshots to prom pictures. With tuition then $3,350 a year, Bishop Gorman was the costliest four-year high school in Las Vegas when Kenny enrolled as a freshman in the fall of 1989.

School offered a refuge after a summer that blazed too hot for the boys who hung out on Geronimo Way. Every Fourth of July, they launched bottle rockets along the 18-hole golf course that circled Kenny's cul-de-sac block and surrounding streets. Director Martin Scorsese showcased this neighborhood of half-million dollar homes in his film *Casino*, set in 1973 Las Vegas.

Although the kids in that neighborhood called their Fourth of July ritual a fight, and the commotion annoyed the doctors and lawyers of Paradise Palms, the flying bottle rockets did no real damage—until that summer of 1989. The firecrackers ignited the shake roof on the Tioga Way home of two women, ages 79 and 77. All three local TV networks filmed the inferno that night. The house that burned was next door to Dan Etter's home, and police charged his older brother Tim with possession of illegal fireworks. He was fined $155, but the bigger legal mess was the civil suit the women filed to recoup $170,000 in damages to their home. A private detective found witnesses who claimed they saw Kenny Kimes, just 10 minutes before the fire, headed to the Etter's carrying a bag with bottle rockets and other firecrackers. The civil lawsuit added Kenny to the defendants. In March 1993, the case was settled for an undisclosed sum.

Skinny, with braces on his teeth and acne breaking out on his cheeks, Kenny in those days bounced around the hallways of his new high school in a hyperactive whirl, remembered classmate Jason Benatz. While Kenny worked out with weights and did some wrestling, he was not a jock like Jason, a linebacker on the freshman football team. Their common bond was alternative music, which in that era meant the punk rock sounds of the Dead Kennedys or Seven Seconds, a local band from Reno. "They were kind of like a theme music between all of us," said Jason. "One cut, 'I Want to Stay Young Until I Die,' that was one we all liked." With his father's resources, Kenny bought new albums from the East Coast before they went on sale locally. "He was cutting edge, always a few steps ahead of anyone else," Jason remembered. His fashion was also cool, thick silver bracelets, and stone rings; his favorite was a tiger's eye that he wore on the middle finger of his left hand.

He still had that short attention span of his early childhood. Bright, Kenny liked math and science, but if he were bored with a subject, he faltered. "He had the trademark characteristics that would lead me to believe now that he had either attention deficit disorder or hyperactive disorder," said Jason. "I would say hyperactive, the short attention span, wanderlust, the wacky spasticness. He'd be into one thing one week, and one week another. One week he bought guitar equipment and then dropped it shortly thereafter."

One constant was his father.

"He had a deep admiration and love for his father," said Jason. "I think in fact he wanted to be very much like him. He considered his dad very successful but worried about whether he was in good health or not."

Kenny's shot at normalcy was about to end. Paroled on December 11, 1989, his mother came home after four years in prison. "He never wanted to talk to her even when she called from prison," said neighbor Sandra Raho. "He dreaded her return. He wept! I saw him crying when he found out she was going to be back." The tug of war for his soul began in earnest. It was more difficult for Sante now, dealing with a teenager headed for manhood instead of the small boy she had dominated. When Sante tried to impose curfews and stop him from seeing his new friends, Kenny balked and called her a "bitch" to his friends, Etter said. "After she got back, everything changed," said Dan Etter. "She kept him in the house more, and she tried to keep more control over him. He being the life-of-the-party type, he didn't want any part of that."

Apparently he was still a dutiful son when it came to lying for her, according to an affidavit of a process server who tried to hand legal papers to his parents on March 21, 1990, three days before Kenny turned 15. Las Vegas attorney Jeff Albreghts was suing the Kimeses for $20,000 in unpaid legal fees. He was among six Las Vegas attorneys who claimed the Kimeses stiffed them, according to lawsuits on file at Clark County District Court. Knowing the reputation of the Kimeses for ducking process servers, Albreghts hired sharp-eyed Thomas Jackson, who "was familiar with their patterns and manner of avoiding service of process."

Jackson rushed up to the Geronimo Way home when he spotted their reddish-brown Lincoln sedan pull into the driveway at 6:23 P.M. Seeing the subpoena, Kimes said, "Nope" and ducked back into his car. "That's not Mr. Kimes, honey, that is my son," Sante said. Jackson, who met Kimes before, responded, "He is older than you." Sante stammered and said, "Well, that's not him, it's his brother, he's inside." She also got back into the car. Then as Jackson and his wife, Cindy, were leaving, a teenager in the car fitting Kenny Kimes' description, walked over and "very politely" said they could not accept the papers because the couple in the car were not Sante and Kenneth Kimes. He tried to place the papers in Jackson's car, but they fluttered onto the street.

For his 15th birthday on March 24, 1990, Kimes rushed construction of a new pool and let his son host a big party. The parents left that evening to give the party-goers some freedom. Upon their return, 40 kids were still running around the house, and Sante seethed underneath the tight smile on her face. "Just that night, she was really upset but was trying to be friendly," said Dan. "It was kind of Kenny's last hurrah, and he knew it. It was right after she got back and she was so controlling and he didn't know how far he could go. Kenny always liked to push the limits as far as he could."

Soon Sante asserted herself, pulling Kenny out of Bishop Gorman, away from his new friends. He transferred across town to Green Valley High, a public school in Henderson, on the southeastern fringe of Las Vegas. Academically, this school paled next to Bishop Gorman. Then Sante insisted they spend more time in Hawaii, where Kenny reverted to private tutoring. He was so lonely, his mother must have realized she had gone too far and picked out a friend for him. Blonde and tanned, Kara Craver-Jones was a year older than Kenny and met the Kimeses when they considered buying her family's small boat, a raft with a hard bottom and outboard motor they were selling for $1,400. Instead, Sante chose Kara, with her parent's consent, sending a limousine for the girl to visit her son. At least several times a week during the spring and summer of 1990, Kara rode the 50 miles in luxury from her home on Oahu's north shore to the Kimeses' Portlock Road home on the south shore. Sometimes Kenny would visit her. At first sight she pegged him as "kind of a dork," but he was so delighted with her and she liked the adventure of being around these eccentric people.

They talked of paying for her and Kenny to attend Punahou, an exclusive prep school in Hawaii, and bringing her on their planned trip to the former Soviet Union, even buying her Russian language tapes and maps. She was their dinner guest in fancy restaurants where Sante blew in and announced, "Gimme a phone, gimme a drink." Recycling an old lie, Sante claimed Kimes had been a foreign ambassador. Kenny didn't bother to correct her. In fact, Kara hardly heard him say anything, good or bad, about his mother and thought she had stepped into the middle of an uneasy truce. Polite but cool around his mother, Kenny seemed like a stranger in his own home. Kara never saw him kiss or have any physical contact with his parents. Away from his home, Kenny greeted Kara's parents with a big hug and seemed to relax. "At his house he would never say, 'Cool, Right-on,' or 'Peace,' but at my house, he would use normal kid lingo," Kara said. "In one of the pictures I have, he was flashing a peace sign. He would never do that with his mom."

Kara believed that Sante controlled Kenny's movements, spying on them by always hovering within earshot. Once she asked why his mother wore so many wigs. Kenny started to talk about her undergoing chemotherapy, stopping short as Sante sang out,

"Oh, time to eat, you guys." Another time, as Kara and Kenny headed to the store for bread, Sante called ahead, told the merchant to put the bill on her tab, and send the kids back in five minutes. A surfer girl, Kara wanted to ride the waves, but Kenny would say he wasn't allowed. He also couldn't talk to the punk-rocker-type kids who skateboarded on his street. One night, Kara and Kenny slipped out of the house and ran to the ocean, but he wouldn't swim. "He was like, 'Oh, no. It's dark. We can't be wet.'"

When Sante allowed the teenagers to visit a mall, Kenny acted as though he were boarding a spaceship instead of the No. 52 bus for a 90-minute ride to the Pearlridge Shopping Center. Awestruck, Kenny, 15 years old, had never ridden on a bus before. "Wow," he said of his first taste of public transportation. At the mall, he tried to kiss Kara, but she made it clear theirs was a platonic friendship. After arson demolished Kenny's Hawaii home on September 16, 1990, the second suspicious blaze there in 12 years, Kara never saw him again. He called her for about six months from Santa Barbara and Las Vegas. When she asked about the fire, he alluded to someone chasing his father.

By May 1991, the Kimeses were living in yet another home, a Spanish-style rental with a red-tile roof at 3692 Happy Lane, set on a small horse ranch near singer Wayne Newton's spread in the rural eastern part of Las Vegas. Sante told Kenny she didn't want his old friends hanging around anymore. "It always seemed ironic that the street they lived on was called Happy Lane," said Dan Etter. "I was only out at that house once. I remember we went to his house normally in and out the front door, but his mother came home and she wasn't supposed to see any of us. So we opened his window and got out the first floor and ran away. We had parked the car down the street. Kenny had told us not to park in front of the house."

The friends used the same cloak-and-dagger tactics when Kenny drove to Paradise Palms to see Dan Etter or Tory Raho. He'd park his car around the corner just in case his parents stopped by the neighborhood.

Sante also tried to choose Kenny's female friends, according to attorney Gustav Bujkovsky, who worked for the Kimeses in the early 1990s. He saw Sante yell at Kenny when he wanted to see a girl she didn't like. "She was a domineering mother," Bujkovsky said. "The son would have to get permission to do things. He had wanted to go out with a girl that Sante felt was below his status, and there was a bit of an argument between them, and she raised her voice with her son and told him there's no way he could go out with her. He went to his room."

Realtor Charles Gallagher, who was a guest of the Kimeses in Las Vegas, also saw friction between the teenaged Kenny and his mother. "Sometimes he would move out of the house and live in a friend's house and not come home at all," Gallagher said. "He was running with people she didn't want him to run with. Sante wanted to pick his friends. She said it. Everybody knew it. His friends knew it."

Typical for Sante, her family's stay on Happy Lane brought a tangle of legal action. She and Kimes sued the home's 71-year-old owners, alleging breach of contract. Their countersuit accused the Kimeses of fraud, forgery, and impersonation, reading like a blueprint for the charges Sante would later face in the alleged home swindle of 82-year-old Irene Silverman. At first, Paul and Phyllis Richards thought their new renters, the Kimeses, were charming and went out to dinner with them several times. "They make themselves so well liked, you can be fooled," Paul Richards said. The Kimeses paid $15,000 to rent the house from May to October 1991. As the lease was ending, the Kimeses negotiated to buy the property for $315,000 but then sued, claiming the rent and the sale price were too high after discovering building-code violations.

In a countersuit, the owners alleged that Sante and Kenneth impersonated them to get a building department inspection and services from a plumber and the water authority—all billable to Richards. They claimed the Kimeses forged the rental agreement by inserting a bogus option to buy.

Sante and Kenneth blasted the forgery claim, saying they "stand by the integrity of the document." They placed a lien on the property, preventing Richards from selling the house to anyone else. After the Kimeses missed several deadlines to close on the property, Richards, a retired building contractor, became convinced they were trying to take advantage of him. "They weren't willing to buy it, but they were attempting to hassle me in every which way they could," he said.

He claimed the Kimeses chopped down Italian cypress trees on the one-acre ranch, stayed an extra five months without paying rent, and tried to break in after moving out in the spring of 1992 to a nearby rental in the suburb of Henderson. Then the Kimeses turned on their own lawyer who had filed the lawsuit against Richards. In a criminal complaint to the Henderson police, Sante accused this attorney of bursting into their home, yelling, threatening, and pushing her away to ransack through business records. This case was closed when Sante failed to follow up.

Richards never got the $7,625 for the five months the Kimeses allegedly squatted, but considered himself lucky. "We had a happy ending," he said. "We were able to extricate ourselves from their clutches." It cost him $5,000 to hire a lawyer to defend against the lawsuit and thousands to fix the place after the Kimeses called the building department on him. He also had to pay the plumber they had hired while allegedly pretending to be him. The courts eventually dismissed the lawsuit for inaction.

Kenny seemed to be having a rough time around his mother. She whisked him off to the Bahamas, where he finished high school at St. Andrew's, an Episcopal school in Nassau. About a year later, Kenny returned on a visit to Las Vegas, and all his problems with his mother seemed over. He told Tory Raho and other friends that he loved his mother. "I remember talking to him; he seemed like he was doing good," said Dan. "And later he called Tory, and he was telling Tory that he loved his mother now. It was a complete 180."

By the fall of 1993, Kenny, age 18, was ready for college, and Sante allowed him to attend her alma mater, the University of California at Santa Barbara. Campus police had their hands full with 18,000 students, yet Sante managed to cajole and charm one cop into looking out for her boy. Alan Katje had retired after 20 years as a California highway patrol officer and took another job manning the phones as a dispatcher for UCSB's security. One day a frantic mother lit up the phone line about her freshman kid who lost his plane tickets for a spring break trip to New York. Katje found Kenny's tickets at the local Federal Express office. Grateful, Sante then kept calling for more favors, some a bit wacky. She wanted Kenny's room at the Santa Cruz Residence Hall sterilized after another student caught mononucleosis.

"I said, no, this is ridiculous, Mrs. Kimes," Katje said. "Then she called me a few weeks later for something else. She told me she felt I was Kenny's guardian angel." Katje even agreed to drive some of the kid's stuff back to Las Vegas, and Sante paid him for his trouble.

Academically, Kenny flopped during his first quarter at UCSB, averaging below a C. Even with a lighter class load than most students—12 credits instead of 16—he still pulled only a D in American government and politics, another D in a sociology course called social organization, and a C+ in human anatomy. His 1.43 grade point average automatically landed him on probation, forcing him to eliminate the Ds by repeating the political science and sociology courses. The next quarter he improved a bit, raising his political science grade to a C. For a lover of cutting-edge music, Kenny easily scored a B in music and pop culture. His best grade was a B+ in "Religion and the Impact of the Vietnam War," the most popular course at UCSB, which featured testimonials from veterans and antiwar activists.

By the spring of 1994, he carried a full course load for the first time: four classes worth 16 credits. His busiest quarter, it was also the time of his biggest tragedy, an event that would shape the rest of his life, though he didn't learn about it until months later. The father he had idolized died on March 28, 1994, four days after Kenny had turned 19. Kimes had been the steady hand amid Sante's whirlwinds. The couple had stayed together for nearly 25 years. As Kimes wrote once to Judge McKibben, love for Kenny kept him from leaving the troublesome Sante, sticking with a relationship constantly rocked by crises and lawsuits.

Others who knew Kimes said the bond with Sante was deep, a complicated dependency full of love and mistrust. Mercurial Sante acted sweet and loving around Kimes, especially toward the end of his life when heart disease weakened him. Bookkeeper Sherry Meade worked for the Kimeses in 1993 and 1994 in Las Vegas and saw affectionate exchanges between the couple. She primarily worked on Kimes' finances and would hear him praise Sante, saying proudly, "She keeps me alive." Once Meade walked in on the couple in the kitchen and saw her feeding Kimes. "I think it was her way of showing affection," said Meade. "I think he liked it, and she liked doing it, but she didn't want me to see. She said, 'Don't you have things to do?'" At the same time, Kimes ordered Meade never to tell Sante details of his stock portfolio. When she insisted on getting this information, Meade held her ground and said Sante fired her.

Although Kimes died just three miles away from the UCSB campus, Sante kept his death a secret from Kenny, waiting to break the news after his school term so he wouldn't miss classes. For weeks, she made excuses why Papa couldn't come to the phone. For help with arrangements, she summoned her older son, Kent Walker, by now married with kids of his own and living in Las Vegas. At the time, Kenny knew nothing of the scene Sante created on a public street in front of the Wells Fargo Bank in Goleta as she screamed at the paramedics who couldn't revive Kimes.

He was beyond their help. An aneurysm the size of a man's fist exploded inside his abdominal aorta, spilling approximately 60 percent of his entire blood supply, about 3 to 3.5 liters, into his stomach area. Thrown into irreversible shock, his brain deprived of oxygen, Kenneth Kimes could not be saved despite two hours of exhaustive CPR in the ambulance and in the emergency room at Goleta Valley Hospital.

Sante was hysterical, ordering doctors to "place him on life support or take him to the operating room," according to a 14-page coroner's report prepared when she later threatened to sue the paramedics and hospital staff. "Mrs. Kimes was quite adamant about these wishes and was extremely distraught that these wishes were not carried out," wrote deputy coroner Larry Gillespie. "She raised hell with us," he said years later. Sante was desperate to revive the man who had supported her for more than 20 years. "It was obvious/apparent that she did not have a true understanding of what 'life support' meant and that her interpretation was along the lines of being able to keep the 'body' (brain) alive while surgery and or other medical treatment was carried out to correct the 'problem,'" the report said. "She did not comprehend that in the case of her husband he had already gone beyond that point . . ."

Late in the morning of Monday, March 28, Sante left the Wells Fargo Bank at 122 North Fairview Street in Goleta to find her 77-year-old husband slumped over the steering wheel of their car. She had just gone to the ladies' room and at first told paramedics that Kimes was alone for about 10 minutes, according to the coroner's report. Three days later, she claimed he was by himself only one minute while she rinsed with mouthwash in the bathroom. She charged paramedics took a half hour to transport her husband to the hospital, wasting time treating him for a possible heart attack while ignoring her cries that he had a history of internal bleeding. "She states (admits) that she was overwrought at the sight of her husband lying on the ground being attended to and that she was hysterical in her demeanor and in her demands to paramedics/emergency personnel."

The couple had arrived in Santa Barbara the evening before, presumably to visit their son, and checked into the blue-roofed Hotel Miramar, tucked between the 101 freeway and the famous "Gold Coast" oceanfront. They went to the bank the next morning after breakfast. The morning she found him, she told paramedics that he was unconscious, unresponsive, and barely breathing. A few days later in a phone call to Gillespie, the deputy coroner, she depicted a touching last scene. "She states (now) that her husband was still breathing and that she either clasped his hand or he reached out to her when she called his name. Shortly thereafter his grasp slackened. He did not respond verbally to her."

Gillespie performed a limited autopsy on Tuesday March 29, just to confirm the diagnosis of an exploding aneurysm. Kent Walker and Sante opposed an autopsy but agreed to an exam restricted to the abdominal cavity, to fix the cause of death. Given Kimes' history of heart disease and the size of the aneurysm found during the autopsy, Gillespie concluded that the millionaire died of natural causes. "The development of aneurysms in the aorta is a natural phenomenon usually due to arteriosclerotic vascular disease, which did exist in this patient." Gillespie listed the cause of death as a massive hemorrhage from a ruptured abdominal aortic aneurysm. There was no foul play or negligence found.

Sante did everything she could to hide Kimes' death from the world. He was quietly cremated the day after the autopsy. No death notice or obituary was published. The Welch/Ryce Mortuary told Gillespie that Sante wanted the autopsy report sent to them so she would not receive any correspondence identified as coming from the coroner's office. She instructed Welch/Ryce to forward the report to her in a plain envelope. Sante told Gillespie to keep their conversation confidential and conceal news of Kimes' death from the media. He told her no reporters had asked about him. "She didn't want anybody to know," said her friend, Carolene Davis. "Because of lawsuits and people trying to take this and that away from her, and the house. They were always being sued."

Inaccuracies, most notably the wrong social security number, fill Kimes' death certificate. By listing an incorrect number for that key identifier, a whole host of banks and government agencies were unaware that the millionaire had died, including the Social Security Administration. Also on the certificate, his parents' names are wrong. His father's first name, Charles, is instead listed as Keith, which is Kimes' middle name. His mother is listed as "Naomi Wardshaw" a misspelled combination of her first name "Neoma" and his Aunt Alice's married name "Wardchow." The listing for his home is actually a mail drop.

A week before Kenny's school term ended in June 1994, Sante told campus security dispatcher Alan Katje the truth about Kimes, swearing him to secrecy. "She said Papa would want him to finish the year and get through finals, he would be so devastated by this death and wouldn't finish," said Patricia Katje. "It may sound right, but you don't do that. She just didn't want anybody to know he was dead."

Finals week was tough enough for Kenny, who didn't really like studying, according to a classmate. As students all around him pulled marathon cram sessions, Kenny blasted his music, annoying the kid next door, said Katje. One day the other guy burst into Kenny's room, shouts turned into punches, and both students ended up banned from the dorms next term. Still, it was his best quarter academically. Introductory oceanography brought him his first A, and he scored an A– in introductory communications. In the required English composition course, he earned a B– and pulled his grade from a D to C+ in the sociology course he repeated.

When that school year ended, Katje drove Kenny to the airport, where he thought he was headed for a Hawaiian vacation with his parents. Katje kept the secret of Kenneth Kimes' death. "Where's Papa?" Kenny asked after meeting his mother at Los Angeles airport for a connecting flight. Sante was carrying an urn filled with Kimes' ashes, and Kenny broke down crying, according to the story he told Carolene Davis several years later. "He was very, very upset. I think he called her a few names and said, 'Why didn't you tell me! How could you do this to me! He was my father.' " In a boat in Hawaii, Sante asked Kenny to help scatter his father's ashes among the waves. Wailing and crying, Kenny jumped into the water himself as if trying to touch his father's spirit, Sante told Carolene. "She said it was a really bad scene."

Carolene Davis, a customer-service manager for First American Title Insurance Company in Santa Barbara, and her husband Tim, a construction worker, got a rare inside look at Sante and Kenny in the late '90s. At Sante's invitation, the couple and their four-year-old son, Tyler, moved into her Las Vegas home for several months in the summer of 1994 when they temporarily relocated after the construction business hit a slowdown in northern California. They returned to Santa Barbara, but Sante kept in touch with Carolene over the next four years.

Carolene met Papa Kimes once when the couple arrived at her office in early 1994. They had come for paperwork on the 28.35 acres of undeveloped land he owned in Santa Maria, about 75 miles north of Santa Barbara. From that moment, Sante always said Papa called Carolene "the daughter they never had."

After that initial meeting, Sante kept telephoning Carolene, then 33, asking for more title deeds and other real estate forms. Learning that Carolene and Tim were planning a weekend in Las Vegas in April 1994, Sante insisted they stay with her. She took the younger woman shopping, buying her a $190 black cocktail dress for a party that weekend. She confided in Carolene, tearfully admitting that Kimes Sr. had died. Sante extolled Las Vegas as the place of unlimited opportunities just waiting for the younger woman. Sante said money was important, "you need to be successful." Carolene grew to cherish her friendship with Sante, dropped everything and handled her requests when she called First American, visited her in the Bahamas, heeded her advice, and even called her "Mom." "She was like a second mother to me," Carolene said.

Tim Davis found Sante turned bossy and imperious when Carolene wasn't around. Sante lectured him not to talk with a formerly homeless man she hired as a cook and cleaner in her Las Vegas home. "She said, 'Don't become friendly with him,' " said Tim. ' "Don't talk to him. He's a servant, you don't associate with servants. I'm training this guy to run my house in the Bahamas.' " Sante yelled at Tim for keeping the servant away from the house for four hours as the two men unloaded a moving van.

Kenny, however, was a pleasure to be around, Tim said. Kenny brightened like a kid headed to Disneyland when allowed to work on a plastering job with Tim in Santa Barbara that summer of 1994. Stuck for two hours in Rte. 15 traffic as they drove back from the job to Las Vegas, Tim said Kenny, then 19, opened up about his family. He grew teary-eyed talking about trouble with his mother. The years she spent in prison, "he told me were the best four years of his life, because it was like a normal life," said Tim. "He had friends, people could come over to the house. His father would take him and his friends out to dinner, rent movies and have them all over. I was thinking, wow, I felt sorry for the guy, his mother was running his life."

Tim's boss, Bob Gulvin, hired Kenny and even let him and Tim live in his home in Goleta, California, for two weeks as they finished plastering a two-story Spanish-style house in Santa Barbara. Kenny's soft hands quickly blistered dragging a 200-foot plastering hose, but he never complained. "He wasn't used to hard work, but he gave it his all," Gulvin said. Sante even offered to pay Gulvin to keep her son working, but he refused, saying the polite, friendly teenager earned his pay. He never told

Kenny about this conversation, not wanting to embarrass him.

When September rolled around, the dorm rooms at UCSB remained shut to Kenny because of the fight with the other student. With her usual litigious vigor, Sante hired a lawyer to fight the ban, but that effort dragged and Kenny needed housing fast. The Katjes agreed to take him in as a boarder despite the finagling Sante put them through over the rent. When Alan quoted her $425 a month, she went behind his back to his wife Patricia, who unaware of the first offer said they'd rent the room for $350.

The couple said they grew to love Kenny like a brother. Inheriting his father's mess sergeant genes, Kenny showed a flair for cooking and fixed roasted chicken and other dishes for the Katjes, their daughter, 8, and son, 14. He paid attention to the kids, going with Patricia to her daughter's baton-twirling class, and roughhousing with their son. "He was fantastic, a sweetheart; he just fit in with the family," said Patricia Katje, a medical assistant who worked in UCSB's health-services department. "Kenny became a member of our family. He baby-sat my kid; I'd give him my ATM card to get money out of the account if he needed cash, he never abused that."

Able to bench-press 240 pounds, Kenny lifted weights several times a week with Alan Katje often spotting for him. He took only two classes at UCSB in the period after his father died, earning a B+ in contemporary American history but failing microeconomics. Looks were important to Kenny, who had a nose job in October 1994 to fix the hook nose he inherited from his father. "He liked himself, looked in mirrors a lot," said a classmate Brian Sanger.* "He walked around shirtless and had cut muscles and a flat stomach." Alan Katje liked Kenny's macho en-

---

*Not his real name.

ergy, treating him like the younger brother he never had. "When he was with us, he was a typical college kid, he was fun to be around," said Katje. "He'd have a big smile that would light up the room."

His mother brought the storm clouds. No more than two weeks would pass, and she'd arrive for another visit. The Katjes heard the two yell at each other from behind his closed bedroom door. "They didn't fight all the time, but she was really a controlling person," said Alan Katje. "He'd say things like, 'sometimes my mom just bugs the hell out of me.' Or he'd express his frustrations and say, 'but I know she's only thinking about me. I know she loves me.' "

At the time, Sante frowned on Kenny's long-distance romance with a girl attending college in Los Angeles. Smitten, Kenny pushed the speed limit on two-hour drives to see her and burned up the phone lines between visits. Sante bad-mouthed the girlfriend, Patricia Katje remembered.

Tim Davis said Sante even asked him to steal Kenny's silver Camaro and torch it in a wild insurance scheme, which he refused. "Sante did not want anybody to get that close to Kenny," Davis said. The pressures probably didn't help his grades, which stayed mediocre. He still hadn't declared a major and floundered around in liberal arts classes, earning just a C in western civilization, a C– in general psychology, a pass in the philosophy of law. His only good grade was an A-, for nutrition and fitness, a snap for a bodybuilder.

Sante gave Kenny money to play around with on the stock market when he was in college, and they also traveled to Cuba. He became enthusiastic about the island's economic potential, full of grand plans to develop real estate there. Alan Katje said Kenny even started a Web page to sell Cuban cigars—via the Bahamas to comply with America's ban on direct exports from Castro's Cuba. "I expressed my concern

about him selling Cuban cigars, and he said it was
perfectly legal because it was out of the Bahamas,"
Katje said.

His classmate Brian said Kenny would finger the
gold ring of his father's that he now always wore
and dream out loud about earning millions on his
own. He knew he lacked discipline. "He always said
he was changing his ways and going on the straight
and narrow," said Brian. "He wanted to make his
dad proud." By the close of his sophomore year, he
had improved his grades, earning an A– in religious
studies, a B– in academic writing, and a pass in biol-
ogy. His top grade from that quarter would later embarrass him on national television. "I see from your
transcripts you got an A in acting," said *60 Minutes*
reporter Steve Kroft while interviewing Kenny and
his mother on March 10, 1999. The jailed pair had
agreed to appear on the famed investigative show to
refute their image as grifters who killed Irene Silverman. Mother and son insisted they were honest
folks, not con artists who go around fooling people.
Kenny's acting skills undercut this positive spin.
"Cut," yelled one of their lawyers, immediately ending the interview.

Kenny's third year at UCSB was his last. Now a
junior, he left the Katjes' home for an off-campus
rental. Five housemates shared the $1,920 monthly
rent at a gray wooden duplex at 6795-A Trigo in Isla
Vista, an oceanfront enclave about a mile from campus that was dotted with frat houses. By then, Sante
was renting a seaside cottage just 15 minutes away
in pricey Montecito.

Early into the school year, Kenny had his new
home in an uproar. Another student at UCSB, Carrie
Louise Grammer, claimed Kenny reduced her to a
crying, shaking heap, so frightened she couldn't catch
her breath, according to her application for a restraining order against him. "At one time I had

thought Ken to be a decent person," she wrote in papers filed in Santa Barbara Superior Court on October 25, 1995. "He is very charismatic, but over the past few months, I have realized that his charming behavior is an intentional cover to hide his true abusive personality."

Carrie's boyfriend was one of Kenny's housemates while she lived elsewhere. She and Kenny had argued over something downright laughable, except it produced a stream of character assassinations and a thick court file, depicting Kenny as a nasty hothead and Carrie as a stalker. It all started when Carrie claimed she was baby-sitting Kenny's cat in her place, where the animal soiled her roommate's bed, ruining $70 worth of linen.

When Carrie and her roommate, Lauren Schmalbach, went to Kenny's house for the money the weekend of October 13, 1995, one of his housemates said he was instructed to give them only $35. Carrie wanted the full amount and asked if Kenny had locked himself in his room to avoid her. Suddenly he flung open his door. "I walked in to see Ken sitting at his desk counting money," Carrie said in court papers. "I could see that he had well over $100 in large bills. Ken was putting on a show for me. Ken is financially well-off and he was flaunting the money in an attempt to anger me." Pressed for the money, Kenny turned ugly, Carrie said. "He said he was not going to pay and told me that if our friendship was worth only $35, then I can 'fuck off.' I said to Ken that he was being an 'asshole.' Ken immediately jumped out of his chair. He came at me in a threatening manner with an infuriated expression on his face. His eyes were squinted, his jaw stuck out, his lips were pinched, and his face was red."

Wagging his finger in her face, cursing wildly, muscle-bound Kenny towered over the five-foot, 115-pound Carrie who felt like she was about to get

hit and ran from his room, according to her statement. The living room at 6795-A Trigo rocked with
shouts. "He called me a 'classless bitch,' a 'slut,' a
'little whore who turns tricks' and many other de-
grading things," she claimed. "Ken told me that he
'had more class than (I) ever would.' I then asked
him why he had tried to make out with me (his
friend's girlfriend). He screamed that I was a 'little
whore if (I) was going to hold that against him to
break up his friendship with Pat (her boyfriend).' "
Her roommate Lauren said she heard Kenny let loose
a stream of obscenities such as "greedy bitch" and
"cussing and swearing and uttering many other pro-
fanities, which shocked me." Lauren grabbed Carrie
and took her out of there. "I was shaking and crying
for hours afterward," Carrie said. "I had not done
anything to Ken that would provoke or deserve such
abuse. I told my boyfriend Pat what Ken had done
to me. Pat and I had heard Ken curse out his own
mother in a similar fashion."

The next afternoon Carrie's boyfriend visited
Kenny in his room, as she waited in the living room.
She claimed to hear Kenny scream that she was the
one who had pounded her way into his room the
day before and hit him. "This is not true," she wrote
in her application for a restraining order. "I know
that Ken did not directly threaten me, but he is very
cunning. Ken only does things when he won't get
caught. He is very good at not getting caught." She
concluded her complaint, saying, "I feel in my heart
of hearts that Ken will abuse me again. Whether it
be physical or verbal, I don't know. However, verbal
abuse hurts just as much, if not more than physical
violences. [sic] I am scared of Ken. My roommates
are afraid as well."

Kenny fired back with his own court papers, denying all her charges, claiming Carrie hit him in the
chest with a clenched fist and depicting her as some

pathetic stalker out of the film *Fatal Attraction*. He borrowed his mother's technique of lobbing sexually charged allegations. "Carrie has for over a year constantly approached me in private and in public," Kenny's four-page affidavit said. "She has a history of being overly flirtatious and sexually aggressive, even in the presence of her own boyfriend. She would at various times say to me, 'Ken you know that you're the one I really want and how come you have never tried to kiss me.' She would even come and bother me at work while her boyfriend was out and flirt with me there. Numerous people are witness to these actions. I am not interested. I have my own friends, and Pat was my friend."

In his version, the smaller Carrie was the physically aggressive one, bursting into his room while he was seated at his desk studying for midterms. "Carrie then leaned over me and took her finger, pointed it at me, and screamed, 'you're such a fucking asshole.' At this point, I stood up and demanded she get out of my house. She yelled that 'she didn't have to,' and began striking me in the chest with a clenched fist. I told her to keep her hands off me and to get out. She ran out of my room screaming at me, 'I am going to tell Pat (Lieneweg) that you said you want to kiss me!''

In affidavits that echo with some of the same phrases, four of Kenny's housemates seemingly back up his version of the spat with Carrie. Curiously, a Las Vegas notary public stamped the documents, declaring that the students appeared before her personally on November 6, 1995, a Monday when they had classes at UCSB. One housemate's name is spelled two different ways on the affidavit, "Kristen" Gillis and then "Kristin." In *Scarlet Letter* tones unsuited to most young college women, she allegedly wrote: "My boyfriend will testify also that Carrie came on to him and that she has no honor."

A homeless man working for Sante further trashed Carrie's reputation with his own affidavit. While bartending at a party for Kenny's friends, he claimed Carrie wore a skirt so short he could see her underwear, took at least three different guys with her to the bathroom, and grabbed onto Kenny's belt and pulled him toward her. "I have never attended an alleged party scantily dressed, flirting, dancing, and hugging every guy in the place," Carrie responded in court papers. "These are just plain lies."

Carrie obtained a temporary restraining order against Kenny on October 27, which forbade him from threatening, striking, watching, following, or telephoning her. The court scheduled a hearing on the matter for November 17. The day before the hearing, Lauren claimed Kenny telephoned her roommate Carrie, violating the temporary order of protection. Carrie was out, so he left her a message to be "neutral in court on Friday," according to Lauren's report to the Santa Barbara sheriff. At the next day's hearing, Judge Thomas Adams issued a mutual restraining order telling both sides to avoid each other for the next three years. Sante tried to head off a proposed hearing in January on Kenny's alleged telephone threat with a letter to the judge curiously signed "Sante Kahn." She claimed Carrie had placed telephone calls to her son in early January. Mother submitted three unsigned, undated affidavits from the housemates, all sounding alike and claiming Carrie was the one calling and harassing. "I have rushed here from the Bahamas to try and clear up this matter," Sante wrote. This mess of countercharges apparently ended with no other action taken, according to the court record.

During this saga, Kenny's grades fell back into the basement: a D+ in psychology, a C– in communications research methodology, and a C in introductory law and society for the fall 1995 quarter. Now midway through what should have been his junior year, he stuck to 12 credits a quarter, meaning that it would take him five years to graduate. Even with this lighter course load, his grades were mediocre. For the winter of 1996, he got a C+ in all three of his classes: Latin literature in translation, theories of communications, and introduction to literature.

Sante wasn't holding his grades against him when he turned 21 on March 24, 1996. Inviting his college friends to the Bahamas, she hosted a coming-of-age birthday party for her boy. Her antics embarrassed the guests. Gathering the girls around her, she distributed 21 fresh new $100 bills for the birthday boy, to be presented with a big kiss. When one guest's efforts fell short of Sante's ideal wet kiss, she ordered the girl to try harder. "That's not a real kiss, give him a real kiss," she said, according to classmate Brian Sanger. An uncomfortable silence fell over the party. "We weren't all too thrilled with a mother saying that," Brian said. "We were all grossed out." Soon thereafter, the hostess and Kenny abandoned their guests during what was supposed to be a week in Nassau. The pair left their visitors alone in the Nassau house and visited Cuba for a few days. "The kids weren't that happy," said Patricia Katje. "They were sort of stranded there."

That spring 1996 school term was the last time his Santa Barbara friends ever saw Kenny. Dropping out after three years, his last report card again suggested he was smart but lazy. He got a B+ in language communications processes and a B in American military history but plummeted to Ds in issues in mass communication and Spanish communication. Right before he left school forever, Patricia Katje saw him one last time in her medical office. On May 1, Kenny was driving on Mesa Road in Santa Barbara when another car making a left turn broadsided him. Patricia remembered it as a fender bender, but Sante pushed

Kenny to visit a chiropractor as a step toward pursuing legal action. In a lawsuit eventually filed against the driver, and later dismissed by the courts, Kenny claimed he "experienced pain and suffering and may have permanent and ongoing injuries" that cost him in excess of $10,000 in medical bills. "It was her idea," said Carolene Davis. "Oh, God, it was just ridiculous. It was just an ongoing thing, and Kenny was going along."

Three weeks after this alleged accident, he looked robust while jumping about 10 feet into the air on national TV for a contest taped on May 24, 1996. As MTV hostess Jenny McCarthy cheered him on, Kenny leapt higher than two other young men vying for a leggy blonde on the dating show, *Singled Out*. Kenny flashed a smile full of shiny white teeth for the TV cameras and made a pitch to the blonde, "Hey, Kandace, my name is Ken. I want to be the big guy in your life." Another guy won the date.

Patricia Katje saw Kenny right after the Santa Barbara fender bender. Sitting in her medical office in early May 1996, the physically fit young man before her seemed depressed about making a big deal of the accident.

"I've never seen Kenny look so down," she said. "I told him, you have to make up your own mind. He said, 'I can't. I have to do what my mother says.' "

CHAPTER 13

"We found nothing. Absolutely nothing."

In the Bahamas, the locals like their grouper grilled with onions, garlic, and green pepper, the white fish moist and juicy. The dish is a favorite at the Androsia Steak and Seafood Restaurant in Nassau, a two-room bistro tucked into a strip mall. Hard to find, the restaurant draws people fleeing waves of parents and sunburned kids vacationing at the nearby 700-room Radisson Cable Beach Golf resort. The night he vanished, banker Syed Bilal Ahmed had reserved a table for three at one of the resort's main dining rooms, The Forge. He never claimed his place. Instead, that Wednesday evening September 4, 1996, he ate at the secluded Androsia, where his dinner companion, Sante Kimes, was a regular. She walked in that evening with her son Kenny, whose muscular frame always caught the admiring eye of Betty Vonhamm, Androsia's owner.

Mother, son, and Ahmed sat in the back of the restaurant, a Chinese screen shielding their booth. A Muslim who watched his diet, Ahmed chose the grouper, while Sante and Kenny ordered the surf and turf. After a few cocktails, Sante paid the bill in cash and as usual wouldn't sign the guest book. "I asked her all the time to sign the guest book, but she wouldn't sign her name to anything," said Betty. About 10 that evening, the three walked outside. Except for car headlights flashing by, their road was black. And few travelers drove down that way, that time of night.

An hour later, a Radisson chambermaid turned down the tropical print coverlet on Ahmed's double bed in Room 507. Through the room's sliding glass door lay a terrace overlooking a tropical pool. By now the happy mix of calypso music and kids splashing had quieted. Ahmed's business suits hung in the silent room, and his soap and shaver lined the bathroom sink, "like he had gone out for a swim and was coming right back," said Violet Smith, the hotel's housekeeping supervisor. The bed stayed empty that night, although by 7:30 the following morning, someone put the key in the lock, according to the hotel's computer system. Just around that time, Ahmed's driver arrived at the resort. Growing impatient, then worried, the driver from Gulf Union Bank kept looking at his watch, as 8:00 A.M. became 8:45 with still no sign of the five-foot-four-inch executive. Ahmed, 48, a precise man who specialized in auditing complicated money transfers, was nowhere to be seen. The driver urged the hotel security staff to search Ahmed's room. His belongings were gone, yet he had not checked out on his own.

The Royal Bahamas police view the Kimeses as suspects, although they have yet to prove anything or even reclassify the case from "missing person" to "homicide." Douglas Hanna, supervisor of the criminal investigations division of the Royal Bahamas police, said, "She definitely had ties to the bank. At one time her husband had a lot of money in the bank. He (Ahmed) came here to do business, check on the irregularities of the bank. The relationship between all of them is something we are still trying to figure out." Through their attorneys, Sante and Kenny Kimes said they had nothing to do with the banker's disappearance. "Our clients have denied everything," said attorney Jose Muniz. "They knew the banker and met him as to opening accounts. We don't even know that he's dead."

Authorities believe the late Kenneth Kimes had squirreled away a considerable sum in Caribbean banks over the years. With all those civil suits from the maids and stiffed lawyers, Kimes probably thought it wise to sink money in the Cayman Islands and the Bahamas. Bank secrecy laws there are so strict, even the detectives investigating Ahmed's disappearance could obtain only estimates of Kimes' holdings in Gulf Union Bank and its parent, First Cayman Bank, in the Cayman Islands. Police estimate his account was in the high six figures. Faxes "signed" by the dead man and "Mrs. Sante Kimes" began arriving at the banks, requesting money be transferred out of his accounts, said the Bahamas police. These faxes did not raise eyebrows, at first. Like the rest of the world, the banks learned only years after the fact that Kimes had died on March 28, 1994.

Gulf Union Bank and First Cayman Bank were on the road to ruin in the late '90s. Their eventual collapse, a year after Ahmed disappeared, shook the foundations of the Cayman Islands, a stable British territory considered the Switzerland of the Caribbean. Only four banks had ever folded there over the past 20 years. Evidence of dummy loans, missing funds, liquidity problems, questionable transfers and fraud led the governments of the Bahamas and the Cayman Islands to close the troubled Arab-owned banks in October 1997. As much as $5 million was feared missing from the accounts. Creditors and depositors were potentially out $29.7 million; unlike American banks, there was no deposit insurance. In the Caymans, the scandal led to a run on another bank and the firing of the government's cultural minister, a member of the First Cayman's board of directors, who denied any wrongdoing.

Sheikh Jabor Mohammed Al-Thani of Qatar, related to that country's ruling family, owned the two banks when Ahmed worked there. When his banks collapsed, he told authorities he had already sold them to a polo-playing multimillionaire named Sheikh Abdus Shimveel Querishi—known as "Shimmy," a Pakistani born businessman with ties to Palm Beach, Florida. However, the Cayman Monetary Authority said it didn't authorize the sale and still considered Al-Thani the owner. The Kimeses knew both men. Al-Thani shared some kind of friendship or business connection with them, and they later rented a home in Florida near Querishi's.

Sheikh Al-Thani squired Sante and Kenny Kimes around the Cayman Islands in the spring of 1996, and they claimed to have visited him in Qatar that fall, after Ahmed had vanished. Al-Thani introduced Sante as "one of our biggest customers," remembered Ahmed's friend, Raafat Khalil, a car dealer in Cayman. She introduced herself as a health-and-beauty executive and gave out a business card that said "Princess Sante International Anti-Aging and Well-Being" in the center with the words "Longevity" and "Rejuvenation" surrounding it. It had a phone number from Cable Beach, Nassau, where she had rented an oceanfront home for many years. Another of her cards said "LONGEVITY NETWORK" Global with her name "Sante" in the top left-hand corner alongside Nevada and Bahamas phone numbers. Police believe she was peddling some kind of anti-aging treatments. "She said she took 18 vitamins a day, lots of tablets," Raafat said. "She explained that she was the president of a medical or vitamin place, and she had to go to conferences and meetings all over the United States."

To look younger, Sante had a face-lift and liposuction, finding her surgeon via an infomercial broadcast in the Bahamas. The same doctor had done Kenny's nose job. However, by the time Raafat met her, Sante was in the process of suing Dr. Joseph Graves, dubbed "Dr. Lipo" in media exposés. Graves was named in numerous malpractice suits. In April 1997, a San Diego jury found he was negligent for allowing a waiter to assist him during a woman's liposculpture. Other suits alleged he had falsely claimed to be an instructor at Stanford University Medical School and had used dirty instruments. California suspended his medical license in 1997 after a psychiatrist said he suffered from manic-depressive disorder and shouldn't be practicing. Graves surrendered his license in July 1998.

While under sedation, Sante claimed she fell from an operating table after her face-lift on October 12, 1994, landing on a toolbox and injuring her eye. A nurse told her about this 13 months later, she said. Instead of being rushed to an emergency room, Sante claimed Graves took her back to her hotel room, pumping her with painkillers. She added a sexual battery complaint, accusing Graves of "fondling her breast and groin while plaintiff was under the influence of pain medication given by the defendant." She filed suit in December 1996, followed by Kenny's complaint two months later. However, mother and son missed court hearings and both suits were dismissed.

Raafat said he dined with Sheikh Al-Thani and the Kimeses in Pappagullos Restaurant in Cayman and took the mother and son sightseeing in February or March 1996. Raafat said his friend Ahmed appeared uncomfortable around the Kimeses then and declined the shiekh's invitation to join the group for a drink at a hotel bar.

Why Ahmed agreed to dine alone with Sante and Kenny Kimes a few months later in the Bahamas remains a mystery. Based in Cayman, Ahmed was the assistant general manager of the sheikh's bank and traveled often to the Nassau branch. Conducting an audit during his last trip, he targeted loans that performed poorly. Raafat said his friend Ahmed sounded agitated during a phone call three days before he vanished. "I called him while he was in a meeting in Nassau," Raafat said. "He said, 'Raafat, I cannot take it anymore,' and he was screaming on the phone. I said, 'Bilal, why are you speaking to me in that tone of voice.' He didn't answer me. Two or three days after that, he was missing."

Ahmed came from a prosperous Indian family who made their way as merchants and money changers for rich Persian Gulf Arabs. By 1993, he had worked for several financial houses in Dubai and Bahrain before settling that year on the Cayman Islands for First Cayman Bank. The month he vanished, he was looking forward to his oldest son's marriage at the family's ancestral home in Trichy, India, on September 29, 1996. Instead, the wedding was canceled, and his eldest son, Arshad Hussain, flew to the Bahamas that month in a futile search for his father. The family hired a British private eye, Graham Howard, who said that Sante and Kenny Kimes flew on the same plane with the Sheikh and Ahmed to the Bahamas on August 29, 1996. Ahmed checked into the Radisson while the shiekh went to the Atlantis Hotel but left for London the next day. The Kimeses as usual stayed at "Rainbows by the Sea," their beachfront rental about two blocks from the Radisson.

With all the intrigue at his bank, rumors swirled that Ahmed's disappearance was connected to its brewing financial troubles, that he was involved in missing money or fraud. Years later, Sam Wallace, director of investigations at the Radisson, still kept a mimeographed picture of the missing man hanging in his office. "It's something that intrigued us for a while, but then we put it in the back of our minds," he said. "Who knows what happened to him? He could have been in on the whole deal, or he could have been killed. Who knows?" Officials at Gulf Union downplayed any notion that Ahmed had fled with the bank's money. They issued a statement in October 1996, saying that no funds were missing and no one had used Ahmed's credit cards or tried to gain access to his personal accounts other than his family, who posted a $25,000 reward for information about him.

Bahamas Detective Sergeant Mosey Evans focused on those apparently forged faxes, and believed Ahmed tried to meet with Sante and Kenny about the Kimes account. Cops discovered that a man and woman resembling Sante and Kenny asked the Radisson front desk for Ahmed's key a day or two before he disappeared but were refused. The police began staking out Sante and Kenny at their beach rental, where a hand-painted rainbow greets visitors from a stone gate at the foot of a winding dirt driveway. Peering through binoculars from a boat offshore, the police saw nothing suspicious through the bay windows on the sea foam green house trimmed in white. Believing Ahmed was buried in the basement of the four-bedroom home, cops tore up the floor when the Kimeses had slipped away from the island. No body was found. Next, police brought in a backhoe to scour the sand around the property and sent divers down around the shoreline. They also dug up the basement of the Gulf Union bank, and divers searched along the waters there. "We found nothing," said Evans. "Absolutely nothing."

During this time, Sante never stepped a foot into the bank. At her beachfront rental, she also didn't answer the phone or the door, according to Monique Capron, a local woman Sante had hired for secretarial work during the three weeks leading up to Ahmed's disappearance. Monique never got paid; Sante said Gulf Union would cut her a check, but the bank knew nothing about it. Monique had to keep the door shut if people arrived unexpectedly at the Rainbow House. "Kenny was always okay, but for some reason Sante was very strange," Monique said. "The lady never answered the phone. She would always keep visitors from coming to the house." Curiously, for someone so secretive, Sante had printed up brochures advertising her rental as a bed-and-breakfast. "Experience old-fashioned Bahamian charm at our big ole' beachfront bed & breakfast," it said. "Private, white sandy beach, steps away from Crystal Marriott Hotel & Casino, Full-time Chef on Duty, All Water Sports Available. The Perfect Getaway!!" "I believe she was up to some crooked thing," Monique said. "She told me never answer the door or the phones and keep windows closed."

Faxes from the late Kenneth Kimes kept arriving at the bank, each succeeding missive sounding a little more desperate. Ahmed's disappearance had brought greater scrutiny to the bank, and liquidators had frozen its assets, so the Kimeses were like all the rest of the depositors—out of luck. On December 3, 1996, a Kimes fax demanded Gulf Union send $40,000 to Nanette Wetkowski in Las Vegas, a notary public who had signed off on those depositions from four college students that echoed with the same phrases in support of Kenny versus classmate Carrie Louise Grammer. Wetkowski's name would later appear on other Kimes documents. Two faxes arrived on April 17, 1997, the first demanding that $63,000 go to an account run by England, Whitfield, and Schroeder Trading Trust, the other requesting $51,200 be wired to a Wells Fargo account in Las Vegas. Another fax the next day wanted $51,120 transferred to another Las Vegas account. "The bank never complies because they are already in liquidation and all the monies are frozen," Evans said.

Sante stayed away from the Bahamas but tried to

dupe a maid into traveling there for her in May 1997, said State Department officials in Miami. They opened a fraud investigation of Sante when a woman named Donna Frances Lawson tried to use stolen identification to obtain a passport for a trip to Haiti. After Lawson was arrested in Miami, she told federal agents she was applying for a passport because her employer, Sante Kimes, really wanted her to go to the Bahamas and clean a house, said Walter Deering, the special agent in charge of the State Department's diplomatic security service in Miami. The passport fraud case remains open against Sante, but closed against Lawson, authorities said.

"This woman Lawson was a pawn," Deering said. She was carrying a letter for passport officials explaining that she needed to go to Haiti to visit a sick relative. Lawson led six federal agents to a Fort Lauderdale motel, where Sante was staying. With guns drawn, the six burst into a one-bedroom rental in the Blue Bell apartments, where they found clothes, legal documents, food in the fridge, and dirty plates on the sink—but no Sante. Once more she jumped one step quicker than the authorities.

It was an especially close call; by that time, Sante was also a fugitive from a shoplifting charge in Miami that had landed Kenny in jail for the first time.

Ever the dutiful son, he got arrested trying to protect his mother. A plainclothes detective patrolling the Federal Discount store in downtown Miami on May 19, 1997, couldn't help but notice the Liz Taylor look-alike in a fishnet blouse and wide black bell-bottoms roaming aisle number six. Carrying Lawson's identification in her purse, Sante fiddled in the aisle with Revlon lipstick containers. Detective Jose Alfonso gave the following account in an affidavit. He said she ripped the wrappings from several lipsticks, distracted a clerk, jammed the makeup into her purse, and went to pay for other items at the checkout.

As she and Kenny walked outside, Alfonso flashed his badge and asked them to go back in the store. Sante instead threw her purse to Kenny, who started running away. Grabbing at the purse, Alfonso stopped Kenny in his tracks, and the two men played tug of war with the bag as Sante screamed, "You're assaulting me! You're robbing me!" Swinging her fists, she jumped on Alfonso, which forced him to release his grip. Kenny, dressed in sneakers and shorts, sprinted into a nearby five-and-ten with Sante at his heels. Alfonso ran after them and grabbed Kenny again. The son struggled with the cop just long enough to let his mother escape out the rear entrance. Then he refused to say one word to Alfonso, especially not his name.

A passerby turned in the wallet Kenny had ditched during the chase, and he was quickly identified. Kenny was carrying $131.88, enough to pay for 30 lipsticks. "I had a gut instinct there was more to these people," Alfonso would later tell the *Miami Herald*. "She was 20 years too old for the outfit and hidden under two inches of makeup. And nobody invokes their right to remain silent over a Revlon bandit." Because he allegedly fought with Alfonso, police charged Kenny with four felonies: strong-arm robbery, resisting an officer with violence, battery on a police officer, and aiding an escape and a misdemeanor obstruction count. The judge allowed Kenny, as a first-time offender, to plead guilty to two of the charges in a deal that could have wiped his record clean. Kenny admitted to violently resisting Detective Alfonso and to the misdemeanor obstruction count. The judge sentenced him to a "withhold adjudication." Under Florida law, this means that even though he pleaded guilty to a felony and has a criminal record, he is not a convicted felon, said Johnette

Hardiman, assistant state attorney, division chief for the criminal intake unit of Miami-Dade County. If he stayed out of trouble for the next 10 years, he could apply to have the conviction expunged. Florida law enforcement still wanted his mother, however, and after learning her real name, they issued an arrest warrant for her on August 11, 1997, charging strong-arm robbery.

During this drama, the Kimeses faxes to the Bahamas still flowed. Two more requests that spring were signed Kenneth and Sante Kimes, as if they were the married couple, not mother and son, said Evans. Three more arrived that autumn with the last one on December 1, 1997. It read, "As you know, we have been aggressively trying to transfer all of our funds for some time. I want them transferred immediately."

Sante also took steps to control 28.35 acres of undeveloped land that the late Kenneth Kimes had owned in Santa Maria, California, records indicate. The property, about 75 miles north of Santa Barbara, was worth at least $1,963,000, its assessed value in 1999, according to county records. A deed on file transferred the property from Kimes to Sante "in consideration of love and affection" on December 23, 1993—three months before he died. However, this document was not recorded until six weeks after his death, on May 4, 1994. Then 21 days later, Sante signed the land over to Aga Khan International Corporation. Her realtor friend, Charles Gallagher, said she asked him to front the company, enabling her to hide assets from other Kimes relatives. "I knew I was taking on a huge risk, but I decided I could not refuse her," he said. "She asked me to be the president and secretary of Aga Khan. Her name doesn't appear on the corporation papers." Nervous over the arrangement, he resigned on September 16, 1994.

On paper, the land changed hands again in a deed recorded on October 18, 1995. It went from Aga Khan

International to C. V. Narasimhan, the same name of the former Undersecretary General of the United Nations who accepted a flag poster from the Kimeses in the early 70s. Reached at his retirement home in Chevy Chase, Maryland, Narasimhan, who turned 84 in May 1999, said he never owned this property and has no connection with Aga Khan.

Another transfer switched the land in February 1998 from Aga Khan to the Atlantis Group, a corporate name that would figure later in Sante's alleged scam in Manhattan. Sante almost ruined her friendship with Carolene Davis when her title company balked at listing Atlantis Group as owner of the Santa Maria land. Carolene said her firm prepared a preliminary title report, a prospectus on the land given to interested developers, which listed the owner as Sante Kimes, a "widow." Carolene never told anyone that Kimes Sr. had died, but a suspicious coworker checked and found a death certificate on file for him and then traced the land's ownership back to the Kimes family. "She came storming into my office, pointed the finger at me, waving it and telling me she was going to get me fired," said Carolene. "She was madder than hell at me. I was scared to death." Carolene said Sante apologized and convinced another title insurance company to change the paperwork.

With Gallagher bowing out of Aga Khan, other people appeared on the list of the corporation's officers. One name with a Bahamas address was R. C. Tanis, which sounds like Sante's childhood friend in Carson City, the late Ruth Thom, whose married name was Tanis. Sante's name never appeared on the corporation's list of officers. In fact in a January 1997 signed statement, she claimed no interest or position in the corporation. That year, a new name popped up as the corporation's president, secretary, treasurer, and director—David Kazden, with a post office box address in the Bahamas. There was a man with an almost identical name, spelled David Kazdin with an *i*, who lived in a Los Angeles suburb and had known the Kimeses for about 20 years. His connection to the motel millionaire and his flamboyant companion would take a turn that none of his loved ones ever expected.

CHAPTER 14

"I told him, 'The only thing they could do is kill you.'"

David Kazdin liked doing favors. Every Thanksgiving he cooked two turkeys, one turning on a rotisserie, the other roasting in the oven, and invited a houseful of friends and acquaintances who otherwise would be lonely on the holiday. When California's foster-care rules forced his son's classmate on the streets simply because he turned 18, David let the suddenly homeless kid move into his home for five months. He also opened his doors for his own son and daughter when adult troubles battered them. Escaping a dead-end job, his son Steven at age 25 moved back home and joined the family's photocopying business. Divorced at age 29, mother of an infant girl and toddler boy, Linda Kazdin and her babies found refuge with her father.

"Dad said, 'Just get on with your life, and if you want, you can stay with me as long as you want and I'll help you with the kids,'" said Linda, a court reporter. Her father made good on his promise. Intending to stay only a few months, Linda lived with her father for two-and-a-half years. David, a divorced bachelor, changed diapers, baby-sat, and started taking his blond grandchildren with him on client visits, shamelessly showing them off. Linda moved out of her father's stone and stucco ranch home in the Los Angeles suburb of Granada Hills just two days before he was fatally shot there on Friday, March 13, 1998. He was 63 years old.

David also came through for acquaintances Sante and Kenneth Kimes when they asked for help. After a jury convicted Sante of enslaving her maids, she rounded up character witnesses to convince her judge that she deserved a light sentence. He gladly gave his name.

"I first met Sante eight or ten years ago," David said in 1986 court papers. "I worked for an insurance company, and she had a first-party loss. Since then I've socialized with her and her husband. She's an excellent mother and wife. When I heard about this, I was shocked. I couldn't understand how she could possibly be involved in anything like that."

The second and last time David knowingly lent his name to the Kimeses became his undoing, authorities believe. As a favor to Kenneth Kimes, Kazdin agreed to be listed as owner on paper of the Kimeses' five-bedroom Las Vegas home at 2121 Geronimo Way. It proved to be a deadly mistake, trapping him in a web of suspected fraud and arson that ended in his murder, according to a felony complaint against the Kimeses in Los Angeles. Homicide detectives later figured that Kenneth Kimes, looking to hide assets, either paid David or promised him money for agreeing to sign the house deed.

"Kenneth Kimes told him that he was a little nervous with the person in whose name the property stood," said David's friend and attorney Phil Eaton, a retired Santa Ana police officer. That explanation conflicts with the paperwork on the place. Since the Kimeses bought the five-bedroom Geronimo Way home on March 18, 1980, the owner on the deed remained Kimes Motels Inc.

Then two changes in ownership were recorded within days in December 1992. Kimes Motels sold the home to Catherine (aka Kay) Astarita, which is the stage name for Sante's friend, lounge singer Kay Frigiano. That deed was recorded on December 3,

1992. Five days later, another deed transferring the home from Catherine Astarita to David Kazdin was filed. It was signed "David J. Kazdin," which is his real signature, including the middle initial "J" that he always used. Then, before a notary, Kazdin signed a second secret document, a "quit" claim deed, giving Kimes back the property, Eaton said. This document the millionaire held but never filed. It was a safety measure so Kimes knew that David wouldn't double-cross him and sell the property.

Soon thereafter, Kimes called for yet another favor. This time he said renters damaged the home, and he wanted David, the legal owner on paper, to meet with insurance adjusters to settle a claim the Kimeses had filed. "It became obvious to David that the adjuster smelled a rat, either a fake or inflated claim," said Eaton. David told Kimes to take his name off the property and assumed the millionaire had.

David then lost contact with the Kimeses. Kenneth Kimes had died on March 28, 1994, and David had spoken rarely to Sante since then. Their strongest connection had been Las Vegas, David's occasional playground. Every May for nearly 30 years, he traveled there for a reunion of "the boys," about a dozen men who bonded while working in the late '60s and early '70s for Consolidated Mutual Insurance Company, where Kazdin had started as an insurance claims examiner in his native Brooklyn and advanced to manager of the trial preparations department in Los Angeles. In charge of cases in litigation, he directed fraud investigations, tried to settle claims out of court, and if that failed, helped prepare the insurance company lawyers for trial.

Among "the boys" he was the cool gambler who didn't bet over his limit. An excellent pool player who had hustled for money while in college, David named and sank his shots as routinely as choosing a TV channel. Heaven for this football and basketball

fanatic was the sports book in Vegas, where he
would pick teams and sit for hours. "He was the best
sports announcer you could imagine," said his
friend, attorney Martin Handweiller. "Before (TV announcer) John Madden said they were offsides, Dave
said it." David also loved the gambling rooms that
showed every racetrack in the country, where he
handicapped the horses all night long. "He was the
first person I knew who could sit down, read a racing
form, and know how old the jockey was and what
he had for breakfast," said his friend, Les Schifrin.
David called his copying service "Exacta" for the
racetrack bet that picks first and second place.

At six-foot-three and 175 pounds, his quick metab-
olism kept him trim, along with the two packs of
cigarettes he smoked each day. With his deep brown
eyes, warm smile, thick head of hair, generous nature, and man-about-town airs, David easily attracted
women 10 to 20 years younger. Divorced since 1974,
he had a succession of girlfriends through the years.
Some of the women lived with him in Granada Hills,
sharing his king-sized water bed, but none of these
relationships evolved into marriage.

For all his generosity, David was no doormat. He
spoke his mind, turning as subtle as an electric shock
when annoyed. If he didn't like someone's outfit, he
said so. If he thought a particular lawyer couldn't
find "his two buns with his hands and a seeing-eye
dog," he said so. While his intuitiveness rooted out
fraud and quickly assessed the merits of insurance
claims, the bluntness that was drill sergeant to his
brains insulted those who didn't know his sweet
side. Once at a management meeting, the Consolidated executives announced cost-cutting measures
that switched company cars from senior management
to field investigators. This change left David without
wheels, and he said sarcastically, "Well, we *are* close

enough to downtown Los Angeles, so I guess you guys are going to get me a 10-speed bicycle."

His style angered enough bosses at Consolidated that they fired him. His former boss at Consolidated, Les Schifrin, moved to another insurance firm and quickly hired David. He stayed a few years at Yosemite-Great Falls Insurance in Los Angeles as a litigation supervisor then became a claims negotiator with Transit Casuality Company. During these years, David decided he wanted to be his own boss and started a mobile photocopying business for medical and legal documents. With a network of 100 lawyers and insurance firm contacts, David could count on steady orders and low overhead. First he started using his own copying machines, later switching to subcontractors. Working from his home, he personally delivered the finished copies, figuring that was the best way to get the next order. He spread around the Bloomingdale's chocolates, bagels, and charm, so secretaries were happy to see him. His business grew.

Born in Beth-El Hospital in East Flatbush, Brooklyn, on New Year's Eve 1934, David Jay Kazdin was the youngest of three sons born to Sadie and Charles Kazdin, Russian Jews who emigrated to the United States as children and later met in New York and married. The couple kept a kosher home, making sure their sons attended temple and made their bar mitzvahs. David attended local public schools, first P.S. 91 and then Samuel J. Tilden High, where he punted for the varsity football team—a skill he would later teach his son, Steven, who won a football scholarship to the University of Miami as a punter.

Sadie Kazdin wanted her youngest son to go to college, but unlike his brothers, David wasn't keen on the idea. He ended up at the Philadelphia Textile Institute in Germantown, Pennsylvania, which specialized in the garment industry, only because a friend of his went there. Later he would joke that it

was the perfect place to shoot pool for three years
and avoid a real job.

His pool game improved but not his scholastic
bent, and he dropped out of school. After bouncing
around in a few jobs, he landed an entry-level position with Consolidated Mutual Insurance Company,
at the time an innovative firm that would send its
people all over the country. While handling a claim
for a hotel in Florida, David met and fell in love with
the front-desk receptionist, a Canadian named Gloria
Mercanti. David persisted in the romance despite op-
position from both families, who objected on religious grounds. Gloria was Anglican. The couple had
two children: Steven Ira born on March 30, 1964, and
Linda Gail born on October 11, 1966. By the time the
kids reached fourth and fifth grades, the marriage
had floundered, David got custody of Linda and Steven by mutual agreement and settled into a one-story
house with a backyard pool at 17253 Orozco Street
in Granada Hills.

Once David lived the cliché of "a man's home is
his castle" to the hilt, when the Santa Ana winds
whipped up an inferno of smoke and fire. Firemen
screamed at people to evacuate that November afternoon in 1985. Just across Orozco Street, trees aflame
in the foothills of Bee Canyon Park brought the fire
ever closer, spewing smoke that turned the walls inside David's home charcoal-gray. David put his then
19-year-old daughter Linda in a car with a friend but
refused to leave himself. Grabbing a hose, he leapt
onto his roof and sprayed the outside of his house,
one man against a fury of wind and fire. He survived
and so did the house.

"He was like a fighter," said Steven. "He was
very determined."

David was a man of action, said his children, and
that trait extended to the delicate area of his love for
them, a total affection they felt but that he rarely

articulated. Crusty on the outside, he was a jellyfish inside, said his friend of 23 years, Kristina Hope.

Steven said his father was a good judge of character and intuitive about most people, except for Sante Kimes. His kids never met Sante or Kenneth Kimes. Steven remembers in the years he moved back with his dad, from 1989 to 1996, his father acted annoyed if Sante telephoned, which happened about three times a year. He would tell his son to say he wasn't home or let the machine pick up the call.

David's friends believe that at first he socialized with the Kimeses on gambling trips to Las Vegas, after meeting them in the late 70s when he handled one of their insurance claims. His attorney, Phil Eaton, said David first mentioned Sante around 1978 in connection with an HMO business she talked about starting in California around the time she was lobbying in Washington, D.C., for Dr. Alfred Caruso, the wealthy Santa Ana doctor who wanted federal contracts. "My recollection is that he was kind of taken with her in the sense that she was an interesting character, not romantically, but he found her to be an engaging person, a little bit out of the ordinary," Eaton said. David asked his friend if he wanted to do legal work for Sante, but the lawyer steered clear of the idea. "You're telling me this woman is wacky, and you want me to work with her?" Eaton told him.

Les Schifrin remembered that sometime around 1990, David asked him to look into about 30 acres of raw land Sante talked about developing in Santa Maria, California. By this time Schifrin ran an insurance adjusting and private investigation firm that did business in the area. "Sante had obviously asked him if he knew anybody who could work on the sale of the property," Les said, adding that David did not join any real estate venture with her. However, a version of his name later appeared on legal papers connected to that land. Besides being listed as head of Aga Khan International in 1997, "David Kazden" was also the signature on a notice of attorney substitution form dated September 29, 1997. This document was part of a 1996 lawsuit brought by land surveyors who say they worked on the Santa Maria property and were stiffed $63,755.38. They got paid just before the matter went to trial.

David's name on the Las Vegas deed haunted him just as he was looking forward to a slower pace of life. His trips to Las Vegas had dwindled. The copying business stalled, and David planned to retire to Florida, near his brother Mort in Boynton Beach. In his Granada Hills backyard, he started growing cherry tomatoes, asparagus, and artichokes, surprising his friends who still thought of him as a playboy, not a homebody. True, he continued to drive a green four-door Jaguar, but his life was changing. Further shattering his old image, he baby-sat his grandchildren and often fell asleep on the sofa while watching TV, his faithful Alaskan malamute Tayla, by his side.

Suddenly his peace shattered. Documents arrived in the mail on January 23, 1998, saying he owed payments on a 30-year $280,000 mortgage with a variable 9.37% interest rate taken out the previous month on Kimes' Las Vegas home. The signature on the loan was an apparent forgery, signed "David Kazdin," missing his "J" middle initial.

David insisted to the mortgage lender, Ocwen Federal Bank in West Palm Beach, Florida, that he never signed the loan papers. "I think you've been defrauded," he said. Ocwen grilled him about Sante Kimes, and he advised them to stop the loan payment, but they had already mailed the check. Prosecutors later traced about $180,000, believed to be from that mortgage, to a bank in the Caribbean. David realized that a few phone calls weren't going to erase a debt that it appeared he owed on paper, so he consulted Eaton.

Then came news of a dangerous twist. An insurance company called David in early February. A suspicious blaze ripped through 2121 Geronimo Way at 11:19 P.M. on January 31, 1998, just nine days after a new Fireman's Fund Insurance policy began covering the house. Flames erupted from two unconnected areas of the house, and Las Vegas firefighters immediately suspected someone had set the blaze. There were no pipes, crawl spaces, vents, or any other openings that would have carried the fire between a second-floor bedroom engulfed in flames and a smaller but growing fire in a ground-floor bedroom. Josie, a gasoline-sniffing yellow Labrador retriever, inspected the home four days after the blaze. So much gasoline had been poured in the house that Josie "alerted" in a dozen places.

"It was definitely arson," said Mike Patterson, chief investigator with the Clark County Fire Department. "We had two separate unconnected areas of origin. Gasoline was used, there was definitely a pour pattern through the room."

On the phone, the insurance agent asked if David knew the new name listed as owner of the house, Robert McCarren, who turned out to be a homeless man Sante plucked out of a Las Vegas shelter. A deed filed on January 21, 1998, had David signing over the house to McCarren. Again, that signature didn't look like his; it was missing his customary "J" middle initial. Next a mysterious gray-haired woman showed up on David's doorstep and said, "You know you are responsible for the loan." Finally Sante herself left several phone messages on David's machine. "David," she said. "I've got to talk with you. I'm here with Kenny. We've got to meet."

David saw this mess in Las Vegas as jeopardizing his plans to retire, leaving him financially vulnerable.

He was just about to put his Granada Hills home on the market for the asking price of $245,000. Eaton instructed him to write down an entire chronology of the Sante Kimes business. Although David said Sante "was crazy and would do anything," he didn't express any fears for his life. His kids and friends all thought this was a civil matter that the attorneys would handle. Linda Kazdin said her dad didn't act afraid, and even slept with his back window wide open. He was a man who could take care of himself. For years, he kept a small revolver in his home for protection and also had his dog, Tayla.

None of his friends thought he was in mortal danger. David himself was more concerned about financial ruin over the $280,000 home mortgage. His friends tried to convince him that such a disaster was not in the cards. His old pal Les Schifrin, a private investigator, had pulled the deed and mortgage documents on the Geronimo Way home and assured David that it was obvious the signatures were not his.

Les shared one last meal with David on Thursday March 12, 1998, the night before he was killed. They headed to their favorite Italian place, Maria's on Ventura Boulevard in Sherman Oaks, and ordered chicken parmigiana with a double order of spaghetti and no vegetables. Les told David the paperwork easily proved forgery. "I told him, 'The only thing they could do is kill you,'" not seriously thinking that was a possibility. David just laughed.

On Friday the 13th of March, David's answering machine began to fill up with messages from people wondering where he was. He missed lunch with his friend Darci. David planned to bring home-cooked food to a hospitalized friend that afternoon. He never arrived. Steven called about a barbecue David was to host in his backyard on Saturday afternoon. That night David was expected at his friends the Wilsons for dinner.

Linda stopped by her father's house on Saturday morning to pick up the last of her stuff, since she and her two children had moved out a few days before to an apartment in Santa Monica. She found the Granada Hills house empty, the silence like a scream. Her father's green Jaguar was gone, the garage door opener was left inside the house, and his dog Tayla roamed the pool area whimpering. The foot-high brick border around the lawn was cracked near the driveway and spattered with flecks of green paint, as if someone was careless in backing out the Jaguar.

At first she wondered if her father was out food shopping. As the minutes dragged like chains, she looked at the light flashing on his phone machine, listened to all the messages, and started panicking. Steven came over with his friends. They sat in a semicircle, placing calls to the California Highway Patrol and area police and hospitals. Tayla crawled into the middle of the group, collapsed on the living room floor, and began hyperventilating.

"I called his friends the Wilsons," said Steven. "He was supposed to have dinner with them at six o'clock. Next thing you know the sun is going down, six o'clock passes. He misses dinner. At first you think there's got to be a logical reason, there's got to be an answer."

Linda and Steven drove over to the Van Nuys police department and kept calling hospitals. Hope all but gone, Linda's cousin then dialed the coroner. The clerk there sounded like he was checking a grocery list instead of giving dreaded news. "The coroner says, 'Oh, yeah, he's here, he was found in a Dumpster,' " Linda said. "They gave out information like it was nothing. It was horrible. I couldn't breathe."

A homeless man searching for aluminum cans

about 10:35 in the morning on Saturday March 14, 1998, found David's body inside a Dumpster in an alley off one of the snaky little side streets bordering the east end of Los Angeles International Airport.

Although shot in the neck with a .22 caliber gun, David looked peacefully asleep to the homeless man who discovered him. His feet were bare, as if he had opened his front door to his killer after just getting out of bed. David's body was clothed in a shirt and jeans. His pockets had been emptied of his wallet and all his papers, so he lay unclaimed and unidentified far into the night. In an eight-line press release the Los Angeles police department sent out at 6:40 P.M. on March 14, David was described as an unknown "male approximately 60 years of age" killed by a "possible gunshot wound." Almost 12 hours after he was found, the coroner identified him through fingerprints on file from his insurance investigating days. Later his green Jaguar, a shoe print on the trunk, was found parked on a nearby street. Scrapes on the car matched the cracks on the brick along his driveway in Granada Hills.

Phil Eaton told homicide detectives about the alleged fraud and arson scheme involving Sante's Las Vegas house that had ensnared David, all because of a favor. "I said, I think I know who your number-one suspect should be," Eaton said, "and I gave them the name Sante Kimes and laid it all out for them."

CHAPTER 15

"I was buffaloed. I look back and go, God, what an idiot I was."

Normally the murder of a law-abiding businessman and loving grandfather taken from his middle-class suburb in a Jaguar and found dumped near an international airport would make the news. For some reason, David's story slipped through the cracks that month in Los Angeles. Nothing appeared in print or on television. While celebrities drive the media in Los Angeles and March belongs to the Oscars, there is usually room for at least a mention of a murder like David's. Perhaps the fact he was found on a weekend and not identified right away put the case on the road to oblivion. After hearing from Phil Eaton and David's friends, the Los Angeles detectives knew who they were looking for and felt no need to publicize their investigation. David's funeral on St. Patrick's Day, Tuesday, March 17, 1998, at the Groman Eden Mortuary in Mission Hills passed quietly. If they had covered the service, reporters would have found good copy in Kristina Hope's take-no-prisoners eulogy of her friend. It made mourners laugh and cry.

"Dearest Dave," began Hope, an art consultant who was 46 years old at the time. "I've known you for half of my life. You've been a good friend always, and sometimes a pain in the ass. You always had a cynical view of things, and you seemed to think that Pollyanna is dead. I have to say that at this moment, I'd have to agree with you.

"In spite of your crusty exterior, I'm going to let the cat out of the bag and say that I know you were truly a sensitive guy. You were probably the most sarcastic person I ever knew, but that was only a façade. You loved your children and grandchildren more than life. The words 'I love you' didn't come easily to you, but you showed it in many other ways. Those of us who were close to you knew it as well."

If David's murder had become widely known, the law might have stopped the Kimeses in Los Angeles that March before they started their journey to Irene Silverman's doorstep. Clues quickly surfaced that almost nailed them even without publicity over David's death. But fate let the pair slip away again.

They were hanging around Los Angeles before and after David's murder and made several visits to comfort Carolene Davis in Santa Barbara that March, after she had surgery. Knowing her friend was bedridden, Sante brought her a gift of white chiffon baby-doll lingerie, "so I could look sexy," said Carolene. "She was very kind and wonderful to me. She was very caring to me."

Mother and son began arousing suspicions on a quiet block in Bel Air Estates, the exclusive enclave of million-dollar homes tucked in the cliffs above Beverly Hills. Calling themselves Sandy and Manny Guerrin, they had answered an ad in February 1998 for roommates at a secluded one-story house at 3221 Elvido Drive, nestled 30 feet behind other homes on the hilly block. A locked iron fence and 12 sculptured pine trees lining the long driveway offered more privacy. It was perfect for the Kimeses. Saying she was a millionaire philanthropist, Sante paid $8,000 in cash for six-months rent, moved in with her son and a manservant she described as a "mute valet," named Robert Carro. She said her son was a student at

UCLA and that her husband was in Paris. Soon her landlady, who herself was only subletting the home, began to think her new tenants were strange. They never parked their car on Elvido Drive, always around the block. They relied on cell phones instead of getting a telephone in their apartment. They whispered constantly and put dead-bolt locks on their bedroom doors. And they brought over other so-called servants with weather-beaten faces who looked like homeless drifters.

Wanting protection, the landlady turned to a girlfriend who rode a Harley Davidson, carried a 9mm semiautomatic, owned a rottweiler dog, and swaggered in leather and chains. Freelance studio gaffer Jill Gardner had the "biker chick" persona down cold, and she knew a resourceful private eye, John Doty. He tracked down the car dealer who sold the new tenants the forest-green Lincoln Continental, with tinted black windows, that they drove fast along Bel Air's winding streets.

Parkway Motors in Cedar City, Utah, had never heard of Sandy and Manny Guerrin. Car salesman Jim Blackner did know Sante Kimes, "Papa" Kimes and their son. They were his wealthy customers from Las Vegas who had just bought the 1997 Lincoln a few days ago, with no problem. Still, the salesman couldn't help but notice some changes with his long-time clients. Usually Papa Kimes handled the deals, but that February 1998, Sante said he was away in Japan and that she was ordering a car. Blackner had no idea at the time that the senior Kimes had been dead for almost four years. Instead of Las Vegas, Sante now wanted the car delivered to the $325-a-night Regent Beverly Wilshire Hotel, across the street from Tiffany's at the foot of Rodeo Drive in Beverly Hills.

Blackner sent retired truck driver Dennis Garrett and his wife, Diane, to Beverly Hills on Friday, February 27, 1998, with the Lincoln that Sante had ordered. The sales price was $27,973.50. Blackner let Sante trade in a 1993 silver Lincoln he had sold Papa Kimes a few years before, so she owed Parkway Motors a difference of $14,973.50. Dusty from the road and wearing jeans, the Garretts felt uncomfortable waiting for almost two hours in the Beverly Wilshire's hotel lobby, where the buffed marble floors shine like mirrors. Amid the Armani-clad women air-kissing each other, the Garretts spotted a man who seemed to be staring at them as he paced back and forth.

Suddenly that guy was gone, and Kenny Kimes finally walked up and apologized for being late. He ushered the Garretts to the hotel's polished redwood bar, where Sante was ensconced on one of the beige velvet couches. She fussed over the Garretts, gave them a $100 tip, and insisted on treating them to dinner at Lawry's The Prime Rib, a Beverly Hills restaurant in business since 1938. Over prime ribs, she invited them on vacations, offered them work managing her property in Santa Barbara, and asked at least six times if they wanted to stay the night at the Beverly Wilshire as her guests. "We really like you two," Sante cooed. "We're going to send a helicopter to pick you up at Cedar City, and we'll come back to Las Vegas, and we'll fly over to either Cancun or the Bahamas." Kenny flashed a lot of money that night, slipping something to the maître d' to get a table for four and giving the waiters $5 each time they filled his water glass.

The Garretts had a new grandson they wanted to visit that night, so they politely broke away from the Kimeses after dinner. Dennis, six-feet-tall and 230 pounds, had only one drink at the bar and a Bloody Mary at dinner, but he was feeling woozy. Two drinks were nothing for a man of his frame. Although she had been sipping a nonalcoholic Fuzzy

Lawyers representing the Kimeses arrive to speak to the press after their clients' arraignment was postponed in the Silverman case. *Left to right:* Attorney Mel Sachs, investigator Les Levine, Attorney Jose Muniz.
(*Daily News* L.P. Photo)

Exterior of Silverman home. (*Daily News* L.P. Photo)

Kenneth Kimes with his Bicentennial poster.
(*Washington Post*; Reprinted by permission
of the D.C. Public Library)

Sante Kimes in her glamour phase with her friend
Carolene Davis. (Courtesy of Carolene Davis)

Sante Kimes, then "Sandy Chambers,"
Carson City High School, 1948.

Kenny at a college party. (Courtesy of Carolene Davis)

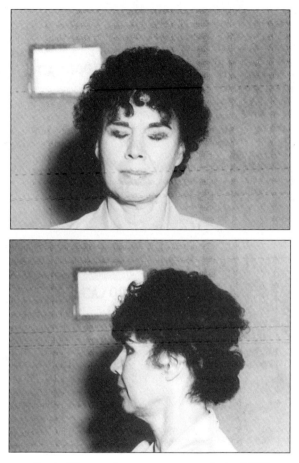

Sante Kimes, slavery case mug shots, 1985.

Kenneth and Sante Kimes meet Betty and Gerald Ford after crashing a Washington, D.C., party on February 26, 1974. (*Washington Post*; Reprinted by permission of the D.C. Public Library)

Missing lawyer Elmer Holmgren.
(Courtesy of Ken Holmgren)

Missing banker Syed Bilad Ahmed.

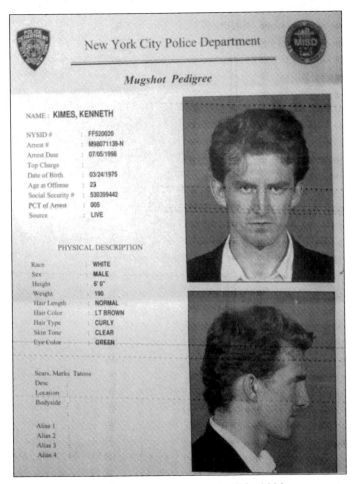

Kenneth Kimes—mug shots, July 1999.
(*Daily News* L.P. Photo)

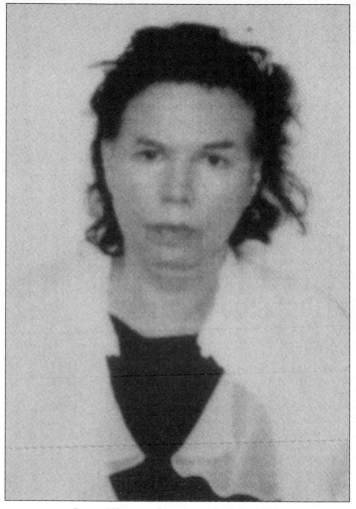

Sante Kimes at her arrest in July 1999.
(*Daily News* L.P. Photo)

Kenny Kimes, at bottom with hands on face,
with school friends in 1989.

Kenny Kimes, as a freshman at
Bishop Gorman High School in 1990
at their Aloha Dance.

David Kazdin *(right)*, murder victim found in a Dumpster at Los Angeles Airport, with his son Steve. (Courtesy of Steven Kazdin)

Irene Silverman.

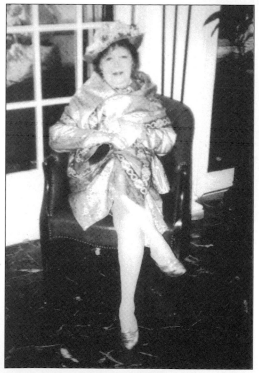

Irene Silverman.
(*Daily News*
L.P. Photo)

Inside Irene Silverman's apartment at
20 East 65th Street, Manhattan.

Navel, his wife didn't feel well either, Garrett later recalled. "Sante kept asking my wife, 'Are you getting tipsy yet?' She must have asked that three to four times." Saying she was too drunk to fill out the car paperwork, Sante had her son sign a nonresident affidavit and the purchase agreement, according to a Utah arrest warrant. Instead of his name, Kenny wrote "AKI R. C. Tanis." AKI International is believed to be a Kimes-controlled corporation and R. C. Tanis, sounds like Sante's high school buddy, the late Ruth Thom Tanis. The address, social security number, and driver's license Sante gave Garrett turned out to match someone else, Nanette Wetkowski, the notary public on the Las Vegas deed transfer that bears David Kazdin's apparently forged signature. Sante used a $14,973.50 Wells Fargo Bank check, purportedly signed by Wetkowski, to pay for the Lincoln.

The mother and son who had tipped big at dinner and talked of flying in helicopters had handed over a rubber check, authorities said. When Blackner learned in March that Wetkowski's account had been frozen, he quickly called back private eye Doty in Los Angeles, who had done some more checking and learned that Papa Kimes had been dead for four years.

Now really scared, the Bel Air landlady had convinced Jill Gardner to move into the Elvido Drive home. Doty thought they needed a lawyer to pursue an eviction, so he hooked them up with his friend, Lawrence Haile, coincidentally the same attorney who opposed Kimes Sr. in an insurance claim years before and went on to represent Linda Kimes. During this time, Jill also tried to get the Los Angeles police interested in the pair, but the cops blew it off as a landlord-tenant dispute.

One day while the Kimeses were away, Jill opened boxes mother and son kept in the Elvido Drive ga-

rage. Among basketball sweatpants and shirts, Jill
found notebooks filled with signatures written over
and over, as if being practiced, and papers belonging
to a David Kazdin. Since his murder never appeared
in the press, his name meant nothing to her. "As
each box opened, it was like another huge 'Oh, my
God' type of event," Jill told the TV program, *20-20.*
"I found the information on David Kazdin—passport, driver's license, the whole deal. I knew something was up that was very, very wrong."

Leaving her papers unattended was a rare security
lapse for Sante. In that house, she played den mother
to a motley crew of down-and-outers and forbade
them from using the phone, answering the door, or
talking to strangers. Her "mute valet "was actually
Robert McCarren, a homeless man whose name appeared as the new owner of the burned Las Vegas
home. He told investigators that he fronted for the
Kimeses in a claim to the Fireman's Fund insurance
company. Other people passed through the Bel Air
rental home at various times: Stan Patterson, the
pizza deliveryman who answered Sante's want ad
and drove her belongings from Las Vegas in late February to a storage facility in Los Angeles; Judy, a
former salesclerk who was living in a Las Vegas
homeless shelter when Sante recruited her as a maid;
and red-haired Sean Little, a drifter with a minor
criminal record who did errands for them.

Dawn Guerin, 23, was an unlikely recruit to this
inner circle. She was a former marine, married to
another former Marine. The mother of a toddler,
Dawn lived in Las Vegas and worked for a firm that
handled paperwork for corporations. While filing
some legal papers, Sante met Dawn in December
1997 at her office and charmed the young receptionist
into working for her part-time as a girl Friday. As
she had 15 years before with tutor Teresa Richards,
Sante came bearing gifts for Dawn: a dress, a vest, a

popcorn tin, and a Bugs Bunny poster. "They seemed so wonderful, they really did," she remembered. "Both of them. Kenny got up whenever I came into the room, gave me a peck on the cheek. She gave me a hug. I thought this was a little odd, and figured some people are more loving than others." Sante also asked Dawn a lot of personal questions, encouraging her to talk about old resentments from her childhood and recent friction with her husband. Sante wanted Dawn to call her Mom, explaining that she had already told Stan Patterson, the pizza guy, that they were related.

Flattered by the attention from this eccentric millionaire, Dawn agreed and pretended around the others to be Sante's daughter and, by extension, Kenny's sister. He also charmed her with compliments about her "pretty eyes," and she developed a crush on him. She said Kenny acted overly protective of his mother, as if she were in danger. "At one point he told me, 'If anyone even thought of hurting my mother, I'd kill them.' " Dawn felt, however, that the balance of power lay with Sante. "I had the impression a couple of times that she had more control over him than he was letting on. It was always 'Kenny go do this and Kenny go do that.' "

For $50 a week, Dawn collected Sante's letters from her mail drop on East Tropicana Avenue in Las Vegas and ran errands. A few weeks into this arrangement, signs emerged that Sante, the supposed millionaire, was cheap with a buck. Hiring Judy, the homeless woman, to clean up a motor home, Sante asked Dawn to oversee the job. "She told me the reason she went to homeless shelters to get these people was because 'you get them at the shelters and you're not going to have to pay a whole lot for them and they'll work paying their room and board and that's the money. You don't actually have to pay a salary.' " The motor home the Kimeses owned needed about $300 in new parts, and Sante asked Dawn, "Don't you have a credit card?"—the same question tutor Cynthia Montano heard 14 years earlier in Mexico. Dawn firmly said she didn't have the money, nor was she charging the equipment on her card.

Dawn agreed to help Judy and Stan Patterson drive the motor home to Los Angeles on March 20, 1998, a week after David Kazdin was slain. At the time, Dawn was unaware that Sante and Kenny had borrowed her last name, spelling it with a second *r*, in renting the home on Elvido Drive. Tensions with the landlady had rattled Sante by the time Dawn arrived. They were out clothes shopping when Kenny rang Dawn's cell phone to say the landlady was headed to the house on Elvido Drive. They rushed back, and Sante began shouting orders. "She said, 'Get everything into the car, any paper, phone number, get it out now. Don't leave anything, not a note, or business card,'" Dawn said. After the mad cleanup, everyone piled into the car, and Sante said, "Isn't this fun?"

Shortly afterward, Robert McCarren bolted while the group ate at an International House of Pancakes about 10 minutes drive from Bel Air. Used as a pawn in the Las Vegas insurance claim, he knew a lot. Mother and son tried to hide their panic at his departure. "They were way too rushed," Dawn said. "They were overreacting. We had to go move the motor home, and then they had to go find him. Kenny said, 'We have to find him.'"

With McCarren gone, the Kimeses sent Dawn back to Las Vegas and quickly cleared out of Bel Air forever, leaving behind some of their papers. McCarren told the LAPD that the Kimeses manipulated him, and they had papers referring to a man whose name he didn't recognize—Syed Bilal Ahmed, the banker missing from the Bahamas.

In hiding, mother and son called Dawn for another favor. Sante convinced her to help Stan Patterson buy a .9mm Glock and a .22-caliber Barretta. Before Kazdin was shot with a .22, Patterson had already given the Kimeses two guns of the same caliber, according to the Bureau of Alcohol Tobacco and Firearms. One they returned to him because it didn't work. The other has never been found. Now the Kimeses wanted more weapons. "She said driving through Los Angeles in a motor home is dangerous," Dawn said. "She wanted a little gun to protect herself." Sante explained she didn't completely trust Stan and wanted Dawn along on the purchase.

On March 29, police believe Kenny used the alias Ken Johnson to wire Dawn $740 to the Barbary Coast Hotel in Las Vegas. Then she and Stan went to Discount Pawn in Henderson, just outside of Vegas, and bought the guns. When the gun shop asked if they were related, they lied and said yes. It's an illegal straw purchase if one person buys guns and another person unrelated to him pays for them. By asking both Stan and Dawn to buy her guns, Sante had tricked them into breaking the law, officials informed them later. "I was buffaloed," Dawn said. "I look back and go, God, what an idiot I was."

After buying the weapons, Stan got nervous handing them over to either the Kimeses or Dawn. Several days later at 11 o'clock at night, Sante and Kenny showed up at Dawn's doorstep in Las Vegas and stayed over. Reluctantly, Stan gave them the guns after they threatened to make him pay for a dent he made while driving their motor home, Dawn said.

During all this time, Sante had been talking to Jim Blackner from Parkway Motors in Utah, assuring him she would make good on the $14,973.50 bounced check. The two played cat and mouse over the phone that entire spring. He would leave a message at her

805 area code answering service in California, and she would call back claiming to be in the Bahamas and other far-flung locales. She kept promising to settle the bill in calls that lasted until the week before her arrest in Manhattan on July 5. At first, Blackner was not going to press criminal charges.

"You know me, I'm good for the money," Sante told Blackner. He let her keep up the charade about Papa Kimes visiting the Far East. In typical Sante fashion, she complicated the simple deal of paying Blackner what she owed. Kenny's 23rd birthday on March 24, 1998, gave her the idea of swapping the green Lincoln for a present, a new black Cadillac. She started complaining that the green Lincoln was unsafe, that its trunk leaked.

In retrospect, Blackner said he thinks Sante might have been surprised that Wetkowski's check had bounced. She might not have realized that authorities investigating the Las Vegas home arson had moved so quickly to freeze Wetkowski's account, where some of the mortgage money had been transferred. "I think from the time she wrote me the check and she found out the account was frozen, she kept buying time," Blackner said.

Sante suggested that Blackner send her a new black Cadillac, let her return the green Lincoln, and pay the difference during a swap April 4 at the Hilton Hotel in Las Vegas. Blackner had no intention of bringing her yet another car. Instead, he contacted a friend on the Cedar City police force, Detective Lynn Davis, and asked him and Dennis Garrett to drive the Kimeses' old silver '93 Lincoln to the meeting. Blackner figured Davis would flash his badge, pressuring the Kimeses to take back their old car and relinquish the green Town Car.

Sante had other ideas. She stood Davis and Garrett up. At the time she was supposed to be at the bar, Sante was sitting on Dawn Guerin's couch, the green

Lincoln Town Car parked outside, a cell phone at her ear. Sante was phoning to change the meeting place to Landry's Seafood Restaurant on West Sahara, about 10 minutes drive from the Hilton.

Fearing they were walking into a trap, Detective Davis called off the rendezvous and returned empty-handed to Cedar City, where Blackner finally filed criminal charges. Utah issued an arrest warrant for Sante and Kenny on April 9, 1998, charging them with two counts of "communications fraud," a second-degree felony.

The last time Dawn saw Sante was April 5, 1998, though she continued to call for weeks afterward. Dawn was trying to patch up her marriage, and it hurt having Sante and Kenny encamped in her home. Her husband Anthony said he was fed up and yelled at the Kimeses to leave. The Guerins claim they caught Sante walking out of their home with his formal white brimmed Marine Corps hat, known as a "cover." Sante blamed the rush of moving for her mistake. Dawn remembered Sante telling her, " 'Now, if the FBI ever asks you about me, you don't know me.' And, I thought, I'm not going to cover for her ass and throw myself in jail. She's not worth it." Throughout the spring, Sante, now vanished from Las Vegas, called Dawn, urging her to still pick up her mail. Dawn said she was too busy, then even lied and said she was pregnant to stop Sante from bothering her. "She just kept calling and calling," Dawn said. "She just wanted to talk, she wanted to be my friend. She said, 'I love you, you are like a daughter to me.' I would hang up on her."

Dawn took a break and visited relatives in Arkansas, where Sante still managed to track her down by phone. "I think I stayed with it longer because when I realized something was wrong, I was curious," said Dawn. "I wanted to know what the hell was going on." Now convinced she was dealing with a strange woman and worried over her own role in buying the guns, Dawn called the FBI from Arkansas. She was still unaware that the mother and son had borrowed her last name and would use it again in New York.

CHAPTER 16

"She liked to hear people say, 'You have a beautiful home.' That was her pride and joy."

"Hey, Brenda!" squawked radio comedienne Elvia Allman. "What is it, Cobina?" rasped actress Blanche Stewart. "I think I'll hang my hair out to dry, Brenda." "Yeah, are those your teeth in my water glass, Cobina?" Named for two real-life debutantes, darlings of the 1938–1939 New York social season, the "Brenda and Cobina" radio program poked fun at the staid world of cotillions and curtsies. The Depression-weary public loved the corny show, a highlight of Bob Hope's radio lineup in the years leading up to World War II. Among the many fans listening on Tuesdays at 10:00 P.M. were two people new to Manhattan, young ballerina Irene Zambelli and her mother, a seamstress from Greece known in Fifth Avenue dress shops as Madame Irene, the finest needlewoman in New York.

In shrill voices, Brenda and Cobina griped each week about their boring love lives. As Irene Zambelli and her daughter listened to the program one night, the characters' phone rang. Brenda answered. "Cobina," she proclaimed. "It's a *man*!" As if on cue, a few minutes later the phone jangled in the Zambellis' tiny fifth-floor walk-up at 47 West 51st Street, across the street from Radio City Music Hall, where Irene danced with the resident ballet corps. Barely five feet tall and 88 pounds, she was the perfectly proportioned doll holding up one end of the chorus line. Zambi, as the other dancers called this doelike beauty, was a favorite with the stage-door Johnnies who clamored for dates after the shows. It was a suitor who had called while mother and daughter had been listening to the radio skit. Madame Irene couldn't resist putting her hand over the mouthpiece and wisecracking to her daughter, "Cobina, it's a *man!*"

So began the tradition of the two Irenes calling each other Cobina, another name they shared, another example of the strong bond mother and daughter forged that lasted a lifetime. They supported each other during the Great Depression, when Madame Irene sewed dresses for $28 a week. She still managed to set aside money so her daughter could take ballet classes from the legendary master, Russian choreographer Michel Fokine, who settled on West 72nd Street in 1923. After 18-year-old Irene landed a steady but grueling job with the Radio City corps at $36 a week in 1934, her mother earned extra money sewing evening gowns for the other ballerinas. Soon they shortened their pet name for each other from Cobina to Coby.

When a man permanently joined their world, they tried calling him Coby, but it just didn't sound right. Ballerina Irene had married Sam Silverman, a millionaire realtor, who ensconced mother and daughter in a posh mansion. It was the same home from which, years later, the widowed Irene Silverman would vanish without a trace.

Mother lived with daughter throughout her entire 39-year marriage to Silverman. He griped good-naturedly to friends, saying the two women formed their own exclusive clique, admitting no one else. "She and her mother were attached at the hip," said Irene's friend Janice Herbert, who danced at the Music Hall in the 1950s. "The stipulation was that the mother came with the package." Madame Irene filled the couple's new home with intricate needlework, so detailed it took 100 stitches per square inch, appliquéd pillows, and petit-point wall hangings. Outliving Sam, who died in 1980, Irene's mother continued sewing into her 80s. Left a rich widow by Silverman's shrewd eye for real estate, Irene wanted to devote her millions to the legacy of her mother, who died at age 95 on October 14, 1985. She started a nonprofit foundation and planned to turn her E. 65th Street mansion into a museum celebrating the sewing arts.

In a 1994 letter to the Internal Revenue Service, Irene wrote, "I would benefit by the satisfaction of knowing that everything I worked my entire life for would be dedicated to the memory of my mother and to the benefit of everyone who would participate in the foundation." Dubbing her dream The Coby Foundation, she posted their radio show nickname on her mansion doorway.

It was a dream she would never live to see.

Born Mary Irene Zambelli in New Orleans on April 17, 1916, she was the only child of Irina Meladakis, an immigrant from Crete, and her husband George Zambelli of Louisiana. Irina, who Americanized her name to Irene, descended from a family of heroes. As recounted in an epic poem, her grandfather George Meladakis, "who had wings on his feet," rose with fellow villagers against invading Turks, who were forcing the Christians of Crete to convert to Islam. On a steep cliff overlooking a gorge, so high they walked among eagles' nests, Meladakis and the other men from the village of Asi Gonia battled the Turks, who had ambushed their mountain hideaway on December 23, 1866. They held fast even as most of Crete lay in ashes. Asi Gonia won the battle, but the villagers eventually had to flee the Turks by ship. In the frenzy of evacuation, Irina's father, Michael, then a baby, was placed naked on the sand-covered ship's deck. Family legend had it that the sand pebbles embedded in his skin forever. By the time Michael was old enough to father his own children, he and his wife Angeliconda were able to return to Asi Gonia, where it's believed Irina was born on November 6, 1890. Church records in the village were destroyed during World War II, so it's not clear if Irina was born there or in the Athens suburb of Piraeus, where her family moved when she was an infant.

Settling in Piraeus, the port city bordering Athens, the Meladakis family had four more children. Their oldest became known at age three as "Irina the Dressmaker" for transforming fabric scraps into an outfit for her imaginary doll. By age 13, she began working for an Athens seamstress who had studied dressmaking in Paris. Irina started humbly, fetching pins that dropped on the ground and threading needles for the veterans. Four years later, the shop gave Irina most of the work because her seams were "the straightest and best," according to a pamphlet advertising the Coby Foundation. Her father and two brothers had emigrated to America by the time Irina turned 24. With the blessing of her mother and two sisters, who waved bon voyage from the docks of Piraeus, Irina and a distant cousin boarded a rickety ocean liner, the *Austro-Americana*, on February 10, 1914, and sailed to the New World. The ship had no cabins. Instead, beds sat side by side, dormitory style, with one deck for women, the other for men. As soon as the ship passed Gibraltar, those decks looked like hospital wards as the passengers en masse began vomiting from seasickness. Hanging on to the railings, Irina and a girlfriend, Sarah, crawled to the top deck looking for the ship's doctor. He and the captain turned out to be molesters, but Irina escaped their groping hands with the feistiness her daughter would inherit.

"So we held on to the railing and went to the hospital," Irina told the authors of *Island of Hope, Island of Tears*, a 1979 book about immigrants. "There was the doctor and the captain of the ship, and the captain said to Sarah, 'Sit on my lap.' And we did not know who was the captain and who was the doctor—they both wore uniforms—she sat on his lap, thinking that she was to be examined. He did examine her, all right. He started feeling her breasts at the same time the doctor was feeling mine. But I fixed him. I vomited on him, and he let me go. We both, Sarah and I, vomited our way back to our cabin. We sailed for 22 days in an awful stormy sea."

Finally on March 3, 1914, Irina looked up to see Lady Liberty gracing New York Harbor. As they docked on Ellis Island, the processing center for all immigrants, Irina's dressmaking panache set her apart from the crowd of peasant women on the ship. They tied handkerchiefs on their heads. Irina wore a hat that matched her custom-made rust brown suit and patent leather and suede shoes.

Carrying $30 between them, Irina and her cousin traveled three days by train to New Orleans, where her father was waiting. The Meladakis family was living above a candy store in a worn-out stretch of the city dotted with brothels and rooming houses.* A Creole woman, Josephine Casanova, took in boarders and sometimes ran a bordello in her place next door to the Meladakis' home. When Irina arrived, a broke gambler, George Zambelli, 24, was visiting his father William in Madame Casanova's. She fixed both men ham and crab gumbo, perfect for a chilly March evening. The next morning, with the hope born of a full stomach, George gazed at the bright day before him, noticing how the light caught the chestnut hair of a woman in the courtyard next door. He stared as she hung laundry out to dry, moving gracefully even

*Some of the facts about Irene Silverman's life are drawn from her unfinished memoir and other writing.

while heaving wet blankets over the clothesline. Her hands and feet were delicate. George didn't understand the strange language she spoke, but he wanted to learn it. He wanted to know everything about this pretty stranger, a dressmaker from Greece. George was gazing at his future wife, Irina Meladakis.

George needed an anchor in his life. His parents had never married and lived apart, a scandal in turn-of-the-century New Orleans. George and his twin brother, William, spent their early years in Catholic orphanages where the nuns were cruel, stealing fruit given to the twins on weekend visits and threatening to hit them if they complained. When their mother, Amila Laurie, took them in, she had trouble paying the rent and they bounced from one cheap rooming house to the next in the French Quarter. Their school was the street where they learned to duck the addicts, drunks, and whores and make pennies by shining shoes or begging. George took to gambling, though he wasn't very good at it. After his twin died of a burst appendix when they were 21, George fell even further into the house of cards, becoming a fixture at poker and dice games. When his luck failed in the gambling halls, he shuffled to the track. At five-feet-six and 120 pounds, he looked like a jockey, but afraid of getting thrown, he turned down a chance to ride the horses.

Finding Irina pushed him to reform. He found respectable work on the fishing docks and in a dry-cleaning shop, and wooed the dressmaker. They married, and their daughter Mary Irene was born two years later on Dauphine Street in the French Quarter. For her baby's christening at St. Louis Cathedral, Irina sewed for more than a month, making the infant a layette from the finest white linen and lace. It had a 40-inch train, two slips and a matching bonnet. The family settled off Jackson Square just two doors down from another brothel. Everyone called the

Zambelli girl "Ah-rene," as it sounded in a Southern accent, forgetting "Mary Irene" in favor of just her mother's name. Mrs. Zambelli allowed her daughter to play with the kids on the block, warning her never to go inside the whorehouse. One day Irene followed the kids inside the brothel, and Mrs. Zambelli threw a fit, even though no customers were there at the time. She demanded that George move the family to a better neighborhood.

Always wanting the best for her daughter, Irina encouraged the girl's love of dance, enrolling her in ballet classes when she was three. George Zàmbelli shared the same last name as a famous Italian ballerina of the day, Carlotta Zambelli. Her people came from Milan while the New Orleans Zambellis hailed from Venice, but it's possible the two families were distantly related. In later years Irene encouraged the connection. As a girl in New Orleans, she read about Carlotta, whose combination of grace and technical prowess made her a star at the Teatro al la Scala in Milan and the Opera in Paris. Invited to dance in St. Petersburg, Carlotta Zambelli became the last visiting ballerina to grace the imperial stage before the Russian Revolution.

Irene studied tap and ballet in New Orleans and dreamed of her own career. For her 14th birthday, her mother took her to Europe for the first time. On route to what her mother planned as a triumphant homecoming in Athens, they spent two weeks in Manhattan and 10 days in Paris. In Greece, typhoid fever struck down the young dancer, and she nearly died in her mother's birthplace. For 45 days, Irene struggled in Evangelismos Hospital in Athens as bacteria invaded her intestines and shot her temperature above 104 degrees. Her mother begged God for her daughter's life. Typhoid fever was known to cripple its victims, so only the Fates knew if Irene would walk, much less ever dance again.

Doctors pumped her with quinine and wrapped her fevered body into a latex sheet jammed with ice packs. After a month like this, fed only liquids, her fever broke but then her temperature nose-dived, dragging her into a coma. As if answering her mother's prayers, she emerged from this fog after 15 days. Too weak to stand, thin like a famine victim, her belly swollen and stinking of the smell of mothballs from camphor treatments, she was carried via stretcher to Kifisia in the hills outside of Athens, a retreat known for healing waters and pine-scented air. For four weeks, the hotel staff pampered her with healthy meals. Slowly she regained her strength. One day, she grabbed a chair, held on and carefully arranged her feet into first position. Her legs worked. She would dance again. "Only those who've almost died really know how to live," Irene would tell friends throughout her life.

When they returned home by 1931, the teenaged Irene resumed her dancing lessons, but her time in New Orleans was ending. Her parents had separated over her father's lapse into gambling. Confident her dressmaking skills would tide them over, Madame Irene in 1934 agreed to take her 18-year-old daughter to Manhattan to pursue her dancing. Just as they had in New Orleans, the Zambellis found themselves living near a bordello, the flat above their tiny apartment on West 51st Street. Elegance, however, surrounded her in ballet class. Slipping into her size-three dance slippers, an awestruck Irene stayed in the back of Michel Fokine's master class. Not only was the choreographer of celebrated works like *Petrouchka*, *The Firebird*, and *Les Sylphides* now her teacher, her classmate was the star Patricia Bowman, who later cofounded the American Ballet Theater.

A butler answered the door to Fokine's mansion on Riverside Drive overlooking the Hudson, ushering students past a marble vestibule and elegant self-portrait of Fokine wearing velvet trousers and a flowing white shirt. He also painted his ballerina wife, Vera Fokina, known as "the pearl of Russia." The students signed for the $5 per half-hour lessons in an open book left on a desk at the base of a marble staircase. "I paid for my lessons by my mother sewing for Fokine when he had private recitals," Irene said in a tape-recorded 1975 interview with dance writer John Gruen, who was researching an article on Patricia Bowman. "She would make costumes. Each time I signed in, I would say, 'Oh, Gosh, how much will this be toward the account?'" Her mother found work with Charles James, a designer for Elizabeth Arden, and also made a believer out of a 38th Street furrier who scoffed when she bought some leftover karakul sheep pelts to make a coat. He offered her a job when she returned showing off the finished product.

Classical dance in America was in its infancy in the mid-1930s. In those days, The Radio City Music Hall Ballet Corps supported the only resident company in the entire country. Their 36 ballerinas danced a grueling schedule of four shows a day on the giant hall's city block-wide stage made of cement and steel. It had no give and turned their toes to mush. On holidays, management often added a fifth show for no extra pay. Also each time the act changed, the dancers had to rehearse in between performances. Blood seeping through satin dancing shoes was a common sight backstage. "It was a tough schedule," said Vivian Smith Shiers, who danced at Radio City with Irene from 1938 to 1942. "We would be rehearsing from 9:00 A.M. until the lunch break, do the first show and after the first show, which took about an hour, rehearse until 10 minutes before the next show. Then we had a dinner break, and very often we would have to rehearse from after the dinner show to the final show. That was four shows a day plus three rehearsals." The pace was so exhausting, one dancer missed her period for two years. The non-union dancers had little recourse. In Depression-era New York, at least 10 girls were waiting to fill any empty slot.

Patricia Bowman became Radio City's first prima ballerina. Just a few inches taller than Irene, the five-foot-two-inch star dazzled the newcomer. For years, Irene wore the same mascara that had turned Patricia's eyelashes long and spidery. She stared at her in Fokine's class. "Just to see that one exercise was a performance by itself," Irene told writer Gruen. "And she was so fragile and pale with gorgeous coloring—she was a strawberry-blonde, with a very pink and white complexion and green, green eyes. I always felt badly that such an exquisite artist should be asked to do four shows a day in a big movie house like Radio City. But then, where could one go? In those days the Music Hall was about the only place for a ballet dancer."

Crowds lined Sixth Avenue for the 50-cent tickets that provided an afternoon of vaudeville, glee club singers, high-kicking Rockettes, Hollywood's latest feature film, and the ballerinas. Legend among the dancers was the story of Rosalie Spatcher, who changed not far from Irene's side of the dressing room. Feeling sorry for a bag lady waiting for tickets in the cold, Rosalie started giving her passes. The woman turned out to be a millionaire who willed her entire fortune to Rosalie. She quit in a flash.

A similar fairy tale happened to Irene, with a husband engineering her escape from the grind of bleeding toes. For Irene, dancing became more of a way to make a living than artistic expression. "I was never an energetic dancer and hardly ever perspired," she said. She turned down a chance to tour Europe with the famed Monte Carlo Ballet Corps because they couldn't give a straight answer about the salary and wouldn't let her bring her mother. "I wasn't ever that interested in dance that I would have just thrown myself into a situation and hoped for the best," she said. So when suitor Samuel Silverman knocked at the stage door, Irene was only too eager to accept his proposal.

In 1941, the Silverman she met was remaking himself from the ashes of his former life in Florida. A 1929 law graduate of the University of Florida at Gainesville, he quit the state bar on September 28, 1937, according to Florida Supreme Court records. Details of this case have been destroyed. His only child, Ronald, said Silverman resigned in disgrace over allegations he had embezzled his clients. His wife, Ronald's mother Bertha O'Koon Silverman, filed for divorce, "because she thought he was dishonest, a crook, and had lied to other people," their son said. Arriving in New York, Silverman was vague when people asked about his background, leading them to believe he grew up on the Lower East Side or graduated from Columbia University. He started a new career in real estate and prospered. Eight years older than Irene, he was a handsome man. At six feet tall, he moved gracefully on a tennis court, looking like a natural blue blood with his light blond hair and blue eyes. "He looked like a good German Aryan even though he was Jewish," said his son. Eight months after his divorce was final, he and Irene married in Manhattan on October 3, 1941. Sam was drafted into the army two years later, and Irene continued dancing at Radio City until Sam returned home, near the end of World War II.

In an era when mortgage brokers were more than retail drones, Silverman was an ace among the freelancers who put together huge land projects. Manhattan's biggest landowners, like the Goldman-DiLorenzo empire that at one time owned the Chrysler Building, called him when they had trouble closing a deal. Silverman helped Columbia University become one of Manhattan's landlord giants, enriching their portfolio by bringing them investment opportunities. Silverman ferreted out deals where Columbia would issue standby commitments covering a loan if a builder needed more financing than the banks were willing to extend. Columbia would charge two to three points to guarantee the builder's loan. Silverman usually picked winners so the university and he grew richer. His scope gradually expanded overseas with investments in Paris and in America's last paradise, Hawaii. Before Japanese money turned Honolulu into a high-rise city, Silverman introduced the island to New York investors. As an adviser to Hawaii developer Chinn Ho, Silverman helped secure financing in the 1950s for the largest condo project to date in Wakiki, a 1,000-unit beachfront building that, at 32 stories, was the tallest building in town. "Sam was brilliant," said Chinn Ho's son, Stuart. "He could reduce complicated thoughts and schemes to simple sentences. In fact, he would write long-term financing commitments in long hand. His basic equipment was a telephone, a pad, and a pencil. Nothing more."

Money lifted both Irenes far from their seedy walkup. The Silvermans would come to spend summers at their country home in Septeuil, a small village west of Paris. They also kept an apartment near the Opera in Paris that was so close to the stage, they could hear the performers and orchestra in their living room. Successful in Hawaii, Silverman bought a beachfront condo in Wakiki, where he stopped on the way to frequent business meetings in Japan.

Silverman began to travel more while Irene expanded her educational horizons. In 1949, he took his first trip to Europe, visiting Paris with Irene. She enrolled in ballet lessons with Carlotta Zambelli in her studio near the Paris Opera and art classes at the

Academie Julian, where she struck up a friendship with painter Emile Sabouraud. The rich Americans bought two of his paintings, arranging for Irene to pose for a portrait the following summer, dressed in a tutu and standing on point. Silverman bought a Pontiac in 1950, and they drove it onto a Norwegian freighter that sailed from New York to Antwerp in 12 days.

Arriving in Paris, Irene began 11 days of three-hour sittings for her portrait. At first Sabouraud proposed painting her three-quarter size, but the 96-pound subject pushed for a full-sized rendering, arguing she was small enough and tired of nicknames like "Peanut," or "Shorty." She posed, draping her hands in front of her while balancing on one foot. As the painting dried, the Silvermans took the artist, his wife, and son on a 17-day driving tour around France, staying in a different village each night. When they picked up the painting, Irene hid her displeasure. In Irene's opinion, the artist had given her thick hips, fat thighs, lost her waist, made her face too thin and hair too short. In New York, Irene doctored the portrait herself with gouache paints, filling out the face, tucking in the buttocks and adding volume to her hair.

That portrait of her wearing a white and light blue tutu against a darker blue backdrop became the centerpiece of the best room in the biggest canvas of her later years, her mansion on East 65th Street. Silverman bought the house for her in 1957 over misgivings that it might be a flop as an investment. "My husband hated the idea of the house," Irene told *New York Times* real estate columnist Christopher Gray in 1994. "He said, 'It's a big white elephant, it will just weigh us down.'" However, Irene was smitten. The mansion sits on one of the best blocks on the Upper East Side. The world's largest synagogue, Temple Emanu-El, which means "God is with us," com-

mands the northeast corner of E. 65th Street and Fifth
Avenue. During High Holy Days, the temple draws
5,000 people. (Manhattan District Attorney Robert
Morgenthau, who would bring charges against
Irene's suspected killers, is a trustee there.) Permanent missions to the United Nations for Pakistan and
the Republic of Congo are both on the block. On
the Madison Avenue side, the Terramare Café sells
cappuccino for $3.50 under a green awning embossed
with gold letters advertising "Truffles and Caviar."

Irene threw her gusto for entertaining, decorating,
and gardening into the landmark town house erected
in 1880 and rebuilt 21 years later in 1901 to accommo-
date advances in electricity, plumbing, and heating.
Following the French classic revival style popular
during New York's golden age, the limestone building features simple straight lines with a few flour-
ishes. It is a rectangle 25 feet wide topped by a
copper mansard roof. Two windows on each of the
five floors overlook 65th street. An arch with a floral
design decorates the top of the second-story windows. Hoisted in the center of the arched doorway
rests the head of a bearded godlike figure who has
wings sprouting from his hair. He looks displeased,
with his mouth open and his nostrils flaring.

When the overhaul was complete in 1904, the family of Edward N. Gibbs, a force in the ubiquitous
New York Life Insurance Company, and his descend-
ents lived there until Silverman bought the home,
according to a historical report Christopher Gray of
the *New York Times* prepared for Irene. The most col-
orful resident was Gibbs' son-in-law, Charles Hitch-
cock Sherrill, minister to Argentina, author of 10
history and travel books, lawyer, member of the International Olympic Committee and college track star
who invented the kneeling crouched start. While an
undergraduate at Yale University in 1887, Sherrill
knelt down at the start of a 100-yard dash. For the

next four years, he beat everyone using this technique, forever changing the way track races begin. Owned by his wife, the mansion mostly lay empty after she died in 1948 until the Silvermans came along.

Irene convinced her husband that this home would impress his clients. She kept the champagne flowing at parties and prided herself on her role as business helpmate. "She said that being able to entertain right is 99 percent of all business success," said her stepson, Ronald Silverman. "Being able to pick the right wine, the right hors d' oeuvres and serve it in the right atmosphere accounted for a lot of my father's success, and she said she was responsible for that." She stocked her freezers with the finest cuts of meat from Piccinini Brothers butchers on Ninth Avenue, suppliers to Manhattan's best restaurants. Guests walked under some 16 chandeliers that dangled from 12-to-16-foot ceilings throughout the town house. Nine marble fireplaces provided a warm glow. Madame Irene's fine embroidery enriched the backs, seats, and arms of antique chairs stitched in rainbow floral patterns with imported silk and wool thread. Irene placed inlaid tables next to overstuffed velvet couches, put thick carpeting on the floors, and filled the walls with antique maps of Paris, oil paintings of African villagers, and still lifes of flowers and fruits. Shelves and tabletops overflowed with memorabilia from travels abroad and her life in the theater. She and Silverman lived in a 3,000-square-foot duplex that overlooked a private landscaped terrace with a fountain facing south. Sunlight from a massive skylight made the spiral staircase gleam. Front and center in the living room, Irene held her pose in Sabouraud's vision. Gold curtains with matching valances ringed the painting and the room, catching rays of sunlight that also grabbed the purple applique pillows and light blue upholstered chairs. More than 300 plants flourished on three floors, including the duplex terrace and the rooftop garden. Like a good Italian, she grew her tomato plants every summer. For a 1983 article on urban green thumbs, Irene told the *New York Times*, "the best way to water is with a gin bottle, but only the kind that's embossed with bumps and won't slide from your hand." Briefly, she toyed with the idea of selling the home for $700,000 in 1968, but couldn't go through with it. "Fortunately, I chickened out," she said.

Silverman was choosy about the tenants who rented the lower floors below the apartment he shared with Irene in the East 65th Street town house. Steady but unassuming, Sam was the flour to Irene's icing. "I think they got on very well in the way that oddly matched couples did," said financier turned writer Michael Thomas, their third-floor tenant from 1975 to 1987. "Sam was a very quiet, self-effacing guy with a lot of sparkle behind it all. He was the type of guy who gave real estate a good name. Irene was a flamboyant character very outspoken." Invited over to the Silvermans' in the mid-1970s, writer John Gruen said Sam sat silent as Irene bubbled with talk of the theater and Europe. However, she kept referring to her husband, and he never took his eyes off his vivacious wife. She found a safe haven in Sam, as well as a partner who accepted and grew to love her mother.

While Irene operated on instinct, Sam acted on research. When he and Mrs. Zambelli were still alive, the tenants at 20 East 65th Street were top-notch and stayed for years. Prominent Washington lobbyist Liz Robbins, a 20-year friend of Hillary and Bill Clinton, rented there. Renowned orchestra leader, author, pianist, and composer Peter Duchin, who's played at every presidential Inaugural Ball since John F. Kennedy's, lived on Irene's fourth floor for three years. With him there was his wife Brooke Hayward, daughter of Broadway impresario Leland Hayward and the actress Margaret Sullavan, and author of the best-selling autobiography, *Haywire.* In one of those only-in-New York coincidences, Hayward had previously been married to writer Michael Thomas and now found herself living one floor above him at Irene's. Investor Arthur Kreizel and his wife Isobella, an interior designer, rented the second floor for five years.

Irene delighted in the comings and goings of her powerhouse tenants and loved her role as chatelaine, a charming but all-knowing one. Trailed by at least three boxer dogs, her "children," she swept into rooms, making her presence known. "She was always around the place, tidying, fixing, and snooping," said Duchin. "She was amusing actually, you could always kid her." Michael Thomas remembered returning from a trip with his third wife to discover that Irene had replaced the linoleum floor in their kitchen without telling them. "Irene was very proprietary," said Thomas. "She took a real interest in her tenants, she got nosy. This was her family, this building. I think it irritated the women. You were likely to come home from a trip and find Irene in the apartment." He thought she got on better with men than women and was secretly disappointed when he married. "I don't think Irene was really happy when I got married," he said. "She liked having me there as a bachelor, liked seeing the variety of women going in and out of there. When I had a party, I would always invite her."

In the years after Sam Silverman's death in 1980, money seemed more important to the widow, even though he had named her sole heir to his $3.2 million fortune. In addition, she owned the mansion, whose worth soared with the booming Manhattan real estate market. Irene stunned Michael Thomas with a letter saying she was tripling his $850 a month rent, effective immediately. He checked with a realtor and learned that since only five units in the building were rented at the time, Irene had the right to charge whatever she pleased. "I remember thinking to myself that Sam would never have done this to me," he said. "Normally they say we can and will raise the rent, but in increments. This went from $850 to close to $2,600 overnight. I remember at the time being terribly surprised because I was really close to her." Peter Duchin said Irene "liked money a lot" and steadily hiked their $3,000 a month rent by $1,000, which prompted them to find another flat. Isobella Kreizel said that while Irene "never threw her money around," she was also generous and gave gifts with flair. Every Thanksgiving and Christmas, she bought the Kreizels champagne and turkey. On Easter, she filled the house with white lilies and brought some for them also. Once when her boxer dogs produced a litter of puppies, she offered them for sale in a newspaper ad. A 12-year-old girl arrived from Long Island, obviously unable to afford the $500 each purebred puppy was worth. Irene just asked the girl to fill up her piggy bank and presented her with one puppy named "Shoe" for the white marking on one foot. Then Irene donated the girl's pennies to the Humane Society of New York. Toward the end of her life, she saw an Ethiopian immigrant delivering groceries with such care, they struck up a friendship. She ended up hiring the man to work in the mansion and made arrangements to send him to college.

While financial success had always impressed the former chorus girl, she admired hard work and academic achievement just as much. "She judged a person on how much money he had," said her stepson, Ronald. "You were either capable and competent, meaning you made a lot of money, or you were something else. There were some who achieved in the world, those who made money, and there were ordinary human beings." When asked why she married Silverman, Irene once said, "I wanted his name, and I wanted his power." However, academics and industrious people had riches of another sort, Irene believed. Inspired by her mother's work ethic and immigrant past, she took history courses at Columbia University and befriended her professors, even touring the south of France with one of them. Arriving on campus in a limousine, Irene had her driver wait there upwards of three hours, until the lecture finished. She was generous to the other students, instructing her driver to take them home and hosting impromptu wine and cheese parties at term's end. The Silvermans had always donated to Columbia, giving the university a condo in Hawaii and a five-by-eight-foot Japanese lacquered screen decorated with birds.

She asked Columbia's oral history professor, Ron Grele, for advice about starting an audio-library of the garment and fashion industry. As her mother advanced into her 80s, Irene began tape-recording interviews with her and writing a history of "Madame Irene's" life in the needle arts. Irene made her mother's last years as comfortable as possible. The older woman lived in a sunny apartment full of her treasured embroidery, pictures of Greece, and a doll collection for the seamstress whose career began by dressing an imaginary doll. At the age of 94, she was still able to walk up a flight of stairs and read for pleasure. When her mother underwent bladder surgery at Mt. Sinai Hospital, staff nurse Louise McNair took extra care of the frail woman, impressing Irene. She hired Louise to work private duty part-time in the mansion, even though Madame Irene didn't require the care of a registered nurse. "She loved her dearly," said Louise. "Irene was just so devoted to her mother. She wanted to be right there in the room every minute." McNair fussed over Madame Irene, giving her baths and massages, thereby allowing her daughter a little break from round-the-clock care.

When her mother died on October 14, 1985, Irene was 69 years old. The person who meant the most to her, her rock, best friend and constant companion was now gone, and the void was tremendous.

The Coby Foundation, the tribute to her mother, became Irene's passion, and she turned every available inch of mansion space into rent-producing income to leave a bigger gold pot for her dream. Moving out of the duplex, Irene established her bedroom in a ground floor office. She hired carpenters to divide the large apartments and created 10 rentals in the mansion, turning it into an upscale hotel with maid service. Carpenter Harry Papaioannou said Irene was happy overseeing the renovations. "She was always in a good mood, always laughing," he said. "She told a lot of stories about the old days, and she used to drink a lot of champagne and offered it to us after we were done." Technically, she was violating the housing code by installing so many rentals; however, she didn't hurt anybody except herself in the end. The mansion's certificate of occupancy allowed only five apartments and a doctor's office. Anything more required approval from the building department, and there are no such permits on file.

Entertainers like singer Chaka Khan and actress Jennifer Grey loved her place. Irene beamed. Friends thought she kept busy to ward off loneliness. "She liked to have people around, she was happy to see people," said Papaioannou. "She was very trustworthy. She liked to hear people say, 'You have a beautiful home.' That was her pride and joy. All the brass in there was like a mirror, and she would say straight out, 'This is my pride and joy.' " Feathered Nest, her rental agent, filled her place with bankers and diplomats and the system seemed to work. Her staff of nine maids and handymen kept the mansion gleaming, and they fussed over their mistress. Sundays, her maid Marta gave her a massage, a manicure, painting her fingernails red, as well as a pedicure for those ballerina feet. Once a month Irene had her hair colored Lucille Ball red.

As she grew older, she began to slow down. She stopped traveling to Europe and didn't take classes at Columbia anymore. Her dinner parties for her university friends and the young clothing designers she mothered tended to end by nine instead of the usual midnight. Arthritis and back pain, which she blamed on her years of grueling dance rehearsals and performances, made her reach more often for the two splits of champagne she always carried in her bag. Whenever he was in New York, Hawaiian developer Stuart Ho visited to reassure himself that Irene was okay and in control of her large staff. Friends said her mind remained sharp, and she read five daily newspapers, two weeklies, and 28 monthly magazines. She also began writing her memoirs and cataloging the hundreds of embroidery pieces she wanted to preserve for the museum. On annual checkups in 1998, she impressed both her doctor and dentist. She underwent successful surgery to correct a tearing eye duct. Following her own drumbeat, she often stayed in her nightgown past noon. If she felt like eating raw oysters and champagne for breakfast at two o'clock in the afternoon, that's just what she did.

Under normal circumstances, she had more good years left. She proceeded as planned toward creating a living memorial to her beloved mother. The IRS granted her foundation tax-exempt status, and she chose a board of directors. In the fall of 1997, she hosted a debut event for the foundation, inviting designers and museum curators to a lecture about embroidery. "Women who sew have an independence," she said in promotional literature for the Coby Foundation. "They are never alone, never lonesome, never wondering what to do next. There is always something to do." At age 82, Irene was busy and pursuing her dream. Surrounded by a devoted staff, her boxer Georgie constantly at her side, Irene was the center of a comfortable world. She thought she had everything under control.

Chapter 17

"Love Thy Neighbor as Thy Self."

Danger sprang from a routine part of life at Irene's, someone on the phone wanting to rent an apartment. Prosecutors allege that Sante Kimes, identifying herself as a secretary named Eva Guerrero, lined up a flat at the mansion for her "boss" Manny Guerrin via long-distance calls beginning in April 1998. In other calls, Sante posed as real estate broker Joy Landis to hire a title search company, which discovered the mansion was mortgage free. Birdlike Irene and her slice of Paris in Manhattan registered on the Kimes radar by chance. Sante had floated through investment seminars in Florida and elsewhere, giving out her longevity-network business cards and trying to drum up interest in developing those 28 acres Kenneth Kimes had owned in Santa Maria, California. Through her networking, she met a Prudential Bache executive based in New York a few years before and asked him to recommend a decent Manhattan rental. He directed her to one of his clients, butcher Rudolph Vaccari, who owned Piccinini Brothers on Ninth Avenue, where Irene had been buying her meat ever since she and her mother lived near Radio City Music Hall. Through the butcher, a personal friend of Irene's, Sante first heard of the East 65th Street mansion.

In the weeks leading to their arrival in Manhattan, Sante and Kenny were suspects in David Kazdin's murder, the car swindle in Utah, and the arson and

mortgage scams in Nevada. They were wanted in
three states. Accompanied by drifter Sean Little, they
bounced around Texas, New Mexico, and Louisiana.
They surfaced in mid-May at a gated community
popular with the equestrian set in southern Florida,
renting a town house in the Palm Beach Polo and
Country Club. Their landlady was the former wife of
Shimmy Querishi, the millionaire linked to Gulf
Union Bank in the Bahamas, where Kimes Sr. had
stashed money. Querishi also lived in the same complex. Combing through a Palm Beach registry, the
Kimeses began checking off the names of rich people
with homes in Manhattan.

Authorities charge they came across the name of
Brooklyn native Max Schorr, at 90, the oldest practicing attorney in Palm Beach, who still played golf
three times a week and attended civic meetings.
Mother and son somehow unearthed personal details
about Schorr, including his social security number,
date of birth, and mother's maiden name, and applied for a Mastercard in his name.

Little, a Californian with a conviction for burglary,
left the Kimeses suddenly. In need of a gofer, the
Kimeses recruited a 24-year-old Cuban immigrant
working in a chicken restaurant in West Palm Beach,
hiring him as their handyman and driver. Jose Antonio Alvarez had been a short-order cook for the Pop-
eye's chain, drove a truck, worked construction, and
accumulated a pile of unpaid parking tickets since
legally emigrating from Cuba in May 1994. Against
his family's wishes, he went off with the Kimeses.

Just as they had used the best hotel in Beverly Hills
as the posh drop off for their Lincoln Town Car, the
Kimeses borrowed the oceanfront splendor of the
Ritz Carlton in Palm Beach for another scam, police
suspect. They convinced a Louisiana dealer to accept
a trade-in of a 1985 motor home, the one Stan Patterson had driven to Los Angeles, for a new 36-foot-

long Holiday Rambler. The Kimeses offered the Dixie
Motor company in Hammond, Louisiana, the older
motor home and agreed to pay $70,000 for the Ram-
bler. Worth $89,000, the white and blue Rambler fea-
tured a 27-inch color TV, a VCR, high-backed captain's
chairs, a microwave oven, and a washer and dryer.
A driver from the Dixie company drove the Rambler
to the Ritz Carlton but never met the so-called buyer,
"Nanette Wetkowski," the Kimeses' ubiquitous notary. Using a fake name, a woman believed to be
Sante met the Dixie employee on Saturday, May 30,
explaining that Wetkowski was resting inside the
Ritz Carlton. Sante took the paperwork inside,
emerging minutes later with the signed sale documents and two checks, for $7,000 and $63,000. The
larger check was signed L. M. Carpeneto, actually a
Los Angeles man who had reported his checks stolen
in Las Vegas. The other check was signed "S. A.
Kahn" on a Bank of America account from Santa Barbara, California, that had a zero balance. Kahn was
the same last name Sante used in a letter to the Santa
Barbara judge handling the feud between Kenny and
classmate Carrie Louise Grammer.

Dixie Motors insisted on payment by certified
check. They got checks bearing an impressive "Certified," probably from a stamp available in most office
supply stores, said Manalapan, Florida police detective Tom Clark. By Monday when the checks
bounced, the Kimeses were a weekend ahead of the
game. The motor home people reached Sante by
phone, and she apologized about the checks and
promised to take care of the problem, the same script
Utah car dealer Jim Blackner had heard that spring.
Unconvinced, Dixie contacted Detective Clark. Three
weeks later, he found the Holiday Rambler in a Wel-
lington parking lot, minus its vehicle ID numbers and
a "Dixie RV" decal. "It was neatly stashed in the
corner to be used at a later date, I strongly suspect,"

Clark said. "The Kimeses talked a good story, dropped the names of horse people, and used them as authorization to keep their vehicle in the area." In the window, they left a note saying the equestrian manager gave them permission to park there and listed a Las Vegas number for any questions.

With Alvarez driving the Lincoln Town car, Kenny up front, and Sante napping most of the way on the backseat, the trio headed north in mid-June. Kenny Kimes, alias Manny Guerrin, was due to occupy Apartment 1B in Irene's on Sunday, June 14. Arriving in Manhattan the night before, Sante thought hotel prices were too high so they drove back to New Jersey, settling in the $59-a-night Starlight Motel in Jersey City. Kenny checked in under the alias Manuel Guerrero then sneaked in Sante and Alvarez. Crowds dancing the merengue, waving red, white, and blue flags and shouting "Viva Puerto Rico" took control of Irene's neighborhood the next day. The Kimeses didn't realize they were driving into the heart of the 41st annual Puerto Rican Day Parade, where two million revelers, undaunted by rain, gyrated and sang their way up Fifth Avenue from 44th to 86th Street. The trio had trouble finding a parking space near Irene's. Finally pulling into a spot, Sante and Alvarez drank $5.50 beers in the green-walled bar inside Le Regence Restaurant of the $275-a-night Plaza Athenee Hotel, two blocks from Irene's, while Kenny moved into Apartment 1B.

He was shown into a one-bedroom flat with a spacious oval living room, an ornate fireplace, and a pink-tiled bathroom. Forty plants arranged floor to ceiling filled a rear atrium. Artwork destined for the Coby Foundation brightened the walls, including Mrs. Zambelli's needlework of a Picasso and a vintage American crazy quilt made in the 1860s. Feathered Nest Realtors described the décor as "typical

Irene style" with a mix of velvet couches, antique chairs, and a black-leather love seat.

A subsequent indictment described their alleged behavior:

Kenny smuggled in his mother and Alvarez, police said. They took turns peering through the peephole and jotting descriptions of people going in and out of the mansion. Attaching a listening device onto the mansion phones, the Kimeses began eavesdropping and taping Irene's conversations, according to prosecutors. Mother and son told Alvarez that nobody must know he and Sante were in the apartment and ordered him never to answer phone calls or knocks on the door. Each time he entered the lobby doorway, Kenny slid along the wall ducking the security camera and hid Sante's face.

Immediately, Irene felt uneasy about this new tenant, which only intensified after he refused to hand over his identification to be copied, delayed signing the rental agreement, then flatly refused to fill it out until consulting with his lawyer. However, he was sure to get Irene's signature on a handwritten rent receipt. Never in 41 years of renting apartments did Irene meet a tenant like this. The worst she had encountered was a tenant who held a pot party, which moved her to throw him out. At least that nuisance was understandable.

This new tenant was strange. While keeping people out of his apartment, he started snooping around the mansion, and walking uninvited on upper floors and into the basement kitchen. Fashion designer Zang Toi said he was eating lunch with Irene in the kitchen that first Sunday Kenny was there. "He tried to come in, but as soon as Irene heard footsteps, she told the maid to send this person away."

Kenny was nosy. He asked how many employees were on staff. He convinced one to let him see Irene's sweeping 3,000 square-foot duplex, offering $30,000 for two months there. Irene was appalled. "He'd barricade himself up there, and I'd never get back in," she said. She brushed off a friend's question about her watery eyes, saying she had "bigger problems" with the new tenant. She began comparing the young man with the slicked-back hair to a jailbird.

Prosecutors allege mother and son spent the next three weeks laying the groundwork, on paper, for taking over Irene's mansion. The indictment claims the following: Back on the phone, always using aliases, Sante gathered the documents needed to transfer the mansion to an offshore corporation the Kimeses controlled. Meticulous as librarians, they made notebook entries of their every step. Sante allegedly kept a score card of all her various aliases and with whom she used them. They compiled a virtual textbook on the basics of New York real estate, including questions for the title company, procedures to complete a deed, transfer property, and pay taxes.

According to the indictment, Sante bought a copy of the mansion's deed and got real estate transaction and tax forms. Claiming to be a hotel employee, she purportedly told a real estate lawyer that she needed to quickly transfer a Manhattan property to her firm. She wanted the necessary forms mailed to a private post office box in Manhattan that Kenny had opened under an alias. Real estate taxes had to be paid to complete the transfer, so the lawyer helped her compute the amount for checks addressed to the New York City Finance Department.

They needed Irene's social security number for the paperwork. Posing as a Las Vegas casino worker, Sante telephoned Irene with the news she had won a free gambling trip, according to the indictment. To claim the prize, all she had to do was give her social security number. Irene didn't bite. Kenny asked staff members for the number. Sante tried to pry it from

Irene's former accountant, claiming she was doing a background check on the landlady in preparation for signing a long-term lease at the mansion. These scams failed, so the Kimeses allegedly created a bogus Social Security card, copying Irene's signature from the signed rental receipt. According to the indictment, one of the suspects drafted a deed to transfer the $7 million home for $390,000 to a dummy corporation, forging Irene's signature on that document as well as on a tax form, a preliminary residential property transfer, a power of attorney, and a rental agreement.

By day they worked on these arrangements; by night they treated themselves to dinners and drinks at Manhattan's finest hotels, allegedly charging $565 on the bogus credit card bearing Palm Beach attorney Max Schorr's name. Sante charged an additional $113 for soaps and toiletries at the Chanel boutique. Sometimes accompanied by Alvarez, they dined at the stately Pierre Hotel on 61st Street and Fifth Avenue, just four blocks from Irene's. Headed to the Pierre, mother and son passed the headquarters of the Union of American Hebrew Congregations, on the southeast corner of Irene's block, 65th, and Fifth Avenue. Etched in 15-inch letters on the building's limestone façade are these quotes from the Old Testament: "DO JUSTLY LOVE MERCY WALK HUMBLY WITH THY GOD, MICAH 6:8" and "LOVE THY NEIGHBOR AS THY SELF, LEVITICUS 19:18." Kenny recited a version of this golden rule while defending himself and his mother on *60 Minutes*. "I've had many friends," he said. "I've had many relationships. Always kindness. Kindness is very key. Do unto others as you would have done unto yourself."

After moving into Irene's ground-floor rental, mother and son apparently used the secretary-boss routine to try and lease commercial space in another building just across the street from the mansion. This building had a clear view of Irene's upper floors. A newspaper advertisement about a $2,000-a-month office rental at 3 East 65th Street brought a phone call from a woman saying her boss wanted to look at the place. Calling himself Athanasio Tsoukas from Beachwood, Ohio, Kenny filled out a lease application for realtor Bob Hammer of David Frankel Realty on June 30. He claimed to be president of "Gulf Stream Inc.," a computer firm based in the Bahamas. "My secretary spots him as a phony right away because, as he's filling out the application, we ask for tax ID information, and he says, 'Oh, we don't pay taxes,' " Hammer said. "When it came to filling out the social security number, he excuses himself to go to the bathroom. Obviously he couldn't remember the number." When the realty firm ran a credit check, they discovered the real Tsouskas was recuperating from surgery in an out-of-state hospital. "It was all phony," said Hammer. "Even his corporation was phony. It has some jet-age, space-age name, and he said it was based in the Bahamas, but he kept saying he would provide all the information later. He was a very charming man, but you could tell he was full of baloney."

By early July, the Kimeses had gathered all their paperwork. Now all they needed was the seal of a notary public to complete the mansion transfer. Sante looked for someone willing to illegally notarize documents without witnessing the signature, promising to pay hundreds of dollars, according to the indictment. In New York the usual fee to notarize a document is $2. On their first try the Kimeses encountered a tired but sharp man, Don Aoki, a full-time manager for a midtown drugstore who notarizes documents on the side. Mother and son found him by calling the Hilton Hotel, which keeps his store on their referral list. He worked a late shift so it wasn't until 11:20 P.M. on Wednesday, July 1, 1998, that he met a Mr.

Win at the bar of the Plaza Athenee Hotel. This Mr. Win, dressed in a blue blazer, dungarees, and an open collar shirt, was Kenny. He walked Aoki back to Irene's. Apartment 1B was dark when Kenny ushered Aoki into a room where a woman wearing a nightgown and a nightcap lay in bed with papers by her side. Aoki glimpsed some real estate terminology on the document, but there was one big problem. "It was already signed, and I said, 'I'm sorry this has to be signed in front of me,' " Aoki said.

The woman in bed said she didn't realize it was wrong to sign the papers before the notary had arrived. Aoki suggested she write her name on another piece of paper and he would compare that with the signature on the real estate document. "I guess she wasn't ready to do that," Aoki said. "Honey, I think we should wait," the woman in bed said to Kenny, and he asked Aoki to step outside for a minute. In voices loud enough for Aoki to hear, the pair debated the merits of going through with the signing at this time. "They made it appear as if it was a family thing they had to work out," Aoki said. The woman, who prosecutors say was Sante, never got out of bed. Kenny emerged from the room, apologized to Aoki, and gave him $20 for cab fare home. According to the indictment, the next day the pair tried again with another notary, a woman. Kenny called his mother "Mrs. Silverman" in front of this notary, and the pair somehow tricked her into putting her seal on the documents. Prosecutors allege she notarized a deed bearing Irene's forged signature, which transferred her beloved mansion to a dummy corporation called The Atlantis Group, Limited. It listed a post office box address on Third Avenue but was chartered in Antigua.

Only a few more details remained. Mother and son allegedly had arranged for a financial company in Bermuda to mail them an $8,000 check made out to a Manuel Guerrero, a real person unlike the Manny Guerrin identity Kenny used in the mansion. Guerrero, a Blackfoot Indian, was a drifter who had a minor arrest record in Idaho and had worked for the Kimeses in California. Kenny had a birth certificate, Florida state identification card, and a social security card all bearing Guerrero's name, police and prosecutors said. The ID card had Kenny's picture on it. Guerrero, who was born in 1970, was also listed as vice president of Atlantis Group, Limited, the company that on paper now owned Irene's mansion. Using Guerrero's identification, Kenny posed as him and tried to cash the $8,000 check at the main branch of Chase Manhattan Bank on Thursday July 2, but the bank refused. Instead, they agreed to cut two checks made out to the city finance department totaling $7,214.30, the cost of switching the mansion's title from Irene to the Atlantis Group. In return, according to the indictment, mother and son gave Chase another check for $8,000. Later that same day, the pair appeared at another Chase branch in lower Manhattan, claiming that the city finance department refused to accept the two checks. In that second branch, Kenny again posed as Guerrero while Sante hid behind a large hat and dark sunglasses.

Irene was unaware of all this plotting. However, she grew more suspicious of the new tenant and began keeping notes on him. She challenged him when he ducked the security cameras, and he mumbled something about not being in jail. Noticing his limp, Irene asked him if he had been brawling. She drew a picture of him with arrows to different parts of his body alongside comments that noted his limp and crooked nose, possibly broken in a fight. "He smelled like jail," she told her staffers. Her staff knew Manny Guerrin was hiding someone in his room because they heard a woman's voice telling them not to come in. They also spotted him on the security monitors hiding Sante and Jose from the camera. When the staff knocked on the entrance to Apartment 1B, a woman's voice answered at times, claiming to be Manny's secretary and refusing to open the door. Sometimes she just wouldn't answer the door or phone, and on at least one occasion she hid when a staff member managed to get inside Apartment 1B. When a maid found an antique smashed inside Apartment 1B, Irene asked her business manager to try to get rid of this tenant.

Never did Irene think the new tenant would get the best of her, but the whole ordeal seemed to fatigue her, said her friend and former tenant for five years, Isobella Kreizel. She visited Irene just three weeks before she disappeared and thought her old landlady looked tired. "She was very distressed and very worried," said Isobella. "She never said anything particularly. She was frail and was suddenly getting so old. She just said something about, it's a lot of work having the tenants, or something like that. Me, not knowing anything was wrong, I let it pass."

Investigators believe mother and son thought the lazy July Fourth weekend, when people were away, was the perfect time to try and take over the mansion. They began to assemble their own staff. Cuban immigrant Jose Alvarez had quit, so they needed other workers. Sante arranged for handyman Stan Patterson in Las Vegas to manage the town house. By this time authorities had squeezed Patterson for selling guns to the Kimeses, and he reluctantly agreed to secretly cooperate in trapping them. Unwittingly, Sante laid her own trap by phone. She bought Patterson a ticket on an America West red-eye from Las Vegas arriving in New York early Sunday morning, July 5. Calling herself "Ellie," Sante then telephoned a Salvation Army homeless shelter in Long

Island City, Queens, on Friday, July 3, and spoke with a hulking resident. She told this Vietnam War veteran, who towered nearly six-feet-six, that she wanted him to work as a superintendent for a high-rent building. In his Manny Guerrin tenant guise, Kenny asked one of Irene's staffers how many people would be working at the mansion on Sunday. For safekeeping, Sante put the notarized deed transferring the mansion to their corporation into a black canvas bag and checked it with a bellhop at the nearby Plaza Hotel at 59th Street and Fifth Avenue. When Sante met Patterson, she ordered him to fire all the employees at Irene's, evict the tenants, and take over the place, police said. Instead, he led her into the arms of the law.

CHAPTER 18

"What have we done?
What are we doing now?
What do we have to do?"

Detective Tommy Hovagim was just about to dig into a fine Italian meal delivered to the squad room at the 19th Precinct. Usually cops on the Upper East Side can bank on Sunday evenings in July being quiet. So Hovagim and Detectives Tommy Ryan and Tommy DiDomenico decided to treat themselves to spaghetti and meatballs, a side order of fried cala-mari, and dinner salad from Arturo's Restaurant on York Avenue. Each man threw down $12 to pay for the full-course feast, rare for guys who normally grabbed a slice of pizza on the run.

The rich neighborhood they cover empties out on summer weekends, especially over the July Fourth holiday, as people flee to the Hamptons, and other beach and mountain spots. Sunday, July 5, 1998 had been beautiful, with early morning clouds dissolving quickly. Temperatures reached a high of 82 degrees by mid-afternoon. Only a skeleton crew of three de-tectives was working the four p.m. to one a.m. shift that day. Twice that many detectives covered the 19th on a normal weekday. However, that Sunday, Hovagim was the only designated "catcher," the de-tective there to handle any new cases, while the other two Tommys concentrated on old burglaries. Like most other family men celebrating the holiday, Ho-vagim had been hosting a barbecue with his wife and friends earlier that day at his home in the suburbs of West Haverstraw, 40 miles north of Manhattan.

They were having such a good time, his wife Tracy even urged him to call in sick. "I can't, I'm the only one," he said.

Hovagim, 32, had never caught a murder case before, though he had assisted other detectives on homicides. Baby faced despite a black mustache, he had just earned his gold detective shield in January, following three years of investigative work as a patrol cop assigned to the squad. The son of an Armenian-American photo engraver, Hovagim had applied to the police department on a lark in 1984, and was surprised when they called him three years later.

And now, the young detective was about to catch one of Manhattan's all-time "heavies" or "capers," nicknames cops give high-profile cases weighted with attention from the bosses and the media. "The kind where you don't go home," Hovagim said.

It started with a routine notification from patrol cops who had visited 20 East 65th Street on a "missing elderly." Detectives don't automatically respond to missing-persons calls; however, the habits of Irene Silverman clashed with any notion that she had just walked away from her home of 41 years. A careful soul, she had refused to venture outside alone in 15 years, a precaution she insisted on after once falling on the sidewalk and fracturing her arm. Beyond some trouble with her eyes and arthritis, she was healthy, with no history of mental illness. Hearing all this from her worried maid and rental agent, the patrol cops immediately called the detectives.

"Aw, you know what, we should respond over there," Hovagim said. "It could be something." Ryan and DiDomenico drove the five blocks from the precinct to the mansion without Hovagim, because somebody had to stay in the squad room. Since most calls like this turn out to be false alarms, Hovagim left their food in the paper bags, optimistically figuring that the Tommys would return soon. "I'll wait to eat until you guys get back," Hovagim said.

The meal grew cold in the bags. "The next day it was still in the bags and a week later it was in the fridge and I ended up throwing it out," said Hovagim.

At the mansion, the detectives heard about the new tenant on the first floor, Manny Guerrin, who had been acting suspiciously. He hid his head from the security cameras and spied on everyone through his apartment-door peephole. Sometimes a mysterious Latino man walked in with Guerrin. The new tenant left the mansion in mid-afternoon after uncharacteristically asking the maid to clean his apartment. She refused because it was Sunday, and he left in a huff. By evening, he hadn't returned.

A search of the mansion and calls to area hospitals and morgues failed to turn up Irene. Their shift ending, the two other Tommys returned to the squad and Hovagim replaced them at the mansion, where he manned the phones all night. Behind Irene's desk in her first-floor office, he notified supervisors and checked with patrol cops, who found nothing in their canvass of the neighborhood. Irene's boxer Georgie had been her shadow. Now she wouldn't let Hovagim out of her sight, stirring from her chair anytime the detective moved.

Driving to work early Monday morning July 6, Deputy Inspector Joseph Reznick checked with the office on his cell phone, heard about the missing-person case, and headed straight to the Upper East Side. As Hovagim and the others filled him in, he asked his trademark questions, "What have we done? What are we doing now? What do we have to do?" The cops expanded the search for Irene and focused on Manny Guerrin, interviewing the mansion staff and calling around to Irene's friends to see if anyone knew this Guerrin. Reznick ordered his de-

tectives to take Irene's staff down to One Police Plaza
so a police artist could interview them and prepare
a sketch of Guerrin. At age 46, Reznick had spent 25
years, more than half his life, with the NYPD. As a
detective boss, he was the veteran of close to 700
murder investigations, and he always tried to visit
each crime scene. Taking in the polished marble
floors and art-filled rooms of Irene's mansion, "a lot
of questions were answered," he said. "Like, this is
the motive, at least we had a motive. Here it is."
What nobody yet knew was the role of the missing
tenant in what looked like a kidnapping or, worst
case scenario, a murder.

From his trimmed mustache to his silvery-gray
hair cropped close on the sides, but elevated an appropriate two inches on top, to his spotless white
shirts, Reznick looked neat. He liked order, hung
clipboards with crime statistics in neat rows on his
office walls, allowing his steel-blue eyes to quickly
find the most obscure piece of data from his region
in seconds. A workaholic, he was known to appear
at the office at 4:30 A.M. or on his days off. He said
he was catching up on paperwork, though his cynical
gumshoes felt he liked surprising them. Anything
that disrupted the steady progress of solving a case
drove him into fits of screaming. Slackers soon heard
the deep-throated voice, heavy with a classic New
York accent, call them on the carpet. Yet if somebody
succeeded, he would stride into the squad room and
say "nice job," on one of his six-to-eight trips to the
coffeemaker each day.

Mastering details served him well when chaos
rained down around him earlier in his police career.
From 1987 to 1993, he commanded the 34th precinct
detectives in Washington Heights. They worked more
murders than any other squad in an era when crack
ruled and drug dealers turned streets into shooting
galleries. Overseeing 587 homicide cases in the Do-

minican neighborhood underneath the George Washington Bridge was a homecoming for Reznick, the son of a maintenance man, whose heritage is Ukrainian and Czech. It was the same area the squad commander had patrolled as a rookie in 1974, his first assignment after training in the Police Academy.

Like most detectives, it was a new experience for Reznick to try solving a homicide without a body. One of his most wrenching cases before this was just the opposite—a body but little else. Baby Hope was the name his 34th precinct detectives gave an unidentified 25-pound girl found beaten, starved, sexually abused, bound, smothered and stuffed into a picnic cooler on July 23, 1991, off the Henry Hudson Parkway. Reznick, the married father of three sons, delivered her eulogy when his men bought the little girl a white dress and buried her two years later, still without a name. So far, she still doesn't have one.

He had paid his dues with a stint as a boss in the "rat squad," the nickname given the Internal Affairs Bureau, which investigates corrupt cops. Payback came in 1997, managing the 225 detectives in Manhattan North, as a deputy inspector. His detectives nicknamed him "D. I. Joe," but only the senior and best among them dared call him that to his face. In charge of solving all murders above 59th Street to the northern reaches of Manhattan, Reznick managed some huge cases before the Silverman mystery. His detectives deftly made arrests in the shooting of high school teacher Jonathan Levin, son of Time Warner CEO Gerald Levin, the throat-slashing of a Columbia University law student from Korea, and the slaying of a man gutted in the stomach and found floating in a lake in Central Park.

Monday July 6, 1998, brought nothing but dead ends when it came to finding Irene Silverman or Manny Guerrin. On her block, nobody saw anything suspicious that sleepy Sunday morning she disappeared. As had been the custom for the previous 16 years, about 100 homeless people lined up across the street at the giant limestone Temple Emanu-el for a free Sunday lunch. Two cross-town buses rumbled by on the eastbound one-way street every 20 minutes or so. Still there were no witnesses. Usually people sipped cappuccinos at five sidewalk tables right next door to Irene's, but the Terramare Café was closed for the holiday. Perhaps a tourist saw somebody leaving the mansion with a heavy duffel bag, but that could have looked like a person on his way to the beach or airport.

Reznick asked his supervisors for permission to hold a press conference that Monday evening to try and drum up leads. Displaying a police artist's sketch of Guerrin and a photograph of Irene, the inspector appealed to the public for help in solving the mystery. On his feet now for two days running, Hovagim looked bleary-eyed at the TV cameras during the press conference. He would finally get to go home for some rest that night. His spirits lifted when his partner, Tommy Hackett, the fourth and last Tommy in the 19th squad, swung back into work on Monday afternoon. "The place was buzzing," said Hackett, 36, who like his partner wears his hair neatly spiked, sports a mustache, and has soft brown eyes. "Oh, we had a caper," the others told him. "A missing old lady."

When Hackett arrived at four p.m., he planned to sleep that night on a cot in the back of the squad room because he was on a turnaround day. Due back at eight a.m. Tuesday, it didn't pay for him to drive two hours roundtrip to his home on the eastern end of Long Island after his evening shift ended at one a.m. At that hour, night-watch detectives manned the squad's phones in case the press conference generated any tips. Hackett told them to wake him if anything important happened.

The call came around six a.m. Tuesday. On the line was a sheepish member of the NYPD-FBI Joint Fugitive Task Force. There was a colossal screw-up. Since Sunday night, they had in custody a mother and son, alleged con artists suspected in a California murder, who were carrying Irene's personal papers. However, no one on the task force thought to check if Irene was okay that Sunday or even on Monday. It dawned on them that she was missing after hearing Reznick's press conference on the news and recognizing that Irene's name matched the paperwork the Kimeses had. Perhaps they dismissed the Kimeses as another state's problem. If the task force had checked on Irene, cops on the Upper East Side would have known right away that the mysterious tenant Manny Guerrin was Kenny Kimes. They might have been able to talk to him or figure out leads to Irene's whereabouts. That crucial two-day delay jinxed the search for Irene's body, detectives believe.

Hackett quickly bolted wide-awake hearing about the mother and son. Their arrest and link to Irene was the first and only break in the case. He beeped Reznick, who was headed to an early morning TV show to again publicize Irene's disappearance. Quickly canceling that interview, he ordered Hackett to rush down to 26 Federal Plaza and try and interrogate the Kimeses. Reznick, the man who loved order and precision, couldn't believe what had happened. In the following days the 65-foot long hallway from Reznick's Harlem office at Manhattan North Homicide to the squad room rocked with his screams whenever the subject of the Fugitive Task Force came up. Thank God, thought his detectives, it wasn't us.

Sante Kimes did not tell Hackett anything useful about Irene. Neither did Kenny. "I can't divulge (where Mrs. Silverman is), maybe after I speak to my lawyer," said Kenny when Hackett caught up with him in the holding pen in the Criminal Courts building the following afternoon. He was being held on the Utah warrant, which accused him and Sante of bouncing a check to pay for their Lincoln Town Car. Reznick ordered a flurry of search warrant applications for Kenny's clothes, his apartment at Irene's, and the pair's Lincoln Town Car. They ran a check on Sante's criminal history and talked with Los Angeles detectives about the slaying of David Kazdin.

Hovagim and Hackett spent 12 hours in the airless basement garage at FBI Headquarters, taking notes as the forensics experts from the Crime Scene Unit poured over the Kimeses' Lincoln Town Car. They dusted for prints on the car handles, steering wheel, windows, trunk, and roof, took impressions of the tire tracks, and collected fiber samples from the carpet. Finding what looked like a drop of blood on a rear-passenger seat belt, they cut out the strap and sent it to a lab for testing. In the glove compartment they found a microcassette recorder, presumably used to tape Irene's phone conversations. Covering the garage floor with tarp, they carefully opened up the plastic garbage bags jamming the back seat. The bags held clothes and a mountain of clues in the paperwork. Thirteen green, red, blue, and pink spiral notebooks were full of names, including the slain David Kazdin and Syed Bilal Ahmed, the missing banker from the Bahamas. The writings, the subject of a later court battle, detailed the real estate steps for transferring the mansion's title, aliases, notes about Irene, and names and social security numbers for Kimes employees. Cops photographed and cataloged each item, noting where they had been put in the car. Descriptions of the contents filled 115 police vouchers, each form able to list upward of a dozen items. At the mansion, cops discovered that Apart-

ment 1B, which Kenny had rented, had new dead-
bolt locks on the inside bedroom door. Ominously
littering the apartment were giant plastic garbage
bags, larger than the mansion staff used and big
enough for a body. A roll of duct tape lay in a garbage pail.

The evidence haul seemed to douse any hope that
Irene was still alive. Cops found a 9mm semiautomatic Glock pistol, ammunition, gun manuals, plastic handcuffs, the box and receipt for a stun gun, an
aerosol canister of Qualco-brand hot pepper spray,
syringes, a moldy jar with three milliliters of the
sedative flunitrazepam, nicknamed the "date rape"
drug, brass knuckles, and a knife. Another telling
piece of the puzzle was a "to do" list in which the
Kimeses mixed groceries with more chilling items.
It included skim milk, shower curtain, stun gun,
ropes, tape, batteries, cell phone, garbage bags, "a
good area for parking," water, socks, orange juice,
eggs, blanket, and an abbreviation police believed
meant chloroform, the colorless liquid that can
knock you out.

Cops had to wade through a Niagara Falls of paperwork, investigate a coast-to-coast trail of alleged
scams and other missing or dead persons, and find
a corpse that vanished off the face of the earth. This
was shaping up to be one of the most complex murder investigations ever in Manhattan. Reznick picked
his best detectives and called them the Silver Task
Force, drawing upon a core of 17 and supplementing
the ranks when needed from the borough's 22 other
squads. The priorities were finding Irene's body and
amassing a circumstantial case from the avalanche of
paperwork the Kimeses had left behind.

Cops were having no luck searching for Irene's
body. Cadaver dogs, specially trained to sniff for
bodies, couldn't find her among the five stories of
her mansion. Police then combed Central Park, just

a block away. Searchers even knocked down a brick wall in the basement of 3 East 65th Street, where Kenny had tried to rent office space, after the spooked landlady couldn't remember when the wall was erected. They tore through construction sites around the corner and down the street.

As for New Jersey, cops figured on three hours' driving time round-trip from New York and started combing all highways in that radius. State troopers helped search rest stops along the Garden State Parkway. Irene owned six acres of land in Mt. Olive, New Jersey, and cops searched there also. They looked through swamps in the Meadowlands, the traditional dumping spot for mob killings. A vacationing factory worker in New Jersey, away from all the headlines when the Silverman case first broke, contacted cops early in July. He remembered seeing a woman and man in a Lincoln Town Car parked by Berry's Creek in Carlstadt, New Jersey, on July 1 or 2. When a police dog named Boris turned up a bag of social security cards in these swamps near Giants' Stadium, scuba divers then searched for Irene. It was a false alarm. A parking receipt indicated that the Kimes car was in a Manhattan garage on the dates when the factory worker saw the Lincoln. And authorities said it was common to find bogus documents in this area, located near an industrial complex.

Other tips took cops from the cliffs of the Palisades to parking lots at Newark Airport. They also searched near LaGuardia and John F. Kennedy airports in Queens, just to cover all bases. Tracing the path of commerical garbage collected from the Upper East Side, cops inspected a block-long conveyor belt in Pennsylvania, hoping a worker might have noticed something unusual. On a tip, they combed through a recycling plant in the South Bronx only to discover body parts of another murder victim, a Hispanic woman in her 40s. Searchers used an array of equipment, from sophisticated infrared plane sensors that detect heat from decaying flesh to tools as commonplace as weed whackers that cut away brush.

The chronology of that July 5 day left only a short time to dump a body without leaving a trace. Less than three hours elapsed from the moment Kenny last called Irene's maid in the mansion around 2:30 P.M. and Sante appeared at the Hilton Hotel to meet Stan Patterson at 5:00 P.M. Cops believe Kenny and Sante split up for several hours that afternoon. He rejoined his mother at the Sixth Avenue Street fair shortly before 7:00 P.M., after parking the Lincoln Town Car in a garage about 12 blocks from the Hilton. Sante told Patterson, she'd be at the hotel by noon, then arrived five hours later. When she called Patterson, claiming to be stuck on New Jersey's Garden State Parkway, the cell phone relay stations indicated she was in Manhattan during that conversation. Investigators aren't sure if the pair even crossed the Hudson River into New Jersey that day.

Easily overpowered, Irene was either knocked unconscious or killed immediately, detectives theorize, bound with duct tape and wrapped in one of the giant-sized plastic garbage bags found in Apartment 1B. From there she was either stuffed into a car trunk or carried out. Digging a grave seemed unlikely, since there was little time and it would attract attention in daytime. No dirt was found on either suspect or in the car. The leading theory is that the killer threw Irene's body into a Dumpster on the Upper East Side, it got mixed in with the rest of the industrial garbage and shipped to a processing plant in Pennsylvania or Ohio. Another possibility is that her body was dumped in marshland somewhere in New Jersey. Somehow, if the cops are correct, the Kimeses, newcomers to the tri-state area, apparently managed to hide Irene's remains forever.

The people who handled Irene's financial affairs believed she was gone forever. Just nine days after she vanished, the executor of her 1996 will filed papers in Surrogate's Court to declare her an "absentee" and protect her $9 million estate in the likely event she was dead. Under New York State law, a missing person can be declared legally deceased after three years. To oversee her estate, the court appointed The Bank of New York, where Irene had accounts since the 1970s. Valued at $7.5 million, her town house represented the bulk of her fortune. Her land in Mount Olive was worth $83,100. The bank listed her other assets: a lease in Maui, Hawaii valued at $753,000; a temporary administration account totaling $204,448.11; municipal bond holdings reaching $343,595.25; and jewelry and furnishings appraised at $530,000. Her principal outstanding debt, beyond the cost of running the town house, was a personal loan for $240,000.

She willed all her assets to the Coby Foundation, but failed to specify her dream that the museum be housed in the town house. Following the letter of her will, the bank took over the town house, fired all but one member of the staff, phased out the apartment rentals, and installed a new security system. According to the surrogate papers, "the bank is carefully watching the real estate market to decide the most advantageous time, if any, for sale of the property." The bank planned to first sell the New Jersey and Hawaii properties to support the estimated $100,000 annual cost of maintaining the mansion.

As the search for Irene grew more fruitless, detectives focused on assembling the circumstantial case. They had a threefold mission: build a case against the mother and son, disprove that anybody else could be the killers, and establish Irene's schedule and habits to show foul play as the only reason for her disappearance. Reznick divided up the areas: one team on the Kimeses' finances, another tracing all their car and vehicle registrations, a third tracking down their employees, many of them homeless drifters with minor criminal records. Cops found about 30 of these people, checking their alibis to make sure they weren't in Manhattan when Irene vanished. "We found almost everybody who's ever been connected with the Kimeses," said Detective Danny Rodriguez. "They had a knack for picking people who were very gullible and who were very easily misled."

Tracking former Kimes employees gave a big break to Los Angeles cops investigating David Kazdin's slaying. When they arrived in New York to try and question the Kimeses, the pair stayed silent but their habit of writing everything down spoke for them. The notebooks led cops to drifter Sean Little, whose testimony was crucial to a later indictment against mother and son. He reportedly told Los Angeles detectives that he drove with Kenny to Kazdin's Granada Hills home early the morning of March 13, 1998. Told to wait in the car, he heard a single shot from inside the house after Kenny had entered. He claimed that Kenny then called him over, explained he had a problem with the guy, and asked for help in moving his body. Little said he and Kenny stuffed Kazdin's body into the trunk of his green Jaguar and drove toward Los Angeles International Airport.

LAPD now had a witness and a body, making their case arguably stronger than the groundbreaking hurdle New York faced. Manhattan District Attorney Robert Morgenthau, at 78 a wily veteran, was not about to relinquish the Kimeses. Mother and son would stay in the Big Apple and face trial on Irene Silverman. After that verdict, Los Angeles was expected to try them for Kazdin's slaying. By then it would probably be more than two years after he died. LAPD detectives grumbled privately about the delay, but Los Angeles District Attorney Gil Garcetti, who lost the O.J. Simpson murder trial, deferred to Morgenthau.

A huge stumbling block in the beginning of the New York investigation was the identity of the Latino man seen sneaking into the mansion. As a missing link, he could be an accomplice to murder or a valuable witness. If he wasn't found, the defense could always use his presence in the mansion to suggest he killed Irene, not their clients. That July, finding this man was imperative.

The job fell to veteran detectives John Schlagler, a white-haired bear of a man, and Danny Rodriguez, his courtly partner. Together since 1985, each had attained the rank of first-grade, the top pay and prestige bestowed on just 148 of the city's 5,704 detectives. A demolition expert in the Vietnam War, Schlagler worked in the police department's bomb squad from 1972 to 1982, before they used protective bodysuits, in the days when each man, as Schlagler said, "relied on sharp knives and a pair of balls." Twice Schlagler earned the department's Medal of Valor, the highest honor for acts of bravery where the cop emerges in one piece. He defused a pipe bomb on the 19th floor of a Soviet trading company in midtown in 1976. Six years later on a Sunday morning, he removed a ticking gasoline explosive left across the street from thousands of worshipers at St. Patrick's Cathedral. Rodriguez also survived a different kind of danger. He risked his life for five years in deep undercover on antiterrorist work, even posing as a drug dealer and getting arrested in a sting. He helped run surveillance on bomb throwers in the Jewish Defense League, the Weathermen, and the Puerto Rican separatist group, FALN, which stands for Fuerzas Armadas de Liberacion Nacional.

The two men had bonded like brothers by the time of the Silverman case. Schlagler, 50, was the mischievous one, quick to arch a bushy eyebrow and make a crack he really didn't mean. Rodriguez, 52, was the gentleman with the soothing voice, able to coax favors and open doors. With his memory for numbers, Schlagler would have made a good bookie. Rodriguez never forgot a face. Schlagler was a master at calling cold on the phone and coming away with reams of information. Rodriguez excelled at face-to-face meetings, making informants and contacts in other police departments. In the squad, they joke that the steady Rodriguez is headed straight to heaven for dealing with the flamboyant Schlagler. Typically, Schlagler bursts into work with his Brooks Brothers tie undone, itching for the first of the 40 Benson and Hedges he smokes a day. Rodriguez arrives with every hair in place. When both get ready to hit the street, Rodriguez announces, "Okay, son, make your tie," Schlagler complies, and both grandfathers head for the door.

Over 13 years, they caught hundreds of killers, from the seven-foot father who shushed his crying baby to death by placing his oversized hand over the child's mouth, to the robbers who used a hammer to bludgeon two elderly sisters who had survived the Holocaust, killing one. Using Rodriguez's law enforcement contacts, the pair stopped a plane at Santo Domingo airport in the Dominican Republic in 1993 that was carrying a man wearing Bermuda shorts and posing as a tourist. Actually, he had tossed a bomb into a fire truck in Washington Heights, injuring three firefighters. When Rodriguez and a sergeant flew down, all they had to do was put the guy on the next plane back to New York.

The partners became experts at interrogation, with Schlagler pretending not to understand the perps and getting them to offer damning explanations and Rodriguez soothing them into believing they should "do the right thing" and confess. They alternate these good-cop-bad-cop roles. Born in Puerto Rico and fluent in Spanish, Rodriguez, son of a merchant seaman, sometimes played the heavy with Latino perps or let Schlagler, whose father was a cop, use his size to swagger like Numero Uno. Few detectives can top them when it comes to finding someone.

Locating the mysterious Latino man, in a metropolitan area with an estimated Hispanic population of almost three million, was a challenge worthy of this pair. Tracing cell phone records, cops found notary Don Aoki and checked out the Plaza Athenee, his rendezvous site with Mr. Win, actually Kenny. A hotel bartender remembered Sante and the mysterious Latino man downing beers at the bar on the Sunday of the Puerto Rican Day Parade. The bartender, a Dominican, recognized the mystery man's accent as Cuban. Figuring that a foreigner new to the area would seek out his countrymen, Rodriguez suggested they comb through the Cuban enclaves of Union City, New Jersey. They visited restaurants, homeless shelters, bars, and police throughout the city, passing around flyers with a sketch based on a description from the bartender and the mansion staff. For the first few weeks, they had no luck. But their hunch about Union City would prove right.

Reznick was hungry for somebody's idea to pay off. Forensics tests were going as badly as the body search. There were 20 red spots on the sidewalk outside the mansion that appeared to the lab technicians to be human blood, but were too small for comparison. Detectives don't believe these stains are linked to the case, since they were noticed the day after Irene vanished. It's possible but unlikely that all those cops and worried staffers trooping in and out of the mansion the first evening failed to spot the sidewalk stains. The Lincoln Town Car was a wealth of paperwork but full of forensic dead ends; hair on a peach comforter and a black duffel bag and a saliva stain on a pillow did not match samples taken from Irene's hair and toothbrushes. A speck of blood on a rear passenger seat belt strap turned out to be from a man, based on tests that can identify genetic markers. It did not match Kazdin's blood. Cops cut away part of the bathroom wall in Apartment 1B thinking that reddish-brown splatter marks were bloodstains. They turned out to be nail polish.

The lack of progress on the case made the top brass in the police department crazy. Chief of Detectives William Allee had to listen to Police Commissioner Howard Safir ask him about Irene at every staff meeting. Reporters from as far away as Australia were calling about the case. While New York City in 1998 enjoyed worldwide renown for taming crime, becoming the safest large city in America, it still didn't look good not being able to find a frail old lady. "It was massive frustration," said Reznick. "You find yourself thinking about this case like 24 hours a day. Your wife could be talking to you, and you'll turn around and you'll be off on Cloud Nine and it's not Cloud Nine. You're thinking about Irene Silverman, where she could be. Where is this deed? We knew things had happened, but we were just missing the evidence."

Cops suspected that a deed existed which transferred Irene's mansion to the mother and son. If found, it would be the first direct link between the Kimeses and the presumed scheme to take over the mansion. From Stan Patterson, cops knew the Kimeses coveted Irene's $7 million home. From notary Don Aoki, detectives also knew that the pair had some kind of real estate document. Detectives searched city real estate records, fishing for any kind of recent transaction concerning Irene's property. They looked through mail and paperwork at the city's Department of Finance figuring mother and son sent in a document, recording the mansion's title transfer. Nothing turned up. The deed was the final act in their alleged plot and proof of a swindle, more valuable than the mountain of paperwork the detectives had recovered from the Kimeses. Reznick knew it had to be out there somewhere.

Cops almost recovered it early on in the probe. When the Silverman case first broke, Reznick telephoned retired NYPD captain Sal Blando, head of security for the Plaza Hotel. The inspector wanted help in identifying a scrap of paper the Kimeses had containing a number and the word "Plaza." However, for some reason, nobody at the hotel could trace it. Striking out at the Plaza, Reznick sent detectives to about 100 hotels in Manhattan, showing the Kimeses' pictures and hoping to turn up property they might have left behind. "It was a race to find something to connect these Kimeses to Mrs. Silverman, other than they were living there," said Rodriguez. "In the beginning we were looking for hotel rooms that maybe we thought the Kimeses stayed in. Maybe they left a bag there or some evidence. At the beginning we really didn't know that Sante was staying at the Silverman mansion. So we started looking around. We figured, now she's in jail, she didn't know she was going to be locked up, she didn't have a chance to go back. Where is her luggage?"

The Plaza Hotel people were wrong. Sante had been there. On Sunday, July 5, she had checked a black canvas bag with a bellhop at the four-star hotel. He secured it behind a red-carpeted door in a first-floor storage room. Only guests are supposed to check bags at the Plaza, but the staff doesn't want to risk insulting their wealthy customers by asking for identification or a room key. So, in effect, anyone who dresses decently can leave a bag there.

Under pressure and frustrated after 16 days of running down dead ends, Reznick again decided to go to the press. Without specifically mentioning the deed, Reznick asked area hotels to check for unclaimed property the Kimeses may have left behind. Displaying two keys at this press conference on July 21, 1998, he also asked for the public's help in matching them to the post office boxes the Kimeses were believed to have rented. He revealed that a witness remembered seeing a Ford Crown Victoria with the words "Columbia Ambulette" on its rear door parked near the Silverman town house the afternoon of July 5. Cops ran every possible combination of that name and found no ambulance service or any other company that fit. The inspector appealed for help identifying the Spanish-speaking man who had become the obsession of Rodriguez and Schlagler.

Word apparently reached the Rose M. Singer Center for women prisoners at the Riker's Island Correctional Facility. There, Sante was sweating over the black bag in the Plaza, police believe. For days, she had been urging her lawyer's private detective, Lawrence Frost, to pick up the bag in the hotel. The day after Reznick's press conference hit the papers, Frost retrieved the bag from the Plaza's check room. He approached a Plaza bellhop and said he wanted to pick up a bag for a client, without identifying who they were. The bellhop contacted a security guard, who turned over the black bag after Frost signed a release form. Blando learned about this just five minutes after the guard gave Frost the bag, and the retired captain immediately thought it could be linked to the Kimeses. He ran outside looking for the private eye but just missed him. Blando called Reznick, who quickly ordered all his detectives to find Frost. "Everyone flew out of the room," said Hovagim. If not for Blando, Sante might have pulled off a trick worthy of Houdini: fooling the entire NYPD even after she'd been handcuffed.

The sought-after deed was inside the bag, along with other paperwork. Irene's friends and the cops doubted that she willingly signed over her beloved home to a mysterious company called Atlantis Group Limited. Tracing the firm to Antigua, where it was chartered in January 1998, prosecutors charged that it was a dummy corporation, controlled by the Kimeses. Forensic document examiner John Paul Osborn, working for the prosecution, then compared Irene's name on these real estate papers with her genuine signature on 22 of her bank checks, dated June 16 to June 30, 1998. Osborn found that Silverman's name was forged on six documents recovered from the Kimeses, including a residential property transfer, a tax return for the mansion's switch to Atlantis, a general power of attorney form, and a social security card. "These imitations were produced by means of tracing and, in some cases, tracing using a carbon outline," said his report to prosecutors. He discovered carbon lines underneath the writing ink on certain questioned signatures and "clear evidence of a slow and laborious" script, different from Irene's natural flowing signature. Most of the fakes looked like they were copied from Irene's real signature on the rental receipt that Manny Guerrin, alias Kenny Kimes, had requested.

The bag from the Plaza Hotel gave the cops other leads. It contained a loaded .22 caliber Baretta pistol, purchased after Kazdin's murder, plastic handcuffs, hypodermic syringes, two fright masks from the movie *Scream*, a woman's white turban, cosmetics, and more notebooks. In a huge break for Schlagler and Rodriguez, one of those notebooks held the name, date of birth, and social security number for the missing link. He was Jose Antonio Alvarez, the former short-order cook from Florida working as a driver and handyman for the Kimeses. The Plaza Athenee bartender was right, the guy was Cuban,

Rodriguez confirmed in a phone call to Alvarez's family in Belle Glade, Florida. He had lived in a trailer in the depressed town about 40 miles southwest of ritzy Palm Beach. Alvarez, who could barely write his name, had a falling out with his family when he quit working in his father's one-truck hauling business and left behind an unpaid pile of parking tickets. He had no criminal record. Rodriguez told the Alvarez family he was concerned about the young man, given the Kimeses' track record, and urged them to call if he surfaced. There were no signs of him for three weeks, so Reznick again went to the media in mid-August, displaying Alvarez's photo and asking the public's help in finding him.

Late in the afternoon of Saturday, August 22, 1998, the call came while Schlagler and Rodriguez were driving the streets of Union City looking for Alvarez. He had finally returned home after bumming around Miami, working as a car washer and construction hand. Heeding Rodriguez's plea, his stepmother brought him to the Belle Glade police station and called New York. Schlagler and Rodriguez grabbed the first plane south and headed smack into the fury wrought by Hurricane Bonnie, lumbering off the South Florida coast. Pumped up, they didn't care about the weather. "Bam, we were excited," said Rodriguez. "We thought, we got it, we'll break this guy's story and he'll tell us the whole thing."

Landing in West Palm Beach around 11 P.M., it took them almost three hours to cover the 40 miles to Belle Glade. They were barely able to see past the windshield wipers flipping madly back and forth in the "worst thunderstorm I've even seen," said Schlagler. Drenched, they walked into the one-story brick station house, trying to look nonchalant. They found Alvarez to be a friendly young man, honestly puzzled by all the fuss over him. He answered all the questions Rodriguez had. Alvarez claimed the

Kimeses wouldn't pay him, so he left them in late June—almost two weeks before Irene vanished. "I was just working for them," he said. He sounded believable.

Rodriguez did the interview in Spanish and kept giving Schlagler updates. "John, the guy is very straightforward, he's not trying to hide anything," Rodriguez told his partner. After about twenty minutes, both detectives realized the Cuban didn't know what had happened to Irene. "He's not going to be able to help us with the murder," Rodriguez told Reznick. However, by finding Alvarez, the cops eliminated the possibility that the defense could blame him for Irene's fate. "Thank God he wasn't part of it, because, down the road, we figured if we couldn't find this Jose, the defense would say Jose killed Irene," said Schlagler.

Cops grew to consider him one of the many lost souls the Kimeses used. He spent only about a week in the mansion. Not knowing anyone in New York, he slept in Central Park the first two nights after he left the Kimeses. Bumping into Kenny on the Upper East Side, Alvarez stuck to his guns and refused to return to Irene's. Instead, as Rodriguez initially guessed, Alvarez sought out fellow Cubans in Union City. At a bank in nearby Hoboken, he cashed an old paycheck for $244.04 on June 23, 1998, and boarded a bus to Miami the same day. His alibi was tight, confirmed by the check and the bus ticket. While not a witness to Irene's disappearance, he proved valuable in confirming details of the mother and son's alleged spying inside the mansion. Also he placed Sante Kimes in the mansion, living there in secret and posing as a secretary to Manny Guerrin alias Kenny. Alvarez also raised the detectives' hopes when he said Kenny casually pointed out a good place to dump a body as they drove in June past desolate marshland near a New Jersey cemetery. Fanning out in grid formation, using body-sniffing dogs, police searched the weeds near St. Peter's Cemetery on Route 1 and 9 in Jersey City. All they found was a garbage bag filled with chicken bones.

Nothing in Reznick's career, or in the experience of veterans like Schlagler and Rodriguez, approached the scope of the Kimes case. Detectives pursuing a standard homicide, one with a body, witnesses, forensic evidence, and perhaps a confession, usually type 30 to 40 hot-pink forms, called DD5s, detailing their interviews. The Silver Task Force amassed more than 800 DD5s. They traced the Kimeses' path in Manhattan, traveled to Las Vegas, Los Angeles, the Bahamas, Antigua, Louisiana, and Florida, running down leads and interviewing more than 400 people. Not fully computerized, the cops kept track of all these people with an index-card file. Each card contained a contact's name, cross-referenced to the appropriate DD5. Reznick also converted an eight-by-eight-foot office space into the "Kimes war room," filling it with charts, maps, and pictures of key dates and people in the probe.

Mulling over Sante's exploits, the detectives couldn't believe how audacious her alleged plot seemed, how hard it would be in New York City to simply take over a building of tenants with a nine-person staff. Also, it was nervy that the Kimeses left an obvious paper trail. Detectives thought mother and son were poised to leave Manhattan in early July. They speculated that the pair planned to try and get a mortgage with the mansion deed—a repeat of the scam using Kazdin's name on the Las Vegas home. But how could mother and son believe this ruse would work a second time, especially with West Coast authorities now looking for them? Common sense didn't always apply here. Trying to get his detectives to think creatively, Reznick posted a quote about Sante that

Linda Kimes told *Newsday*. It became the unofficial motto of the Silver Task Force.

"You cannot approach this from logic. You have to approach this from the most wild depths of your imagination."

Chapter 19

"As God Is My Witness."

As Reznick and crew plugged away, lawyers for the mother and son proclaimed their innocence far and wide, accused the police of brutality, and bad-mouthed Irene. Sante claimed cops and federal agents beat her with a telephone book. "She said they did it in a way so it would not leave marks," said her attorney, Jose Muniz, on July 9 after a court hearing. An FBI spokesman called the charges lies.

Banging on Irene's front door on July 13, another Kimes lawyer demanded to be let inside to collect Kenny's belongings. He called Irene a crotchety old lady who alienated her staff. This move, just eight days after Irene vanished, suggested a defense strategy of blaming the victim, as well as others, for her presumed demise. "She's a tough lady, she treats her help very abruptly, she's hard on her employees," said Matthew Weissman a lawyer who, after a decade of specializing in real estate, expanded his practice to include criminal cases. The Kimeses were his first big-time criminal clients.

"She has a lot of arguments with them," Weissman said about Irene's relationship with her employees. "She's not the lovely eccentric old lady who's devoted to the arts and other things." Muniz added, "Sante Kimes' position is that there may be others involved. Mrs. Silverman had her own life." Egged on by a TV reporter, Weissman pounded on Irene's door so he could go inside and recover evidence to prove his clients' innocence. Nobody answered his knocks.

The lawyers also publicly named informant Stan Patterson that day, maintaining that the 9mm Glock and ammunition found in the Kimeses' car belonged to the hapless pizza deliveryman. They also claimed Patterson knew David Kazdin. The two men traveled in different circles; none of Kazdin's friends had ever heard of him before, and the LAPD did not consider him a murder suspect. "They gambled together in Las Vegas," said Weissman, "and whether the FBI put the heat on him and he found it appropriate or adept to pass the buck to our clients, we'll find out down the line."

In court hearings that began that summer and rolled into the spring of 1999, mother and son failed in 15 attempts to be released on bail. A tip from a courthouse acquaintance brought Muniz, 41, to the case initially and he asked his friend Weissman, 40, for help. Muniz, a civil rights and criminal defense lawyer, had never handled a case as complex as this one. From rough beginnings on the Lower East Side—his father overdosed on heroin when he was eight, and his older sister was murdered—Muniz had graduated with an award in oratory from New York Law School. Practicing law since 1986, he had represented poor clients for two-and-a-half years at Bronx Legal Services and went on to win a $1.3 million civil judgment for a man Harlem cops had wrongfully arrested.

By the time mother and son had their first court hearing together, Muniz had recruited a more seasoned hand, attorney Mel Sachs, who rarely said something in two minutes when he could stretch it to five. Sachs, 52, loved words, pronounced them slowly, repeated them for emphasis, and had gained a reputation for storytelling that swayed juries. He began coining phrases to deride the case against the

Kimeses, likening it to "building a house from the roof down, without a foundation." Like Sante, Sachs, a trial lawyer since 1972, believed in the importance of image and displayed a flair for theatrics. His gray hair combed back, he looked like a turn-of-the-century barrister wearing his button-down vests, pocket watch on a chain, bow tie, crisp white pocket square, polished cuff links, and custom-made suits. A practicing magician since the age of eight, Sachs loved to perform. A collage filling a wall in his waiting room shows a circus scene with Sachs in a white suit pulling a rabbit from a hat. He once kept a crowd of reporters waiting while he made cigarettes, coins, and pens vanish and reappear from his ear, nose, and sleeve, to the delight of five-year-old Sarah Ross, daughter of *Daily News* court reporter Barbara Ross. "I wonder if his clients did the same with Irene," cracked an onlooker.

His heavyweight clients included billionaire art dealer Alec Wildenstein, accused in 1997 of pulling a gun on his estranged wife when she caught him in bed with another woman. Wildenstein went abroad and the menacing charge against him is pending. Sachs represented magician David Copperfield on contracts and advised civil rights leader Roy Innis, head of the Congress of Racial Equality. However, the Silverman case was Sachs' first that attracted national and international attention. He represented Kenny while Muniz stayed with Sante.

Sachs recruited private investigator Les Levine, another man who cut a memorable figure. At six-feet-two and 225 pounds, Levine looked like a bearded linebacker and drove a white Jaguar with vanity plates that proclaimed "LES PI." Known for digging up dirt on his clients' enemies, Levine helped sportscaster Marv Albert fight sexual-abuse charges in Virginia for biting a woman in the back and handled the Wildenstein case for Sachs. He also worked for

Brooklyn cop Justin Volpe, who later admitted to sodomizing Haitian immigrant Abner Louima with a stick. When he took on the Kimes case in 1998, Levine's high profile led to revelations about his own trouble with the law. He had pleaded guilty in 1989 to bribery for his efforts trying to find a federal witness in a drug trafficking case against his client, a reputed Gambino crime family associate. The Silverman prosecutors would use this conviction in a failed bid to exclude Levine from a defense trip to Irene's mansion on April 28, 1999. Prosecutors also cited his background in arguing against turning over personal information about witnesses. From the start, Levine suggested unnamed others were responsible for Irene's fate. "It's not uncommon for law enforcement to focus on one or two suspects and perhaps ignore other facts," said Levine about the Silverman case. "We might have to find out what happened to Mrs. Silverman. You don't get to be 82 without making a couple of enemies." In the search for other suspects, he said the defense would travel to Los Angeles, Las Vegas, and the Caribbean.

Worldwide, the Kimes case made headlines. From the mystery of Irene's disappearance, to the cold-blooded planning apparently behind her murder to the other people who died or disappeared around the mother and son, the story grew like a Chia pet. Coincidences piled up—too many, it seemed. It was a case of reality outdoing whodunits, said Scott Burns, the Utah prosecutor who brought the bounced-check charges. "It's a Grisham novel," he said. "Twenty different players and five different plots, and the only different thing is this one's real."

Both NBC's *Dateline* and ABC's *20-20* rushed to be first with an extended program on the Kimeses, but neither landed an interview with them. Both programs ended up airing their pieces at the same time, July 17 at 10:00 P.M. Also at that moment New York investigative reporter Jonathan Dienst of WPIX Channel 11 broadcast a scoop, the first live pictures of Sante.

Climbing to the rooftop of a Chinese rooming house behind the Manhattan Criminal Court building, Dienst and photographer Dave Tewes waited in the rain for two hours that day in hopes of catching Sante as guards escorted her back to jail. New York courtrooms ban cameras, so beyond unflattering mug shots, the public hadn't seen Sante's face. Stepping over pigeon bones and trying not to choke on the smell of burned cabbage, Dienst weathered the rain, more worried that TV helicopters hovering above the nearby Brooklyn Bridge covering a traffic tie-up would spot him from the air and blow his exclusive. His patience paid off, as Tewes became the first to film Sante, surrounded by jail guards as she carried a manila envelope with legal papers. She looked like an overwhelmed suburban grandmother. Her dyed jet-black hair arranged in a messy bun, she wore black sweatpants and a top decorated with a pastel bow and a burst of pink and lime-green flowers.

Dienst had been in the courtroom that July afternoon when Kenny and Sante first appeared together in court. Judge Arlene Silverman (no relation to Irene) heard bail arguments on the Utah rubber-check case, the only charge against mother and son at that point. Defense and prosecution presented sweet-and-sour images of the pair—churchgoing do-gooders with a soft spot for children and old folks versus grifters who've left a coast-to-coast trail of scams, arsons, and missing people. Sachs compared Kenny to Richard Jewel, the vindicated suspect in the 1996 Atlanta Olympic bombings. The lawyer extolled Kenny as a high school honor student who attended the University of California at Santa Barbara, worked as an intern for Merrill Lynch, became an "Internet design specialist," and created a Web page called cigarbiz.com. He also found time to volunteer in a hospice and care for the elderly and terminally ill for two years, Sachs said. Muniz described Sante as a widow who, suffering from arthritis, still volunteered for the Salvation Army. She hoped to turn her hobby of writing children's books into a professional career. "She's someone like her son, who's religious," Muniz said. "They have attended St. Patrick's here in New York, where they go to light candles for her deceased husband." Muniz described her slavery conviction as "an immigration matter," adding "there was no violence whatsoever, Your Honor," apparently unaware of the steaming iron Sante had pressed against the hand of maid Maribel Ramirez Cruz 14 years before. Sachs brushed aside the Utah bounced-check charge as merely consumers stopping payment for a defective car.

Assistant District Attorney Carmen Morales shot back, "Your Honor, the defense attorneys would like to portray these two individuals as a choirboy and typical housewife. That is not the case here." Prosecutors guaranteed that mother and son would disappear if granted bail, pointing out Sante's 37-year criminal record and habit of using aliases. Mother and son have shaky community ties, carry around other people's identification, and have resources overseas, prosecutors warned. One of their addresses was a post office box. Another was the Las Vegas home burned in an arson fire linked to the scam that reportedly got David Kazdin killed. "We believe that the source of their money is from out of the country," said Assistant District Attorney John Carter. "We believe they have a lot of money out of the country." In denying bail, Judge Silverman said, "It is no secret that these defendants are under investigation for some rather serious crimes."

Their handholding throughout this 90-minute hearing raised eyebrows in the courtroom packed with reporters and spectators. Sachs later defended their display of affection. "I don't think that the holding of hands shows anything other than a deep abiding love that they have for one another in a situation that they found themselves in," he said.

In her years as a model, official greeter in Sacramento, Washington lobbyist, and millionaire's companion, Sante fussed over her clothes and makeup. Image had always been important to her. Slapping on mascara and foundation, emphasizing her ample bust, wearing beehive wigs, she went whole hog for a brunette Dolly Parton look. She certainly didn't see herself as the frumpy woman captured by Jonathan Dienst's camera or in sketches by courtroom artists. So for her next court appearance on August, 5, 1998, exactly a month after Irene vanished, Sante walked in with full makeup, her hair pinned up, and wearing a fitted jacket instead of bulky sweats. She had wanted to hide her hair under a white turban Muniz bought her, but claimed the guards wouldn't give it to her. The first words she spoke in public were about her appearance, whispering to the courtroom sketch artists to make her look nice. "I'm innocent. My son's innocent. Would it help you if I turned around?" Holding her head high, she then clearly echoed Kenny's "not guilty" as they were arraigned on 17 fraud counts for allegedly using Palm Beach attorney Max Schorr's name to get and use a bogus MasterCard. Outside court, artist Christine Cornell told reporter Dienst that Sante's appeal did get her a more flattering portrait. "I'm looking at her, and I'm thinking, yeah, she's got some warmth to her face," said Cornell. "I did give a little more heart to it, a little more gentleness to her, and she looked better."

"Did she con you?" Dienst asked.

"I'm told she did, and if she did, she's good," Cornell replied.

It was the first of three consecutive days of theatrical court hearings where the Kimeses shattered courtroom decorum by speaking in place of their attorneys, holding hands, touching each other's shoulders and back, waving to journalists, and chatting with courtroom artists. On August 6, Kenny provided the color. Ironically, he walked in carrying the best-seller about a climb of Mt. Everest titled *Into Thin Air*, an apt description of Irene's fate. He schmoozed with the courtroom artists, complimenting them on their work and saying he had ambitions of becoming a painter. "He seemed like a very nice guy, very charming," said sketch artist Jane Rosenberg, who added that Sante "was looking adoringly at her son the whole time." The defense attorneys failed again with bail arguments. "This case cries out—calls out—for remand," said Judge Herbert Adlerberg on Friday, August 7. "These two are drifters and grifters, probably hitting every state in the union. The female defendant has used 23 different names." Sachs derided the fraud charges as minor offenses that would merit bail for anyone except the Kimeses. The system unfairly kept them in preventive detention, trampling their constitutional rights while prosecutors gunned for murder charges, Sachs argued.

Sante also personally spread her message, giving her first interview August 23, in several telephone calls from her jail cell to the home of *New York Post* celebrity columnist Cindy Adams. Breaking into tears and begging for understanding, Sante said she and her son were innocent. Twice she claimed solidarity with "every mother in the world" suffering for their child. In an unusual admission, since she never formally rented an apartment at Irene's, Sante claimed to be fond of the former ballerina and often shared a morning cup of coffee with her.

Sante again played to the courtroom crowd at her next hearing on November 25, 1998, before Acting

Supreme Court Justice Herbert I. Altman. By lottery this judge, a no-nonsense type, was now permanently assigned to their cases. Like the other judges before him, Altman rejected yet another request for bail. "I just wish we had a chance to prove our innocence," Sante said before the hearing. "We're being framed. We're so innocent." Her attorney complained that prosecutors were trying to plant jailhouse snitches on mother and son. He charged that authorities pulled more than 30 inmates from their cells, promising them money or plea bargains if they spied on the Kimeses. "They are making all the efforts they can to get evidence which they don't have," Sachs said. "They don't have a body. They don't have eyewitnesses. They don't have forensic evidence. They don't have any good hard reliable evidence connecting the Kimeses. So now they go to a cell mate, and the cell mate says, 'Oh, I was speaking to Kenneth and Sante Kimes, and they admitted to me what they did.' That would be like giving him the proverbial get-out-of-jail card, Your Honor, that one receives, or place on the Monopoly board that one gets, when they have that opportunity. They take advantage of it."

Sidestepping the jailhouse informant issue, Assistant District Attorney Ann Donnelly announced that Los Angeles had probable cause to arrest mother and son in David Kazdin's murder but were holding off until the New York case concluded. She gave Judge Altman a secret three-page letter outlining evidence of the Kimeses' possible guilt, in a bid to prevent bail and ask for more time to prepare a murder indictment. It worked.

"Very substantial evidence has been presented and a very serious case has been made because we all know what the problems are with the case," Judge Altman said. "As you pointed out, there is no body. It is a difficult case to prove. I have no idea whether they will or won't prove it. However, I will give the

People a further opportunity. I have no doubt that in the event the remand were lifted, the defendants would not be seen again in this jurisdiction voluntarily."

Three days later, mother and son nodded and greeted the press sitting in the empty jury box. Kenny mouthed, "Thank you for the sweater," to a reporter who had mailed him a wool pullover. Sante left court with another message for the crowd, "We just want our constitutional civil rights, please," she said before court officers led her away.

On December 16, 1998, six months and two days after Manny Guerrin first appeared on Irene's doorstep, Manhattan District Attorney Robert Morgenthau announced murder charges against the Kimeses. As inspector Reznick and the Silver Task Force detectives stood behind him in his office at One Hogan Place, Morgenthau released an 84-count indictment. It accused mother and son of second-degree murder, conspiracy, robbery, attempted robbery, burglary, grand larceny, attempted grand larceny, forgery, eavesdropping and possession of weapons, stolen property, and forged documents. If convicted of all charges, they faced up to 131⅓ years in prison. "These two are very competent, very cold criminals," said Police Commissioner Howard Safir, who sat next to Morgenthau at the press conference announcing these charges. "I think in my experience, I have not seen people who have such disregard for other people as we've seen with the Kimeses."

While the half-inch thick document detailed an intricate takeover of Irene's mansion, it said nothing about how and where she was killed. It listed 15 aliases, including Ellie, Ellen, and Ella, which Sante and Kenny allegedly used in their scheme. The indictment also specified that the pair killed Irene the day she disappeared. Morgenthau addressed the core mystery and greatest weakness of his case—no corpus delicti, the Latin term for "body of evidence," which in almost all murder cases starts with a corpse. "The mere fact that you don't have a body doesn't give somebody a walk," he said. "I mean, it's as simple as that. All the facts show that a murder was committed. The fact that you don't have a body . . . I mean obviously it's nice to have a body, but you know, you would never want to send a message out, all you've got to do is hide the body and you walk scot-free. The fact there's not a body does not prevent a prosecution for murder."

To some courthouse wags, the 73-page document reinforced the adage that weak cases produce kitchen-sink indictments, strong prosecutions speak for themselves. Sachs derided the indictment as a Chinese menu of "inconsistent and contradictory theories," pick one and if that fails, switch to column B. He said the indictment careened from the theory of a murder during a robbery, then a murder during a burglary, and "if you don't buy that and those two theories, then what we are going to do is charge them with common law or intentional murder."

Standing outside of Manhattan Criminal Court, Sachs ticked off all the essentials he charged this case lacked. "They don't have a confession," he said. "They don't have a body. They don't have scientific evidence. They don't have any eyewitnesses. They don't have anything. All this case is based upon is a false assumption." Standing next to him was his friend and client Roy Innis, head of the Congress of Racial Equality, who announced his probe into whether authorities denied the Kimeses' civil rights by holding them without bail on minor fraud charges while authorities built the murder case against them.

At their arraignment on January 4, 1999, on indictment No. 10136-98, the defendants exuded confidence, though Sante annoyed Judge Altman with her attempt at oratory.

"I would like to ask a question, if I may?" Sante said when asked for her plea.

"How do you plead," intoned the clerk, "guilty or not guilty."

"I want to ask a question," she insisted.

"You should ask your lawyer the question," Judge Altman said. "Ma'am, do you plead guilty or not guilty?"

"Your Honor," Sante began, "I would like to plead not guilty and pray to be treated equally and fairly as any other citizen."

"Please," the judge told defense counsel, "have her sit down."

Moments later Judge Altman snapped, "Would you please stop holding hands," prompting mother and son to quickly break their customary grasp and place their fingers within plain view on top of the defense table.

At this hearing, Sachs represented both mother and son. Sante's attorney, Jose Muniz, said he dropped the case in October, in part because the Kimeses apparently had no money to pay him. Intrigued by the case, Muniz rejoined the Kimes defense team a few months later at Sante's urging.

Muniz and Weissman have said they hadn't gotten paid since receiving a small retainer in July 1998. Sachs and private investigator Les Levine have declined to discuss finances. While millionaires on paper, Sante and Kenny appeared to be having cash-flow problems in 1998. Like all the bank customers left hanging by the troubles with the shuttered First Cayman and Gulf Union Banks, the Kimeses couldn't get to the account originally opened by Papa Kimes. It was estimated to be worth as much as $850,000. While the 28.35 raw acres in Santa Maria, California is valued at least $1.9 million, unsold and undeveloped, it's actually just a tax burden. Sante's attempts to sell the land in the years before her arrest all fell through, said her friend Carolene Davis. Authorities were still trying to untangle all the ownership changes connected to this land since Kimes died. All the corporations that on paper owned the land were believed to be under Sante's control. And a year after Irene Silverman vanished, cops and prosecutors still were hunting for any other Kimes assets with an eye to freezing them as proceeds of fraud. Whether any of Papa Kimes' fortune remained after years of lawsuits and travel is anybody's guess, although the wily developer did keep financial details from Sante and had a habit of parking money in offshore accounts. Finally, cops seized $36,400 mother and son had with them and in the Lincoln Town Car the day they were arrested.

Before Muniz returned gratis to the case, mother and son were in the unusual position of sharing the same defense team, since both Weissman and Sachs represented Kenny. Explaining that codefendants often have conflicts and are best served by having independent lawyers, Judge Altman asked if the pair were sure they wanted the same representation. "I obviously want to stick with Mr. Sachs, considering the weakness of the charges, sir," Kenny replied. Sante also opted for Sachs, who told the judge, "Their defense is a united defense; there aren't any conflicts." At this stage, prosecutors could forget about flipping one suspect against the other. Flashing a wide smile under her black bowler-style hat, Sante chirped "good morning, take care, we're innocent," as she left the courtroom. After six months in jail, both mother and son looked slimmer. Kenny's dark green suit hung loosely on his shoulders while Sante seemed about 30 pounds lighter under a cream turtleneck and dark gray jacket.

In the new year, Sante expanded her courting of the press, directing a public-relations campaign rare from an alleged killer. They visited six times with

Britain's ITV channel, cooperating with a documentary about their case. Filming was almost canceled when prison officials forbade Kenny from slipping into the $500 suit the ITV people had bought him for the taping. Guards also made him remove a rosary he wore around his neck in memory of his late father. A reporter from the *New York Times* met with the Kimeses five times, three of those with Sante alone. Producers for *60 Minutes* came 10 times, six of those with Sante alone. Fox TV made four visits, all but one with only Sante. *Reuters* and the *New York Post* came once, *Post* columnist Cindy Adams talked to Sante again, and *Daily News* columnist Juan Gonzalez visited twice. Sante squeezed journalists' hands in a motherly gesture, thanked them for listening to her, peered into their eyes over her eyeglasses, and called them at home. She also kept dialing city desks and assignment editors of various outlets. Unhappy with a story in the *Daily News* about the 1991 civil suit with the Richards couple in Nevada over their home, Sante complained to the paper's city desk. Her call was switched to Manhattan court reporter Barbara Ross. "We're being framed," she told Ross. "We need our side to be heard. My son and I are being denied every constitutional right. I'm a mom fighting for her son." She complained of police brutality. "If we didn't sign statements, we got beaten badly."

When asked, over a span of six months, for an interview for this book, Sante has given mixed signals. In March 1999, her attorney Weissman sent a letter to this book's publisher hinting at legal action. In the summer, her lawyers then said she was considering an interview. After a second interview request was sent by certified mail to Riker's Island on July 5, 1999, she asked for guarantees that her interview would not be advertised on the book's cover, according to Weissman. She was unsatisfied with assurances that this book would not be promoted as her or Kenny's authorized biography or version of events. Then she suddenly telephoned this writer on July 22, 1999, from Riker's, and in a brief conversation apologized for causing any imposition. "I hear you're a great journalist, and all I ask for is the truth," she said. "I'm fighting for my innocent son. We've been framed. Everything that has been printed is false. And if we could get good investigative reporters to report on this, it's really . . . it's just a New York law enforcement system that has made the worst mistake, like the documentaries are calling it, in history. And there's no anything to anything.

"I feel bad, I don't want you to think I'm not trying to help," she added. "I just want the truth, and I've read some of your articles, and I think you're fair. What I'm trying to tell you, Miss McQuillan, if you will check even the L.A. ridiculous charges, they're all lies. There's no truth to any of this." When asked if she would sit for an interview, she told this writer to call a new attorney on the Kimes scene, Michael Hardy, who has represented the Rev. Al Sharpton, a New York civil rights activist. Hardy did not return the call before deadline.

Her lawyers fretted privately that she risked incriminating herself by talking to the press. It looked like another high-wire act for Sante, like the time she tried to outsmart a roomful of people by sashaying from the Mayflower piano bar with Mrs. Kenworthy's coat. She told the *60 Minutes* producers that she liked Irene and used to sip champagne with her. Twice now, with *Post* columnist Cindy Adams and *60 Minutes*, Sante had placed herself inside the mansion. Sante tried to suggest to the *60 Minutes* producers that Irene might be traveling abroad since the 82-year-old spoke of visiting Europe. As *60 Minutes* reporter Steve Kroft noted, "Prosecutors say that would have been difficult, since the Kimeses had Silverman's passport when they were arrested."

One thing can be said for Sante's efforts, her timing was good. She wept and complained of being an innocent trapped in a corrupt system, just as two huge scandals battered the police force. The trial of cop Justin Volpe for sodomizing Abner Louima was just getting underway that spring. After Volpe's guilty plea, another cop was convicted and three others acquitted for joining or covering up this sick torture session. Then on February 4, 1999, four white officers killed an unarmed black man named Amadou Diallo in the lobby of his Bronx home, firing 41 times and hitting him with 19 bullets. For six weeks, until the plainclothes cops were indicted for murder on March 31, protesters took to the streets. At Diallo's home, in the canyons of Wall Street and in front of One Police Plaza, marchers demanded reforms and decried the slaughter of an innocent man. Anger at the police department brought out the famous. Led by the Reverend Sharpton, celebrities and politicians joined regular folks who marched on police headquarters for 15 straight days. In sit-ins blocking the entrance to One Police Plaza, 1,175 people were arrested, including former mayor David Dinkins, Harlem Congressman Charles Rangel, Oscar-winning actress Susan Sarandon, and the Reverend Jesse Jackson.

At the height of this police crisis, Sante charged, "We are being framed by a corrupt police force and Gestapo police force gone wild," in a phone call to Fox News reporter Eric Shawn, which aired March 2. "For months, Judge Altman and prosecutors have been intervening and spying on our attorney-client meetings," she said. "Bribed, lying witnesses are being placed in our housing and in our attorney visiting areas to spy on our defense preparation." Continuing this theme of the corrupt system, Kenny, in court with his mother on March 25, read from a written statement, urging Judge Altman to recuse himself. Dressed in a dark blue double-breasted suit, a gold-and-navy-striped tie, his hair neatly jelled back, Kenny could have been mistaken for an earnest young lawyer as he addressed the bench.

"Your Honor, it is with great anxiety and concern that I respectfully ask you to please allow us to have another judge, for I honestly feel that your actions have proven you incapable of any fairness in this case," Kenny began. "In my opinion, Your Honor, you appear to be helping the district attorney build a case that does not exist, and I say this with the comfort from the evidence of your actions, especially your unfairness to deny our attorney visits. We respectfully request and the law requires fairness . . ."

"Who is we?" the judge interrupted.

"Me and my mother," Kenny said, continuing, "from a judge who can be impartial and rise above the impropriety of the failing New York legal system and their uneven inappropriate tactics, whom we, along with countless others, are now victims of. Your Assistant calls us murderers. My beloved father said to me, 'Consider the source.' "

"Okay," said the judge, "have a seat." Muniz then said Sante wanted to talk, but he wasn't sure about the subject. Bouncing to her feet, she began by asking after the judge's health, since he had thyroid surgery, and then said, "Your Honor, the entire world is watching New York."

"What is the subject of this?" asked the judge.

"The subject of this is that we have been held for nine months," she shot back, asking for more chances to meet with her son and their lawyers in trial preparation conferences.

Altman said he would decide the matter in a few days, then denied Kenny's recusal motion, characterizing it as "baseless," and rejected bail for the young man. "I think I have rarely seen a case that calls for remand more than this, people changing identifications, hiding identifications, using forged and phony documents. I have no doubt that these defendants will not return."

His face flushed, Kenny again claimed the system mistreated him and he was keeping a log of the abuses. He alleged that detectives had manhandled him during a fingerprint session earlier in the year. "At this time they caused me physical and mental harm," he said. "They didn't use any punching tactics, but they did jab me and they did certain things to my person that were improper." Attorney Matthew Weissman chimed in that back in July 1998, right after he was first arrested, "Mr. Kimes was stripped naked and handed a blank sheet of paper with a signatory line on it, and was told that his mother had a massive heart attack, and if he signed this paper, they would let him see her for one last time before she died."

"Did he sign the paper?" asked Judge Altman.

"Of course not, Your Honor," Weissman said.

"I would have signed the paper," the judge retorted.

"Well, he doubted the veracity of what he was being told," the lawyer replied.

"Do you know anything about this?" Altman asked the prosecutor.

"I can't imagine it to be so," said Assistant District Attorney Connie Fernandez.

"He was stripped naked," Weissman repeated, "a pressure point was used upon him to inflict pain upon him."

Kenny added, "I also have a witness."

"Based on our experience," ADA Fernández said, "and investigation of defendants' background, they have a history of making false complaints against the police and anyone else on which they seem to have a complaint against."

Muniz then charged that a correction officer improperly examined Sante's personal legal papers in jail. Altman ordered an investigation of all their charges. As the hearing ended, Kenny piped up again. "One thing," he told the judge. "The statements that I made, I meant no disrespect by what I said to you."

"I didn't take it that way," the judge replied.

Juggling offers to appear on national TV shows, Sante chose *60 Minutes.* With her hair swept up in a Katherine Hepburn swirl and peering over grandmotherly reading glasses, Sante faced the cameras with Kenny by her side. They held hands through the interview, conducted by reporter Steve Kroft and broadcast on April 11, 1999. For the first question about why they were taking the risky and unusual step of being interviewed before trial, Kenny turned to his mother and asked, "May I answer that," and she said, "Sure."

"Mr. Kroft," Kenny said, "the reason why we're doing this before trial is because of the unfair portrayal that's been given about us."

His mother added, "The media has so far portrayed us totally like we are not. We're just a mother and son." She said they weren't "drifters or grifters" and lived in the same home in Nevada for 24 years and in one Hawaii house for 12 years. Asked to define herself, she said, "Well, I would describe myself as a mom; I was married to a wonderful man. He was a big old Irishman. Kenny looks a lot like him."

Kenny responded, "I would say that, I'm a son of a very wonderful, beautiful mom. I think she's a beautiful person, spiritually and intellectually and—and physically."

As for Irene, "We don't know where this woman is," said Sante. "Wherever she is, I pray to God she's all right."

Police Commissioner Safir offered this analysis of Sante's public-relations campaign. "I think her view, which I've seen in many criminals but not quite to the extent that she does, is the best defense is an offense. You attack the system and take no responsibility for your own actions and try to portray yourself as a victim. And that's exactly what she's doing. She tried to use current events, playing on the Diallo case and playing on whatever else she could to try and gain sympathy. But, in truth, she's a very unsympathetic character."

Her hair looked noticeably grayer when she smiled at reporters during a court hearing on May 13, 1999. She peered over wire-frame glasses set at the edge of her nose, like a librarian. Her foundation and pink rouge were heavy, but she had toned down the mascara, keeping her grandmotherly image intact. She looked demure in conservative black slacks and black top under a long-sleeved white shirt.

Kenny had the first outburst. "Can't I sit next to my mom?" he asked in a loud voice as three burly court officers with arms folded separated him from Sante.

Mother and son sat at opposite ends of a table, and he passed her a legal pad with a note on it. She whispered back to him, thwarting lip-readers by cupping her fingers over her mouth. After losing an umpteenth bail request, Sante spoke to Judge Altman, asking him to order guards to keep the ankle shackles off her and Kenny. "It's inhuman," she said. And she challenged him to step down from her case. "I'm just really begging you, if this were your son, would you want a fair judge, that was not biased? Listen, if this were your son, would you ask out . . .

"Madam," Altman said.

"All I ask is for a fair, unbiased judge," she said.

"Fortunately for you, you have one," the judge replied.

In her campaign against Altman, Sante even began asking reporters seeking interviews to sign affidavits that the judge was interfering with her attorney visits. At least two reporters refused. However, Sante eventually got her wish for another judge. Altman had been ill and missed several weeks of work after surgery in early 1999 to remove his thyroid. Quietly, on July 20, 1999, Altman left the Kimes proceedings, citing personal reasons "that have nothing to do with the case," said a court spokesman. Altman's replacement was Acting Supreme Court Justice Rena Uviller, a former Legal Aid lawyer, whose last turn in the spotlight was the 1996 trial of convicted subway firebomber Edward Leary. He injured 49 straphangers, including himself, by setting off homemade bombs twice on subways in December 1994. Rejecting his plea for mercy, Uviller sentenced him up to 94 years in jail, calling him evil incarnate.

Altman was still expected to rule on a 55-page defense motion, which ambitiously sought to suppress all the evidence against the mother and son. It claimed the statements Kenny and Sante gave the day of their arrest, July 5, were involuntary. Calling the initial Utah charge over the rubber check a "civil dispute," the defense team argued authorities unlawfully arrested the Kimeses and detained them for months, so all the evidence seized should be thrown out. "That initial warrant was a ruse to hold them, orchestrated by the FBI and Utah officials in conjunction with the New York City Police Department." Defense lawyers charged cops searched the Lincoln Town Car two days before getting a warrant, so the evidence found in the vehicle should be tossed. Forcing grand jury testimony from defense private eye Lawrence Frost, who retrieved the black canvas bag from the Plaza Hotel, violated attorney-client privilege, they argued. Using entries from Sante's diaries broke her right against self-incrimination and contaminated the entire grand jury proceeding. "In a case where there is no corpus delicti [sic], DNA, hair fibers, blood, witnesses to the alleged crime, or proof that Irene Silverman is even deceased, the illegal use of diaries were [*sic*] tantamount to forcing Sante Kimes to testify before the grand jury." Under New York State law, Irene merely was missing, since it takes three years before someone absent can be presumed dead. Also they claimed there was no evidence that the Kimeses were behind the plot to steal the mansion because the deed did not bear their names and wasn't filed with the county clerk.

Ignoring conventional wisdom, Sante insisted to her lawyers that she wanted to testify at trial. Taking the stand could open the door to cross-examination about her criminal record and perhaps grilling about other uncharged acts, and Kazdin.

On August 18, 1999, Kazdin's death quietly changed from an uncharged crime to a thunderous murder case against the mother and son. Sante and Kenny potentially faced the death penalty in California for his slaying. Los Angeles prosecutors filed a felony complaint against the pair, charging they both killed Kazdin "for financial gain." Prosecutors said Kazdin was "a witness to a crime and was intentionally killed because of that fact," an apparent reference to his discovery of the mortgage taken out in his name. Kenny was the one who shot Kazdin, said the complaint which did not detail Sante's role in the murder. Their lawyers attacked the credibility of witness Sean Little, who reportedly told police he helped Kenny dump Kazdin's body. Attorney Jose Muniz argued that mother and son had no motive to kill.

"They got along with Kazdin," said Muniz. "He was a longtime friend for 20 years. Basically Sante's position is, 'We have no reason to knock him off. He was one of my dearest friends.' " New York State law allows prosecutors to introduce uncharged crimes or actions only if they illustrate a specific modus operandi. Laying the groundwork, in case they can't change her mind, Sante's lawyers asked for a hearing to limit cross-examination.

In the People's response, Ann Donnelly, assistant district attorney, said the defendants' statements the day of their arrest were "lawfully obtained," and the Utah warrant was valid. This warrant for the bounced car check couldn't be a law enforcement ruse to hold the Kimeses, because Utah issued it before Irene Silverman vanished. "The Court would have to find that these various agencies concocted a fictitious warrant in another state to trap the defendants for a murder they had not yet committed." She said detectives obtained a search warrant before combing through the Lincoln, even though they didn't need one because the car was stolen. Attorney-client privilege doesn't apply to sending private eye Frost to the Plaza Hotel for a bag filled with incriminating evidence; the defendants' purpose was "to conceal evidence of their crimes and to perpetrate a fraud." Sante's writings don't merit Fifth Amendment protection, since they are notes about crimes, not musing of her innermost thoughts. New York State law allows the fact of murder to be established through circumstantial evidence, and the grand jury minutes detail the plot to swindle the mansion, Donnelly argued. As for a hearing on cross-examination rules, she asked for a postponement. "Immediately prior to the commencement of trial, the People will provide notice of prior uncharged criminal, vicious, or immoral acts they intend to use at trial to impeach the defendants' credibility."

Judge Altman's ruling on September 13, 1999 gave prosecutors almost everything they wanted. Jurors can hear about all the evidence seized when the Kimeses were arrested on the stolen car charge because that Utah warrant was valid as was the search of the Lincoln Town Car, Altman declared. Attorney-client privilege didn't cover private investigator Lawrence Frost's recovery of the black bag from the Plaza hotel; that whole episode suggested to the judge that Kimeses wanted the bag hidden away, "never to again surface." So the jurors could also learn about the allegedly forged deed to Irene's mansion and the .22-caliber handgun in that black bag. Sante had no Fifth Amendment protection regarding her diaries, the judge said. The best the defense got was a future hearing on the legality of the mother and son's statements to cops, and dismissal of the grand larceny charge because the pair failed to complete their alleged theft of the mansion. They remain charged with attempted grand larceny.

Although finding no precedent in Manhattan for a murder case without a body or forensic evidence, Altman determined there was "sufficient circumstantial evidence presented by the People to permit the Grand Jury to conclude that Mrs. Silverman was dead and that the defendants had murdered her.

"This evidence included: . . . the elaborate secrecy and misdirection to which they resorted with the apparent purpose of gaining close proximity to Mrs. Silverman and isolating her; impersonations of the victim by defendant Sante Kimes; the schemes, artifices and many instances of eavesdropping, spying and forgery utilized to defraud the victim and strip her of her wealth; the weapons, chemicals, and instruments of restraint which were in defendants' actual or constructive possession; the personal effects and financial and private documents of the victim found in their possession; the good health and personal habits of the victim, and the circumstances leading to her disappearance. All of this evidence, taken together, strongly supports the inference that defendants caused the death of Irene Silverman in order to further their larcenous purpose. The evidence that defendants conspired to steal Mrs. Silverman's home was strong."

Another legal front for Sante loomed in the spring of 1999, the start of an epic family battle over the late Kenneth Kimes' money. Confident that Sante won't be out of jail any time soon, the late Kimes' daughter from his first marriage, Linda Kimes, moved in Santa Barbara Superior Court on May 10, 1999, to gain control of his estate. Her probate petition maintained that her father was a divorced man, unmarried at the time of his 1994 death. "Our position is, he never married Sante," said Linda's probate attorney Robert Eroen. Fear of Sante kept Linda and her brother Andrew from asserting their rights as heirs in the years following Kimes' death.

Linda Kimes submitted a one-page will, dated July 3, 1963. Her father wrote it while mired in bitter divorce proceedings with first wife, Charloette. According to this handwritten document, Kimes willed his entire estate to his children, Linda and Andrew, and specifically excluded Charloette. To challenge the will, Sante has to prove she did marry Kimes and is entitled to half of any community property. If Linda Kimes' petition is successful, the court could give her subpoena power to track down and freeze any assets belonging to her father. This effort could choke any potential flow of money just as Sante and Kenny go on trial for murder in New York.

As the first anniversary of Irene's disappearance approached on July 5, 1999, Sante granted two extraordinary interviews to *Daily News* columnist Juan Gonzalez. In them, she offered her own eyebrow-raising theory for Silverman's disappearance—that the 82-year-old was running a brothel, a notion cops and Irene's friends totally discount. Sante was back to lobbing sexual allegations, just as she had in years past against an unnamed Los Angeles cop and her late adoptive father, when she was looking for mercy from a federal judge, and then against her tutors, maids, and their lawyer when they sued her.

She'd come full circle, even repeating the same words she used when in trouble before. During her sentencing in 1986 for stealing the mink from the Mayflower, Sante used lines that sounded like the pivotal scene from her favorite film, *Gone with the Wind*, where Scarlett O'Hara vowed with clenched fist, "As God is my witness, I'll never be hungry again." Now 13 years later, in the worst mess of her wild life, Sante was at it again. The pattern stays alive.

"As God is my witness, Juan, we did not do this," she told Gonzalez, later adding, "All I want, as God is my witness, is the truth."

Penguin Putnam Inc.
Online

Your Internet gateway to a virtual environment with hundreds of entertaining and enlightening books from Penguin Putnam Inc.

While you're there, get the latest buzz on the best authors and books around—

Tom Clancy, Patricia Cornwell, W.E.B. Griffin, Nora Roberts, William Gibson, Robin Cook, Brian Jacques, Catherine Coulter, Stephen King, Jacquelyn Mitchard, and many more!

**Penguin Putnam Online is located at
http://www.penguinputnam.com**

PENGUIN PUTNAM NEWS

Every month you'll get an inside look at our upcoming books and new features on our site. This is an ongoing effort to provide you with the most up-to-date information about our books and authors.

**Subscribe to Penguin Putnam News at
http://www.penguinputnam.com/ClubPPI**